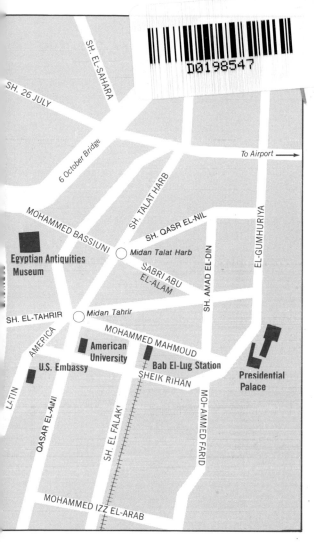

D0198547

SH. EL-SAHARA

SH. 26 JULY

6 October Bridge

To Airport ⟶

MOHAMMED BASSIUNI

SH. TALAT HARB

SH. QASR EL-NIL

EL-GUMHURIYA

◯ Midan Talat Harb

Egyptian Antiquities
Museum

SABRI ABU
EL-ALAM

SH. AMAD EL-DIN

SH. EL-TAHRIR   ◯ Midan Tahrir

MOHAMMED MAHMOUD

AMERICA

American
University

Bab El-Lug Station

U.S. Embassy

SHEIK RIHAN

Presidential
Palace

LATIN

QASAR EL-AINI

SH. EL FALAKI

MOHAMMED FARID

MOHAMMED IZZ EL-ARAB

ARABIC

AT A GLANCE

PHRASE BOOK & DICTIONARY FOR TRAVELERS

BY HILARY WISE, Ph.D.
Lecturer in Linguistics
Queen Mary College
University of London

BARRON'S

BARRON'S EDUCATIONAL SERIES, INC.

Cover and Book Design   Milton Glaser, Inc.

Illustrations   Juan Suarez

© Copyright 1987 by Barron's Educational Series, Inc.

All inquiries should be addressed to:
Barron's Educational Series, Inc.
250 Wireless Boulevard
Hauppauge, New York 11788

Library of Congress Catalog Card No. 86-32272

Library of Congress Cataloging-in-Publication Data
Wise, Hilary
  Arabic at a glance.

  Arabic and English.
  1. Arabic language—Dialects—Egypt. 2. Arabic
language—Conversation and phrase books—English.
I. Title.
PJ6779.W64   1987   492'.783421   86-32272
ISBN 0-8120-2979-8 (pbk.)

PRINTED IN THE UNITED STATES OF AMERICA
6 7 8 9 0 900 16 15 14 13 12 11

CONTENTS

PREFACE

So you're taking a trip to a fascinating part of the world. That's exciting! In more ways than one, this new phrase book will prove an invaluable companion that will make your stay far more interesting and truly unforgettable.

This phrase book is part of a comprehensive series from Barron's Educational Series, Inc. In these books we present the phrases and words that a traveler most often needs for a brief visit to a foreign country, where the customs and language are often different. Each of the phrase books highlights the terms particular to that country, in situations that the tourist is most likely to encounter. With a specially developed key to pronunciation, this book will enable you to communicate quickly and confidently in colloquial terms. It is intended not only for beginners with no knowledge of the language, but also for those who have already studied it and have some familiarity with it.

Some of the unique features and highlights of the Barron's series are:

- Easy-to-follow *phonetic pronunciations* for all words and phrases in the book.
- Compact *dictionary* of commonly used words and phrases — built right into this phrase book so there's no need to carry a separate dictionary.
- Useful phrases for the *tourist*, grouped together by subject matter in a logical way so that the appropriate phrase is easy to locate when you need it.
- Special phrases for the *business traveler*, including banking terms, trade and contract negotiations, and secretarial services.
- Thorough section on *food and drink*, with comprehensive food terms you will find on menus; these terms are often difficult or impossible to locate in dictionaries, but our section gives you a description of the preparation as well as a definition of what it is.

- *Emergency phrases* and terms you hope you won't need: legal complications, medical problems, theft or loss of valuables, replacement or repair of watches, cameras, and the like.
- *Sightseeing itineraries*, shopping tips, practical travel tips, and regional food specialities to help you get off the beaten path and into the countryside, to the small towns and cities, and to the neighboring areas.
- A *reference section* providing: expressions of time, days of the week, weather, countries and nationalities, directions, and information on Islamic festivals.
- A brief *grammar section*, with the basic elements of the language quickly explained.

Enjoy your vacation and travel with confidence. You have a friend by your side.

ACKNOWLEDGMENTS

We would like to thank the following individuals for their assistance on this project: Hala N. Barakat, Hany M. El-Hosseiny, Ashraf Hossein, Ibrahim Gendy, Afaf El-Menoufy, and Eyad Amer; also Dr. Valerie Becker, Anthony Rutgen and Barney Allan of Anthony Rudkin Associates, and Shawki Hussein and Bahiga El-Haggar of the Egyptian Tourist Authority in New York City.

INTRODUCTION

There can be few parts of the world where a foreigner's efforts to speak the language are more appreciated than in the Middle East. Even the ability to exchange greetings and express thanks will arouse interest and establish an immediate bond. The wider your knowledge, the warmer your welcome in countries renowned for their hospitality to strangers.

Who Speaks Arabic?

Arabic is spoken by about 180 million people in more than twenty different countries, from Morocco in the west to Iraq in the east, and as far south as Somalia and the Sudan. As the language of the Koran, the holy book of Islam, it is taught as a second language in Muslim states throughout the world. Arabic originated in Saudi Arabia in pre-Islamic times, and spread rapidly in the wake of the Arab conquests from the seventh century. The languages of northern India, Turkey, Iran, Portugal, and Spain are full of words of Arabic origin.

Modern spoken Arabic varies a good deal from country to country, differing as much as, say, Spanish and Italian. The classical, written language has however changed little over the centuries, and is the accepted literary language throughout the Arab world.

What Kind of Arabic?

As a visitor to the Middle East you have to decide which kind of Arabic is going to be most useful to you. Although Classical Arabic has a standard form, and carries high prestige, it is primarily a written language, used for all literary purposes; it is only spoken on very formal occasions, for example, when someone is making an official speech. Grammatically it is far more complex than spoken Arabic.

Local dialects are used for all everyday communication, at work and in the home, and will clearly be of more practical use to the average tourist or businessperson. But which of the many dialects should you choose?

Egyptian Arabic

Egypt is at the heart of the Arab world, geographically, historically, and politically. With 50 million inhabitants it has by far the highest population of any Arab country, and more than 2 million teachers, doctors, businesspersons, and workers of all kinds are to be found in the wealthier Arab countries. Because Egypt also produces films, songs, and TV serials that are immensely popular throughout the Arab world, Egyptian Arabic has acquired a special prestige, and even in remote areas people are familiar with the dialect.

Other Dialects

Egyptian is similar to the dialects of the eastern Mediterranean — Lebanese, Syrian, Palestinian, and Jordanian — and to Sudanese. The dialects of North Africa, from Morocco to Libya, have features in common, as do the dialects of Saudi Arabia and the Gulf. The main differences in pronunciation, and in some key everyday expressions, are outlined on page 208, so that you will have some idea what to expect if you are traveling in the Middle East outside Egypt.

But if you use Egyptian Arabic you will have no problem being understood, and many people will be able to adapt their own accent to help you.

Using the Book

Most of the expressions in the book are given in Egyptian Arabic, using the Western alphabet. Occasionally an alternative is provided, when a different expression is widely used elsewhere. For instance, the Egyptian word for *room* is **'oh**-Da, but **ghur**-fa is the usual word in many other Arab countries; so both are given, the Egyptian word being listed first: **'oh**-Da/**ghur**-fa. If two words are given separated by a comma, they are both equally common in Egyptian.

In addition, a translation is given in literary Arabic, using the Arabic script. This is so that you can point to a word or phrase, or circle it in pencil, if you want to make sure you've been understood. Or an Arabic speaker may point to the appropriate phrase if *he* or *she* wants to communicate with *you*. The literary version given here in the Arabic script is not the "high" Classical Arabic of the Koran. It is a simplified variety that should be accessible to speakers who may not have had many years of formal education.

If you are going to point to phrases in the book, it's a good idea to make it clear that you are in fact using Egyptian Arabic (**°a**-ra-bee **maS**-ree): otherwise it may be assumed that you are learning literary Arabic and people may struggle to use Classical forms in their own speech for your benefit!

You can manage perfectly well *without* learning the Arabic script, though a guide is provided on page 204 for the really ambitious. With a little effort you will be able to decipher simple notices, street names, and the names of shops. The kind of signs you'll encounter most often are given on page 162-163.

QUICK PRONUNCIATION GUIDE

Most of the sounds of Arabic are similar to sounds used in English; there are just a few that are unfamiliar to English ears, and these can best be mastered by careful imitation of the speakers on the cassette. As with any language, a positive approach is much more important than getting the sounds exactly right.

THE VOWELS

	SHORT VOWELS	EXAMPLES
a	as in *bat*	**ba**-lad (town, country)
e	as in *met*	**ka**-me-ra (camera)
i	as in *bit*	*bint* (girl, daughter)
u	as in *book*	**buk**-ra (tomorrow)
o	as in *dog*	do-**laar** (dollar)

	LONG VOWELS	EXAMPLES
aa	as in *father*	**Daa**-nee (lamb)
eh	as in *met*, but lengthened	*heht!* (bring!)
ee	as in *feed*	*meen?* (who?)
ey	as in *they* but lengthened	*feyn?* (where?)
oo	as in *mood*	*shoof!* (look!)
oh	as in *phone*	*yohm* (day)

All these long vowels should be pronounced "pure," with the lips held in the same position throughout (as in Spanish or French).

COMPLEX VOWELS (i.e., where the lips *do* change position)		EXAMPLES
ay	as in *try*	kub-**bay**-ya (glass)
aw	as in *out*	**daw**-sha (noise)

THE CONSONANTS

The following consonants are pronounced as in English: **p**, **b**, **t**, **d**, **f**, **v**, **k**, **g**, **h**, **j**, **l**, **m**, **n**, **s**, **z**, **w**, **y**.

Notice that **s** is always as in *see*, never as in *his*, and the **g** is always "hard" as in *good*, never "soft" as in *age*. Also:

- **l** is the "clear" British English type, rather than the "dark" American sound.
- **r** is a brief tap of the tongue-tip against the teeth, as in Spanish.
- **h** may be used in positions in which it doesn't occur in English, such as before consonants. Make it nice and breathy: *ah-lan!* (Hi!). (Exceptions are the sequences *oh* as in *yohm* and *eh* as in *heht!*, which always represent long, pure vowels, not a vowel plus aspirate *h*.)

CONSONANT		EXAMPLES
sh	as in *sheet*	*sheek* (check)
kh	a "soft" **k** sound, as in Scottish *loch*	*kham-sa* (five)
gh	a guttural **g** sound, rather like the French *r*	*gha-nee* (rich)
H	a rough, heavily aspirated **h** (as if you've swallowed something hot!)	*Hubb* (love)
q	like **k**, but made further back, so that it has a "darker" quality	*il-quds* (Jerusalem)
' or **"**	a glottal stop, or catch, found in Cockney and Scottish English, replacing a *t*, as in *bi'er* for "bitter," and *Sco'ish* for "Scottish."*	*ma-"ehs* (size)

* Two symbols are used for this sound because they represent two different sounds in some other dialects; *'a-lam* (pain) and *"a-lam* (pen) sound the same in Egyptian, but are different in many other varieties. See pages 208.

CONSONANT		EXAMPLES
c	made by contracting the muscles at the back of the throat. If you use a glottal stop instead ('), you'll still be understood!	^cehl! (great!)

Double Consonants

When the same consonant is written twice, it should be pronounced long. So you should hang on to the *t* in **sit**-*ta* (six) and the *l* in *"ul-lee* (tell me).

"Heavy" Consonants

There are four "heavy" consonants in Egyptian Arabic, represented in this book by **T**, **D**, **S**, and **Z**. They are like **t**, **d**, **s**, and **z**, except that they are pronounced with loose, lax lip and tongue muscles:

LETTER	EXAMPLES
T	**Tay**-*yib* (good, fine)
D	**D**eyf (guest)
S	**Saa**-*la* (hall)
Z	*a*-**Zunn** (I think)

These consonants affect the surrounding sounds; as you'll hear from listening to the tape, the whole word will often have a laxer, "heavier" articulation.

Stressed Syllables

The stressed syllables, which are printed in bold type, should be pronounced more loudly and emphatically than the others (think of the difference stress makes in English **bil***low* versus *be***low**).

It's important to pronounce a long vowel really long (and "pure") in a stressed syllable; for example, *ee* will be longer in *ta-la-***teen** (thirty) than in **bin**-*tee* (my daughter).

There is a tendency to drop some unstressed vowels. For example, the first vowel in *khu-**Saa**-ra* (pity) is likely to be dropped in a phrase like *ya kh-**Saa**-ra!* (What a pity!). When one word ends in a vowel and the next begins with one, the second vowel is usually dropped; so *ma-ᶜa is-sa-**leh**-ma* (lit., with peace; goodbye) becomes *ma-ᶜa s-sa-**leh**-ma*.

A "helping" vowel — usually **i** — is often introduced between two words if one word ends in two consonants and the next begins with one:

shuft (I saw) **+** *mu-**Ham**-mad* (Mohammed) is often pronounced ***shuf**-ti mu-**Ham**-mad*.

THE BASICS FOR GETTING BY

The expressions listed below will help you make contact with people, obtain essential information, and express your needs and views. They are the basic building blocks of everyday conversation, which are needed in most situations. Try to learn as many as you can before you leave; you can then combine them freely with words appropriate to each situation as it arises.

Masculine and Feminine

A distinction is often made between the masculine and feminine in Arabic. For instance, to say "How are you?" you'd say *iz-zay-yak?* to a man, but *iz-zay-yik?* to a woman. And if you are a man you'd say *ʿa-wiz* for "I want," but you'd say *ʿaw-za* if you're a woman. In this book the feminine forms are given in square brackets.

GREETINGS

Hello!	**ah**-lan!	اهلاً
or	**ah**-lan wa **sah**-lan!	اهلاً وسهلاً
How are you?	iz-**zay**-yak? [iz-**zay**-yik?]	ازيك ؟
or	keyf **Heh**-lak?	كيف حالك؟
	[keyf **Heh**-lik?]	
Fine.	**kway**-yis [kway-**yi**-sa],	كويس
	il-**Ham**-du lil-**leh**	[كويسة]، الحمد لله
or	bi kheyr,	بخير،
	il-**Ham**-du lil-**leh**	الحمد لله

Pleased to meet you.	*it-shar-raf-na*	تشرفنا
Goodbye.	**ma-**ᶜ*a s-sa-leh-ma*	مع السلامة

PLEASE AND THANK YOU

Please.	*min faD-lak [min faD-lik]*	من فضلك
Thank you.	**shuk-ran**	شكراً
Thank you very much.	*'al-fi shukr*	شكراً جزيلاً
You're welcome.	ᶜ*af-wan*	عفواً

COMMON EXPRESSIONS

yes	*'ay-wa*	نعم
no	*la'*	لا
fine, O.K.	**Tay**-*yib, oh-**key***	طيب
There is/are, is/are there?	*fee (?)*	(هل) يوجد/توجد
There isn't/ aren't (any)	*ma feesh*	لا يوجد/توجد
Here you are/ do join us/go ahead	*it-faD-Dal [it-faD-Da-lee]*	تفضل/تفضلي
Maybe.	**yim**-*kin*	يمكن، ربما
Never mind.	*ma-*ᶜ*a-lish*	لا باس، حصل خير

What a pity!	*ya kh-**Saa**-ra!*	يا خسارة!
Honest to God! (protestation)	*wal-**laa**-hee!*, *wal-**laah** il ^ca-**Zeem**!*	والله العظيم !
Please ... (excuse me)	*law sa-**maHt***	من فضلك
Sorry.	*'eh-sif ['as-fa]*	آسف [آسفة]
Let's go!	*yal-la!*	هيا!
Just a minute.	*laH-Za*	لحظة
Wait.	*is-tan-na*	إنتظر
That's enough.	*ki-feh-ya ki-da*	كفاية
Great! Wonderful!	*^cehl! mum-tehz!*	عال! ممتاز!
Wow! (amazement)	*ya sa-lehm!*	شيء عجيب
Look!	*shoof! [shoo-fee]*	انظر [انظري] !
I don't mind, I've no objection.	*ma-^can-deesh meh-ni^c*	ليس عندي مانع
I think (so).	*a-Zunn*	اظن
I don't think (so).	*ma-Zun-nish*	لا اظن
I (let's) hope so (God willing).	*'in shaa' al-laah*	إن شاء الله
and	*wi*	و
but	*leh-kin*	لكن
or	*'aw*	أو

PRONOUNS

I (am) — .	**a**-na — .	انا —
You (are) — .	**in**-ta [**in**-tee] — .	انت —
He (is) — .	**huw**-wa — .	هو —
She (is) — .	**hee**-ya — .	هى —
We (are) — .	**iH**-na — .	نحن —
You (pl.) are — .	in-**tum**-ma — .	انتم —
They (are) — .	**hum**-ma — .	هم —

REQUESTS

Bring me — .	**gib**-lee — .	احضر لى —
Give me — .	id-**dee**-nee — .	اعطنى —
■ this/that one	■ da	هذا
I want — .	**ᶜa**-wiz [**ᶜaw**-za] — .	اريد —
I want to go — .	**ᶜa**-wiz [**ᶜaw**-za] a-**rooH** — .	
		اريد أن اذهب —
■ to see — .	■ a-**shoof** —	ارى —
■ to buy — .	■ ash-**ti**-ree — .	اشترى —
■ to eat — .	■ 'eh-kul — .	آكل —
■ to drink — .	■ ash-rab — .	اشرب —

I don't want —.	*mish ᶜa-wiz [ᶜaw-za]* —.	. — لا أريد
■ a lot	■ *ki-teer*	كثير
■ a little	■ *shway-ya, "a-leel*	قليل
■ more	■ *'ak-tar*	اكثر
Is it possible —? Can you —?	*mum-kin* —?	هل من الممكن — ؟
It is possible.	*mum-kin.*	ممكن
It isn't possible.	mish *mum-kin.*	مستحيل
Do you know —?	*tiᶜ-raf* —? [*tiᶜ-ra-fee* —?]	هل تعرف —؟
I don't know.	*maᶜ-rafsh.*	لا اعرف

QUESTIONS

Where is/are —?	*feyn* —?	اين —؟
Where is the bathroom?	*feyn it-twa-litt?*	اين التواليت؟
■ bus	■ *il-'u-tu-bees*	الأوتوبيس
■ telephone	■ *it-ti-li-fohn*	التليفون
What is/are —?	*'eyh* —?	ما — ؟
What's this/that?	*'eyh da?*	ما هذا ؟
What's the matter?	*fee 'eyh?*	ماذا جرى ؟
When?	*'im-ta?*	متى؟

Why?	leyh?	لماذا؟
Why not?	leyh **la'**?	لماذا لا ؟
Who?	meen?	من ؟
How?	iz **zayy**?, keyf?	ازي ؟ كيف ؟
Which — ?	'**an**-hee — ?	اي — ؟
How much?	kam? bi kam?	كم، بكم؟
How many?	kam?	كم ؟

TIME AND PLACE

here	**hi**-na	هنا
there	hi-**nehk**	هناك
up(stairs)	foh"	فوق
down(stairs)	taHt	تحت
in(side)	**go**-wa	في الداخل
out(side)	**bar**-ra	في الخارج
near	"u-**ray**-yib	قريب
far	hi-ᶜeed	بعيد
now	dil-**wa**"-tee	الآن
later	baᶜ-**deyn**	بعد ذلك
soon	"u-**ray**-yib	قريباً
today	'in-na-**har** da/il-**yohm**	اليوم

tomorrow	**buk**-ra	غداً
yesterday	'im-**beh**-riH/'ams	امس
usually	^ca-**da**-tan	عادةً
never	'**a**-ba-dan	اندأ

COMMUNICATING

Do you speak
English? — bi-tit-**kal**-lim [bi-tit-kal-**li**-mee]
in-gi-**lee**-zee? — هل تتكلم الانجليزية ؟

Does anyone here
speak English? — fee Hadd **hi**-na bi-yit-**kal**-lim
in-gi-**lee**-zee? — هل يوجد شخص يتكلم
الانجليزية ؟

Do you understand? — fi-**himt** [fi-**him**-tee] ? — هل فهمت ؟

I don't understand. — mish **feh**-him [**fah**-ma] . — لم أفهم

Please speak slowly. — kal-**lim**-nee bir-**raa**-Ha — أرجو ان
min **faD**-lak. — تتكلم على مهلك

I speak a little Arabic. bat-**kal**-lim ^ca-ra-bee **shway**-ya. — اتكلم العربية قليلا

■ Egyptian Arabic ■ ^ca-ra-bee **maS**-ree اللهجة المصرية

What's — in Arabic? **tib**-"a 'eyh — bil-^ca-ra-bee? — ماهو — بالعربية؟

Please could you
help me? — min-**faD**-lak, **mum**-kin من فضلك،
ti-sa-^c**id**-nee? — هل يمكن ان تساعدني ؟

| Please show me the phrase in the book. | min **faD**-lak, war-**ree**-nee il-**gum**-la fil-ki-**tehb**. | من فضلك أشر إلى الجملة في الكتاب |
| Please write it down. | ik-tib-**hoo**-lee, min **faD**-lak. | اكتبه لي، من فضلك |

PROBLEMS

Go away!	**im**-shee!	امش!
Leave me alone.	**sib**-nee fi **Heh**-lee.	اتركني
Behave yourself.	ᶜeyb, iH-**ti**-rim **naf**-sak.	احترم نفسك
Please help me.	min **faD**-lak, sa-ᶜ**id**-nee.	أرجو أن تساعدني
I'm lost.	**a**-na tuht.	ضللت الطريق، تهت
Nonsense.	ka **lehm** feh-righ!	كلام فارغ!
I'll get the police.	ha-**gib**-lak il-bu-**leeS**.	ساطلب لك البوليس

SOME USEFUL ADJECTIVES

good, nice	**kway**-yis, **Tay**-yib	جيد، طيب
beautiful	Hilw, ga-**meel**	حلو، جميل
bad, ugly	**wi**-Hish	سيء

awful	*fa-Zee^c*	فظيع
expensive	**gheh**-lee	غالي
cheap	ri-**kheeS**	رخيص
old (people)	ki-**beer**	كبير
(things)	"a-**deem**	قديم
new	gi-**deed**	جديد
young, small	Su-**ghay**-yar	صغير
big	ki-**beer**	كبير
noisy	daw-**sha**-gee	صخاب
quiet	**heh**-dee	هادىء
full	mal-**yehn**	ملء
empty	**faa**-Dee, **feh**-righ	فارغ
long, tall	Ta-**weel**	طويل
short	"u-**Say**-yar	قصير
thirsty	^caT-**shaan**	عطشان
hungry	ga-^c**ehn**	جوعان، جائع
tired	ta^c-**behn**	متعب
ill	^cay-**yehn**, ma-**reeD**	مريض
angry, upset	za^c-**lehn**	غاضب
happy, pleased	mab-**SooT**	مبسوط
kind	**Tay**-yib, la-**Teef**	طيب، لطيف

generous	ka-**reem**	كريم
mean	ba-**kheel**	بخيل
easy	sahl	سهل
difficult	Sa⁣ᶜb	صعب
correct	maZ-**booT**	تمام ، مضبوط
incorrect	mish maZ-**booT**	غير مضبوط
early	**bad**-ree	باكر
late	**wakh**-ree, mu-ta-'**akh**-khir	متأخر

NUMBERS

0	Sifr	٠
1	**weh**-Hid	١
2	it-**neyn**	٢
3	ta-**leh**-ta	٣
4	ar-**ba**-ᶜa	٤
5	**kham**-sa	٥
6	**sit**-ta	٦
7	**sab**-ᶜa	٧
8	ta-**man**-ya	٨
9	**tis**-ᶜa	٩
10	ᶜ**a**-sha-ra	١٠

11	*Hi-**daa**-shar*	١١
12	*it-**naa**-shar*	١٢
13	*ta-lat-**taa**-shar*	١٣
14	*ar-ba^c-**taa**-shar*	١٤
15	*kha-mas-**taa**-shar*	١٥
16	*sit-**taa**-shar*	١٦
17	*sa-ba^c-**taa**-shar*	١٧
18	*ta-man-**taa**-shar*	١٨
19	*ti-sa^c-**taa**-shar*	١٩
20	*^cish-**reen***	٢٠
21	***weh**-Hid wi ^cish-**reen***	٢١
22	*it-**neyn** wi ^cish-**reen***	٢٢
etc. . . .		
30	*ta-la-**teen***	٣٠
40	*ar-bi-^c**een***	٤٠
50	*kham-**seen***	٥٠
60	*sit-**teen***	٦٠
70	*sab-^c**een***	٧٠
80	*ta-man-**yeen***	٨٠
90	*tis-^c**een***	٩٠
100	***mee**-ya*	١٠٠
200	*mee-**teyn***	٢٠٠

300	*tul-tu-**mee**-ya*	٣٠٠
400	*rub-ᶜu-**mee**-ya*	٤٠٠
500	*khum-su-**mee**-ya*	٥٠٠
600	*sut-tu-**mee**-ya*	٦٠٠
700	*sub-ᶜu-**mee**-ya*	٧٠٠
800	*tum-nu-**mee**-ya*	٨٠٠
900	*tus-ᶜu-**mee**-ya*	٩٠٠
1000	*'alf*	١٠٠٠
2000	*'al-**føyn***	٢٠٠٠
3000	***ta**-lat a-**lehf***	٣٠٠٠
4000	***ar**-baᶜ ta-**lehf***	٤٠٠٠
5000	***kha**-mas ta-**lehf***	٥٠٠٠
6000	*sitt a-**lehf***	٦٠٠٠
7000	***sa**-baᶜ ta-**lehf***	٧٠٠٠
8000	***ta** man ta-**lehf***	٨٠٠٠
9000	***ti**-saᶜ ta-**lehf***	٩٠٠٠
10,000	*ᶜ**a**-shar ta-**lehf***	١٠٠٠٠
100,000	*meet 'alf*	١٠٠٠٠٠
1,000,000	*mil-**yohn***	١٠٠٠٠٠٠

WHEN YOU ARRIVE

Visitors will need a visa for most Arab countries; these are sometimes obtainable at the point of entry; but it is usually simpler to get them before you leave. If you are touring the Middle East, and expect to come back to the same country, check on the possibility of getting a multiple-entry visa, and also whether you will need an exit visa.

PASSPORT CONTROL

My name is—.	'is-mee —.	اسمي —
I'm <u>American</u>	a-na am-ree-**keh**-nee [am-ree-keh-**nee**-ya] .	أنا امريكي [امريكية]
■ British	■ bri-**Taa**-nee [bri-Taa-**nee**-ya]	بريطاني [بريطانية]
■ Canadian	■ **ka**-na-dee [ka-na-**dee**-ya]	كندي [كندية]
■ Australian	■ os-**traa**-lee [os-tra-**lee**-ya]	استرالي [استرالية]
My address is —.	ᶜin-**weh**-nee —.	عنواني —
I'm staying at —.	a-na **neh**-zil [**naz**-la] fi —.	أنا أقيم ب —
Here are (is) —.	it-**faD**-Dal —.	تفضل —
■ my documents	■ il-'aw-**reh**"	أوراقي
■ my passport	■ il-bas-**boor**/ ga-**wehz** is-sa-far	جواز سفري

■ my identification card   ■ *bi-**Ta**"-ti ish-shakh-**See**-ya*   بطاقتي الشخصية

■ my embarkation card   ■ *il-**bor**-ding kard*   بطاقة الصعود

■ my disembarka-tion card   ■ *kart il-wu-**Sool***   بطاقة الوصول

I'm (traveling) —.   *da **sa**-far —.*   انا مسافر [مسافرة]

■ on business   ■ *shughl*   في عمل

■ on vacation   ■ *'a-**geh**-za*   في عطلة، اجازة

I'll be staying —.   ***ha**"-ᶜud —.*   سأبقى —

■ a few days   ■ ***ka**-za yohm*   عدة أيام

■ a week   ■ *'is-**boo**ᶜ*   اسبوع

■ two weeks   ■ *'is-boo-ᶜ**eyn***   أسبوعين

■ a month   ■ *shahr*   شهر

■ two months   ■ *shah-**reyn***   شهرين

I'm traveling <u>alone</u>   ***a**-na mi-**seh**-fir [mi-**saf**-ra] li **waH**-dee.*   انا اسافر وحدي

■ with my family   ■ *ma-ᶜa ᶜ**eyl**-tee/ 'us-**ri**-tee*   مع اسرتي

■ with my wife   ■ *ma-ᶜa m-**raa**-tee/ **zohg**-tee*   مع زوجتي

■ with my husband   ■ *ma-ᶜa **goh**-zee*   مع زوجي

BAGGAGE AND PORTERS

Where is the baggage claim?	il-*ᶜafsh* **feyn**?	اين مكان إستلام الأمتعة؟
This bag (these bags) are mine.	ish-**shan**-Ta dee (ish-**shu**-naT dee) bi-**ta**ᶜ-tee.	هذه حقيبتي (حقائبي)
This is mine.	dee bi-**ta**ᶜ-tee.	هذه لي
Is there a baggage cart?	fee **trol**-lee?	هل توجد عربة امتعة؟
Is there a porter?	fee shay-**yehl**?	هل هناك شيال؟
Be careful!	**Heh**-sib!	احذر !
I'll carry that.	a-na ha-**sheel** da.	ساحمل هذه الحقيبة
I'm missing one bag.	fee **shan**-Ta na"-Sa.	فقدت حقيبة
I've lost my luggage.	Daaᶜ **min**-nee il ᶜ**afsh**.	فقدت امتعتي
How much do I owe you?	ᶜ**a**-wiz **kam**?	كم تريد؟
Thank-you.	**shuk**-ran.	شكراً
That's for you.	da ᶜa-la-**sheh**-nak.	تفضل، هذا لك

CUSTOMS

I have nothing to declare.	a-na fi Hu-**dood** il-mas-**mooH**.	انا في حدود المسموح

I have <u>one carton</u> of cigarettes.	*ma-ᶜeh-ya <u>khar-Too-shit</u> sa-geh-yir.* معي خرطوشة سجائر
■ two cartons	■ *khar-Toosh-teyn* خرطوشتين
I have one bottle <u>of whiskey</u>	*ma ᶜeh-ya "i-zeh-zit <u>wis-kee</u>.* معي زجاجة ويسكي
■ of wine	■ *ni-beet* نبيذ
■ of perfume	■ *ᶜiTr* عطر
I have nothing else.	*ma ma-ᶜeesh Ha-ga tan-ya.* لا يوجد معي شيء آخر
These are gifts.	*dee ha-deh-ya.* هذه هدايا
They are for my personal use.	*dee li-'is-tiᶜ-meh-lee ish-shakh-See.* إنها لاستعمالي الشخصي
It isn't new.	*dee mish gi-dee-da.* إنها ليست جديدة
Do I have to pay duty?	*leh-zim ad-faᶜ ga-meh-rik?* هل يجب ان ادفع ضريبة؟
Where do I pay?	*ad-faᶜ feyn?* اين ادفع؟
Can I pay with dollars?	*mum-kin ad-faᶜ bid-do-laar?* هل يمكن ان ادفع بالدولار؟

Bureaucracy

Dealings with government officials over visas, customs clearance, residence permits, and so on may be slow and frustrating. Showing impatience and irritation usually has an adverse effect, however. Try to get the official(s) on your side by a warm and friendly but courteous approach.

Make use of any contact you have in the office or Ministry, however tenuous. Ideally, go with someone who is familiar with the procedures involved. If a particular bureaucratic process is known to take forever, take along a stack of post-cards to write or a book to read.

OTHER AIRPORT INFORMATION

Can I book a hotel room from here?	*mum-kin **aH**-giz 'oh-Da/ **ghur**-fa min **hi**-na?*	هل استطيع حجز غرفة بفندق من هنا؟
Is there a post office in the airport?	*fee **mak**-tab ba-**reed** fil-ma-**Taar**?*	هل يوجد مكتب بريد في المطار؟
Is there a bank open?	*fee bank **feh**-tiH?*	هل يوجد بنك مفتوح؟
Can I make a phone call from here?	*mum-kin a^c-mil ti-li-**fohn** min **hi**-na?*	هل استطيع إجراء مكالمة من هنا؟
Where can I rent a car?	*mi-**neyn** a-'**ag**-gar ^ca-ra-**bee**-ya/ say-**yaa**-ra?*	من أين أستطيع إستئجار سيارة؟

GETTING INTO TOWN

Where can I get a taxi?	*a-**leh**-"ee **tak**-see feyn?*	أين أجد تاكسي؟
Is there a meter?	*fee ^cad-**dehd**?*	هل يوجد عداد؟

Is there a bus into town?	*fee 'u-tu-bees li wiST il-ba-lad?*	هل يوجد أوتوبيس لوسط المدينة؟
Where is the stop?	*il-ma-HaT-Ta feyn?*	أين المحطة؟
When does it leave?	*bi-yiT-laᶜ 'im-ta?*	متى يرحل؟
How much will it cost?	*ha-yeh-khud kam?*	كم الأجرة؟
How long does it take?	*ir-riH-la bi-teh-khud "ad-di 'eyh?*	ما مدة الرحلة؟
I want to go to the — Hotel.	*ᶜa-wiz [ᶜaw-za] a-rooH 'u-teel —.*	أريد الذهاب، إلى فندق —
I want to go to this address.	*ᶜa-wiz [ᶜaw-zu] a-rooH il-ᶜin-wehn da.*	أريد الذهاب إلى هذا العنوان
I am with a group.	*a-na ma-ᶜa mag-moo-ᶜa.*	أنا مع مجموعة

BANKING AND MONEY MATTERS

The basic currencies in the major Arab countries are as follows:

dinar (*dee-naar*):Iraq, Algeria, Tunisia, Jordan, Libya, Bahrain, South Yemen, and Kuwait.

riyal (*ree-yehl*):Saudi Arabia, N.Yemen, Oman, Qatar.

gineh (*gi-ney*):Egypt and the Sudan.

lira (*lee-ra*):Syria and the Lebanon.

dirham (*dir-ham*):Morocco and the United Arab Emirates.

These are, of course, all independent currencies. They are all further divided into a hundred units. In Egypt a **gineh** is made up of 100 **piastres** (*"irsh*),which is also the smaller unit of currency in the Lebanon. Sometimes the smaller unit is further divided; in Egypt one piastre is worth 10 **millimes** (*mil-leem*). In Jordan there are 1000 **fils** (*fils*) to the dinar.

Sometimes paper money is used for very small denominations, being worth as little as a few cents.

Check on currency regulations before you leave; often there are restrictions on taking local currency out of the country. It may be necessary to prove you have spent a certain amount during your stay, so keep receipts of all exchange transactions. In Egypt a fixed sum has to be exchanged on entry into the country and, confusingly, more than one "official rate" exists. It pays to do some homework before you leave!

bank	*bank*	بنك
branch	*far ᶜ*	فرع
exchange	*taH-weel, Sarf*	تحويل، صرف
When do you <u>open</u>?	*bi-tif-**ta**-Hoo 'im-ta?*	متى تفتحون؟

■ close?	■ bi-tiⁿ-**fi**-loo?	تغلقون ؟
bank clerk	mu-**waZ**-Zaf Hi-sa-**beht**	
		موظف حسابات
cashier	Sar-**raaf**	صراف
window, counter	shib-**behk**	شباك
check (checks)	sheek (shee-**keht**)	شيك (شيكات)
checkbook	**daf**-tar shee-**keht**	دفتر شيكات
amount	**mab**-lagh	مبلغ
Please give me a receipt.	id-**dee**-nee waSl min **faD**-lak [min **faD**-lik]	اعطني إيصالا من فضلك
I'd like to open —.	‘a-wiz af-taH —.	اريد ان افتح — .
■ a current account	■ Hi-**sehb** geh-**ree**	حساب جاري
■ a deposit account	■ Hi-**sehb** wa-**dee**-‘a	حساب وديعة
What is the interest rate?	si‘r il-**fay**-da kam?	كم سعر الفائدة؟
(About) five percent	(Ha-**weh**-lee) **kham**-sa fil-**mee**-ya	(تقريبا) خمسة بالمئة
■ ten	■ ‘a-sha-ra	عشرة
I want to rent a safe.	‘a-wiz [‘aw-za] a-’ **ag**-gar **khaz**-na.	اريد استئجار خزنة

I'd like to see the manager, please.	‘a-wiz [‘aw-za] a-shoof il-mu-deer, min faD-lak.

أريد أن أرى المدير، من فضلك

(For more banking and commercial terms see the mini business dictionary, page 186)

EXCHANGING MONEY

Is there <u>a bank</u> near here?	fee <u>bank</u> "u-ray-yib min hi-na?

هل يوجد بنك قريب؟

■ a money exchange	■ mak-tab Sarf	مكتب صرافة

Where is the American Express office?	feyn mak-tab il-a-me-ri-kan eks-pres?

أين مكتب اميريكان إكسبريس؟

Can I change —?	mum-kin a-ghay-yar —?

هل يمكن أن أغير —

■ cash	■ fi-loos na"d	نقد
■ dollars	■ do-laa-raat	دولارات
■ travelers' checks	■ shee-keht si-yeh-Hee-ya	شيكات سياحية

Can I cash a personal check?	mum-kin aS-raf sheek khaaS?

هل يمكنني صرف شيك خاص؟

I have a credit card.	‘an-dee kri-dit kard.

عندي بطاقة إعتماد، كريدت كارد

What's the <u>dollar</u> exchange rate?	*kam si^cr id-do-laar?*	كم سعر الدولار؟
◾ sterling	◾ *il-'is-tir-lee-nee*	الاسترليني
Is that the official rate?	*da is-si^cr ir-ras-mee?*	هل هذا السعر رسمي؟
Is there a black market rate?	*fee si^cr soo" soo-da?*	هل يوجد سعر سوق سوداء؟
Do I fill out a form?	*leh-zim am-la 'is-ti-maa-ra?*	هل يجب ان املا استمارة؟
Where do I sign?	*am-Dee feyn?*	اين امضي؟
Here's my passport.	*it-faD-Dal il-bas-boor/ga-wehz is-sa-far.*	تفضل ها هو جواز السفر
I'd like to change <u>100</u> dollars.	*^ca-wiz a-ghay-yar <u>meet</u> do-laar.*	اريد تحويل ١٠٠ دولار
◾ 200	◾ *mee-teyn*	٢٠٠
◾ 300	◾ *tul-tu-meet*	٣٠٠
◾ 400	◾ *rub-^cu-meet*	٤٠٠
◾ 500	◾ *khum-su-meet*	٥٠٠
◾ 600	◾ *sut-tu-meet*	٦٠٠
◾ 700	◾ *sub-^cu-meet*	٧٠٠
◾ 800	◾ *tum-nu-meet*	٨٠٠
◾ 900	◾ *tus-^cu-meet*	٩٠٠
◾ 1000	◾ *'alf*	١٠٠٠

■ into local currency　■ lil-ᶜ**um**-la l-ma-Hal-**lee**-ya

للعملة المحلية

Can you give me <u>small bills?</u>	**mum**-kin tid-**dee**-nee ' aw-**reh**" Su-ghay-**ya**-ra?	

هل تستطيع ان تعطني اوراق صغيرة ؟

■ large bills?　　　■ ' aw-**reh**" ki-**bee**-ra?　　اوراق كبرة

■ some small change?　　　■ **fak**-ka?　　　فكة

(See page 17 for numbers.)

AT THE HOTEL

In the major cities the usual international hotels are to be found, at international prices. More interesting places to stay are the few remaining grand hotels of a more leisurely era, such as the Cecil in Alexandria and the Old Cataract in Aswan. But with the help of the local tourist office you can find a room in any price range; generally speaking, you will get what you pay for.

CHECKING IN

Do you have a room? *ᶜan-du-kum 'oh-Da/ghur-fa?*

هل عندكم غرفة؟

I have a reservation. *ᶜan-dee Hagz.* حجزت

I have no reservation. *ma-ᶜan-deesh Hagz.* لم احجز

I'd like a
  single room.
*ᶜa-wiz [ᶜaw-za] 'oh-Da/ghur-fa
bi si-reer weh-Hid.* اريد غرفة مفردة

I'd like a
  double room.
*ᶜa-wiz [ᶜaw-za] 'oh-Da/ghur-fa
lit-neyn.* اريد غرفة مزدوجة

I'd like a room
  with twin beds.
*ᶜa-wiz [ᶜaw-za] 'oh-Da
bi si-ree-reyn .* اريد غرفة بسريرين

■ with a shower ■ *fee-ha dush* بها دش

■ with a bathroom ■ *bi Ham-mehm* بحمام

■ with a TV ■ *fee-ha ti-li-viz-yohn* بها تليفزيون

■ with a refrigerator ■ *fee-ha tal-leh-ga* بها برادة/ ثلاجة

■ with a balcony ■ *fee bal-koh-na* لها بلكون/ شرفة

■ with air
conditioning

■ *fee-ha tak-yeef
ha-wa*

بها مكيف هواء

■ with hot water

■ *fee-ha may-ya
sukh-na*

بها ماء ساخن

■ with a good view

■ *min-ha man-Zar
ga-meel*

مطلة على منظر جميل

■ (not) facing
the street

■ *(mish) ᶜa-la-sh-sheh-riᶜ*

(غير) مطلة على الشارع

■ facing the garden

■ *ᶜa-la
g-gi-ney-na*

مطلة على الحديقة

■ on the sea

■ *ᶜa-la l-baHr*

على البحر

Can you try another
hotel for me?

*mum-kin ti-shuf-lee
'u-teel teh-nee?*

هل تستطيع ان تجد
لي فندقا آخرا؟

May I see the room?

*mum-kin a-shoof
il-'oh-Da/il-ghur-fa?*

اريد ان ارى
الغرفة

I like it.

ᶜa-ga-bit-nee.

تعجبني

I don't like it.

ma ᶜa-ga-bit-neesh.

لا تعجبني

Can I see another?

*mum-kin a-shoof
'oh-Da tan-ya?*

هل استطيع ان ارى
غرفة اخرى؟

■ larger

■ *'aw-saᶜ*

أوسع

■ smaller

■ *'aS-ghar*

أصغر

■ quieter

■ *'ah-da*

اهدأ

■ cheaper	■ *'ar-khaS*	أرخص
■ better	■ *'aH-san*	أفضل

This is nice.	*dee kway-yi-sa.*	هذه جيدة
I'll take it.	*ha-khud ha.*	سآخذها
What floor is it on?	*dee fee an-hee dohr?*	في اي طابق هي؟
Is there an elevator?	*fee 'a-san-Seer?*	

هل يوجد مصعد / أسنسير؟

What's the rate?	*il-'oh-Da bi kam?*	كم السعر؟
Does it include <u>service?</u>	*da <u>bil-khid</u>-ma?*	

هل يشمل الخدمة؟

■ taxes	■ *biD-Da-raa-yib*	الضرائب
■ breakfast	■ *bil-fi-Taar*	الافطار

How much is <u>bed and breakfast</u>?	*bi kam il-'oh-Da bil-fi-Taar?*	كم السعر بالافطار؟
■ full board (3 meals)	■ *bil-'akl*	للاقامة الكاملة

Is there a reduction for children?	*fee tukh-feeD lil-'aT-faal?*	هل يوجد تخفيض للاطفال؟

Can you put another bed in the room?	**mum**-kin ti-**HuTT** si-reer **tch** nee fil-'oh-Da?	

هل تستطيع وضع سرير آخر في الغرفة؟

I will stay <u>one night</u>.	*ha"-ᶜud <u>ley-la waH</u>-da.*	

سابقى ليلة واحدة

two nights	leyl-**teyn**	ليلتين
a few days	**ka**-za yohm	عدة أيام
a week	'is-**boo**ᶜ	اسبوع
two weeks	'is-boo-ᶜ**eyn**	اسبوعين

I don't know exactly how long.

maᶜ-**rafsh** "ad-di 'eyh biZ-**ZabT**

لا اعرف المدة بالضبط

BREAKFAST

I'd like breakfast in the room.

ᶜa-wiz [ᶜaw-za] il-fi-**Taar** fil-'**oh**-Da.

اريد الافطار بالغرفة

| for one | li **weh**-Hid | لشخص واحد |
| for two | li 'it-**neyn** | لشخصين |

Please send up —.

min **faD**-lak **gib**-lee —.

ارجو ان ترسل —.

coffee	"**ah**-wa	قهوة
tea	shayy	شاي
toast	tust	خبز محمص، توست
(with jam/honey)	(bil-mi-**rab**-ba/bil-ᶜ**a**-sal)	(بالمربى / بالعسل)
fruit juice	ᶜa-**Seer**	عصير فاكهة
eggs	beyD	بيض
(scrambled/fried/boiled)	(maD-**roob**/**ma**"-lee/mas-**loo**")	(مضروب / مقلي / مسلوق)

■ an English language newspaper ■ *ga-ree-da in-gi-lee-zee* جريدة باللغة الانجليزية

HOTEL SERVICES

Where is the elevator?	*feyn il-'a-san-Seer?*	اين المصعد/الاسنسير؟
■ the bathroom	■ *it-twa-litt*	التواليت
■ the restaurant	■ *il-maT-ᶜam*	المطعم
■ the phone	■ *it-ti-li-fohn*	التليفون
■ the bar	■ *il-baar*	البار
■ the swimming pool	■ *Ham-mehm is-si-beh-Ha*	حمام السباحة
I need a chambermaid.	*ᶜa-wis [ᶜaw-za] shagh-gheh-la.*	احتاج لخادمة الغرفة
■ a bellboy	■ *far-raash*	لفراش
■ a hair dryer	■ *sish-waar*	لمجفف شعر
■ a reading lamp	■ *a-ba joo-ra*	لمصباح للقراءة
The room is dirty.	*il-'oh-Da wis-kha.*	الغرفة قذرة
There are mosquitoes.	*fee na-moos.*	يوجد ناموس
Please spray the room.	*rush-shi-lee l-'oh-Da min faD-lak.*	ارجو ان ترش الغرفة

Please bring me <u>towels</u>.	*min **faD**-lak **gib**-lee **fo**-waT*.	أرجو ان تحضر لي مناشف، فوط
■ soap	■ *Sa-**boon***	صابون
■ a pillow	■ *mi-**khad**-da*	مخدة
■ a blanket	■ *baT-Ta-**nee**-ya*	بطانية
■ ice	■ *talg*	ثلج
■ mineral water	■ ***may**-ya ma^c-da-**nee**-ya*	مياه معدنية
■ hangers	■ *sham-ma-^ceht*	شماعات
■ toilet paper	■ ***wa**-ra" twa-**litt***	ورق تواليت
■ an adaptor	■ *mu-**Haw**-wil*	محول
■ a light bulb	■ ***lam**-ba*	لمبة
■ (bath) plug	■ *sad-**deh**-da*	سدادة
■ (electric) plug	■ ***fee**-sha*	فيشة
Just a minute!	***laH**-Za waH-da!*	لحظة واحدة!
Come in!	***ud**-khul!*	ادخل!
Thank you. Put it here.	*shuk-ran. **HuT**-Too **hi**-na.*	شكراً. ضعها هنا
Please put a board under the mattress.	*min **faD**-lak HuTT **lohH** taHt il-mar-**ta**-ba.*	احتاج للوح تحت المرتبة
There is no <u>(hot) water</u>.	*ma-**feesh may**-ya (**sukh**-na).*	لا يوجد ماء ساخن
■ electricity	■ *kah-**ra**-ba*	كهرباء

The <u>air conditioning</u> isn't working.	it-tak-**yeef**^caT-**laan**.	لا يعمل التكيف
▪ toilet	▪ it-twa-**litt**	التواليت
▪ fan	▪ il-mar-**wa**-Ha	المروحة
▪ faucet	▪ il-Ha-na-**fee**-ya	الصنبور/الحنفية
▪ light	▪ in-**noor**	النور
▪ radio	▪ ir-**ra**-dyo	الراديو
▪ TV	▪ it-ti-li-viz-**yohn**	التليفزيون

Can you fix it <u>soon</u>?   **mum**-kin ti-Sal-la-Hoo bi-**sur**-^ca?

هل تستطيع إصلاحه سريعا؟

| ▪ at once | ▪ **faw**-ran | فوراً |

Can you open this?   **mum**-kin tif-**taH**-lee da?

هل تستطيع فتح هذا لي؟

I have lost my key.   il-muf-**tehH** Daa^c **min**-nee.

ضاع المفتاح مني

This is to be <u>laundered</u>.   da lil-gha-**seel**.

هذا للغسيل

| ▪ pressed | ▪ lil-**mak**-wa | للكي |
| ▪ cleaned | ▪ lit-tun-**Deef** in **nah**-shif | للتنظيف الجاف |

When will it be ready?   hay-**koon geh**-hiz 'im-ta?

متى سيكون جاهزاً؟

This isn't mine.   dee mish bi-**ta**^c-tee.

هذا ليس لي

Are there any <u>messages</u> for me?	*fee ri-**seh**-la ᶜa-**sheh**-nee?*	هل هناك رسائل لي؟
■ letters	■ *ga-wa-**beht***	خطابات
■ packages	■ *Tu-**rood***	طرود
Can you make a phone call for me?	***mum**-kin tuT-**lub**-lee ti-li-**fohn**?*	هل تستطيع ان تطلب مكالمة لي؟
I want to speak to <u>Mr. —</u>.	*ᶜa-**wiz** [ᶜaw-za-] a-**kal**-lim is-**say**-yid—.*	اريد ان اتكلم مع السيد —
■ to Mrs. —.	■ *ma-**dehm** —.*	السيدة —
Please give me an outside line.	*id-**dee**-nee il-**khaTT** min **faD**-lak.*	ارجو ان تعطني خطاً خارجياً
Do you have a telex machine?	*ᶜan-**du**-kum ti-liks?*	هل عندكم جهاز تلكس ؟
I'd like to send a telex to —.	*ᶜa-**wiz** [ᶜaw-za] ab-ᶜat ti-liks li —.*	اريد ان ارسل تلكس لـ —
Call me when you have a reply.	*kal-**lim**-nee **lam**-ma y-**gee**-lak radd.*	اتصل بي عندما يصلك رد
I'd like to put this in your safe.	*ᶜa-**wiz** [ᶜaw-za] a-**HuTT** dee fil-**khaz**-na.*	اريد ان اضع هذا في الخزنة
I'd like my things from your safe.	*ᶜa-**wiz** [ᶜaw-za] 'eh-khud il-ha-**geht** bit-ta ᶜ-tee min il-**khaz**-na*	اريد اشيائي من الخزنة من فضلك

CHECKING OUT

I'm leaving <u>today</u>.	*a-na mi-seh-fir* [*mi-saf-ra*] *in-na-**haar**-da/il-**yohm***.	سأرحل اليوم
■ tomorrow (morning)	■ *buk-ra* (*iS-**SubH***)	غداً (صباحاً)
I'd like the bill, please.	*id-**dee**-nee il-Hi-sehb min **faD**-lak.*	أريد الحساب، من فضلك
My room number is —.	*il-'**oh**-Da **nim**-ra —.*	رقم غرفتي —
There seems to be a mistake.	*fee **gha**-laT.*	يبدو هناك خطأ
What is this amount for?	*il-**mab**-lagh **da** ᶜa-shehn 'eyh?*	لماذا هذا المبلغ؟
Please check it again.	*law sa-**maHt** reh-giᶜ ᶜa-**leyh** teh-nee.*	أرجوك راجعها ثانية
Can I leave my luggage here till <u>noon</u>?	*mum-kin a-seeb ish-shu-naT hi-na li Hadd iD-**Duhr**?*	هل استطيع ترك أمتعتي هنا حتى الظهر؟
■ evening	■ *il-mi-seh'*	المساء
Please have my luggage brought down.	*min **faD**-lak **naz**-zil ish-shu-naT.*	أرجوك انزل أمتعتي
I'm in a hurry.	*a-na mis-**taᶜ**-gil [mis-taᶜ-**gi**-la].*	انا مستعجل [مستعجلة]

Please call a cab.	*min **faD**-lak uT-**lub**-lee **tak**-see.*	
	أرجوك اطلب تاكسي	
I'm going to the airport.	*a-na **reh**-yiH [**ray**-Ha] il-ma-**Taar**.*	
	انا ذاهب الى المطار	

OTHER ACCOMMODATIONS

I want to rent <u>a house</u>.	*^ca-wiz [^c**aw**-za] a-' **ag**-gar **beyt**.*	اريد استئجار بيت
◼ an apartment	◼ *sha"-"a*	شقة
◼ an (un)furnished apartment	◼ *sha"-"a (mish) maf-**roo**-sha*	شقة (غير) مفروشة
◼ a furnished room	◼ *'oh-Da/**ghur**-fa maf-**roo**-sha*	غرفة مفروشة
◼ a houseboat	◼ *^caw-**weh**-ma*	عوامة
Do you know a good boarding house?	*ti^c-raf pin-si-**yohn** **kway**-yis?*	هل تعرف بنسيوناً جيداً ؟
Do you know a good real estate agent?	*ti^c-raf sim-**saar** kway-**yis**?*	هل تعرف سمساراً جيداً ؟
I need <u>one</u> (two) bedroom(s).	*^ca-wiz [^c**aw**-za] '**oh**-Dit ('**ohT**-teyn) nohm.*	اريد غرفة نوم (غرفتين نوم)
◼ a living room	◼ *'**oh**-Dit gu-**loos***	غرفة الجلوس
◼ a good bathroom	◼ *Ham-**mehm** **kway**-yis*	حمام جيد

How much is it <u>per week?</u>	*kam* <u>*fil-'is-**booᶜ**?*</u>	كم إيجارها في الأسبوع؟
■ per month	■ *fish-**shahr***	في الشهر
■ per year	■ *fis-**sa**-na*	في السنة
I'll be staying <u>two weeks.</u>	***ha"**-ᶜud* *'is-boo-**ᶜeyn***	سابقى أسبوعين
■ one month	■ *shahr*	شهر
■ two months	■ *shah-**reyn***	شهرين
■ (about) three months	■ *(Ha-**weh**-lee) ta-lat-**tush**-hur*	(حوالي) ثلاثة أشهر
Do you need a deposit?	*ᶜa-wiz ᶜar-boon?*	هل تحتاج لمقدم؟
Shall I pay in dollars?	***ad**-faᶜ bid-do-**laar?***	هل ادفع بالدولار؟
Do you take key money?	*bi-**teh**-khud khu-**luww?***	هل تريد وديعة/خلو؟
Can I use the kitchen?	***mum**-kin as-ta-**ᶜmil il-**maT**-bakh?*	هل استطيع إستعمال المطبخ؟
Is there hot water?	*fee **may**-ya **sukh**-na?*	هل هناك ماء ساخن؟
Is there a youth hostel in town?	*fee beyt sha-**behb** fil-**ba**-lad?*	هل هناك بيت شباب في المدينة؟
Can I park the car here?	***mum**-kin **ar**-kin il-ᶜa-ra-**bee**-ya **hi**-na?*	هل استطيع ترك السيارة هنا؟

Can I leave it
here overnight?

***mum*-kin a-bay-*yit*-ha *hi*-na?**

هل استطيع ترك السيارة هنا ليلا ؟

THE BAWWAB

If you stay in an apartment building for any length of time you will discover the live-in doorkeeper (the *baw-wehb*) who is in charge of the overall security and daily maintenance of the building. It is important to establish good relations with this key individual; if willing, he can prove invaluable by taking and passing on messages, running small errands, acting as a go-between with local tradespeople and repairmen, and so forth.

You will contribute to his official monthly salary, but he should be tipped modestly for any extra services he performs. Find out from the neighbors what sums are appropriate. (Note: Foreigners are usually expected to be more generous than locals!) If you are on good terms, he can also be a fascinating source of gossip about the building and the area generally.

TIPPING

The usual rules for tipping apply in Arab hotels and restaurants as well. It is not customary in most Arab countries to tip taxi drivers, although it is increasingly expected of foreigners, and is certainly appreciated!

In the poorer Arab countries you sometimes find people anxious to perform small services for you: find a cab, carry your bag, clean your windshield. It is often less hassle to accept this with a good grace than to fend people off continually. Keep a supply of small change for the purpose.

In the major tourist centers — in countries like Morocco and Egypt — you will be approached by people wanting to act as a guide. If you decide the person has enough English — and useful local information — to be helpful, agree on a fee for his services in advance. Small boys can often be helpful in showing you out-of-the-way sites or guiding you back to civilization when you get lost. Again, it's often simpler to adopt one young "guide" at the outset; he will then repel rivals, and you will be left in relative peace.

If you are determined to go it alone, reply to overtures with a firm "No thank you," indicating that you have a guidebook and know where you are going. Above all, don't shout or get upset. Everyone has to earn a living. Judging when to tip can be a delicate matter, since people will often show great kindness and hospitality with no thought of reward. Then a small gift is much more acceptable than money, though you might persuade someone to accept the latter by insisting it's "for the children" (*ᶜa-shehn il-'aw-lehd*). Do it quietly and discreetly if possible.

GETTING AROUND TOWN

Taxis tend to be inexpensive (once you get to know the rates!), whereas buses are crowded and slow. Minibuses are faster because they fill up early on the route and don't stop to take on new passengers. In some of the larger cities streetcars still run.

Within some cities, and between most, there is a system of shared taxis. The intercity ones will leave from a specific part of town — often near the railway or bus station. The taxi will leave once it's full (if you're in a hurry, you can pay for the remaining seats).

Shared taxis in town either operate along fixed routes like buses, or, hopefully, you hail a passing cab with the name of the place you want to get to. If it's going in that general direction, you'll be taken on board. The big hotels often have their own limousine service, which is comfortable and efficient but naturally a good deal more expensive.

In some of the countries in the Gulf it's best to use a taxi agency, since the freelance taxi drivers may not have much idea of local geography. Ask the advice of someone who has lived in the town for some time.

Do you have a map of the city?	*ᶜan-dak kha-ree-Ta lil-ba-lad?*	هل عندكم خريطة للمدينة؟
Where is — ?	*— feyn?*	أين — ؟
How far is — ?	*— ᶜa-la buᶜd "ad-di ' eyh?*	كم تبعد — ؟
■ the bus station	■ *maw-"af il-'u-tu-bee-seht*	محطة الاوتوبيس
■ the railway station	■ *ma-HaT-Tit is-sik-ka l-Ha-deed*	محطة القطار

■ the airport bus terminal	■ *maw-"af'u-tu-bees* il-ma-**Taar** موقف أوتوبيس المطار
■ the museum	■ il-**mat**-Haf المتحف
■ Qasr ElNil Street	■ *sheh-ri*^c *"aSr in-neel* شارع قصر النيل
■ Tahrir Square	■ *mi-**dehn** it-taH-**reer** ميدان التحرير

I want to take
a cab to —.

^ca-wiz [^caw-za] 'eh-khud
tak-see li —. أريد أن آخذ تاكسي إلى —

I want to go to —.

^ca-wiz [^caw-za] a-rooH —.
أريد الذهاب إلى —

Can I take a
bus from here?

mum-kin 'eh-khud 'u-tu-bees
min hi-na?
هل استطيع أن آخذ الاوتوبيس من هنا؟

Which number
is the bus?

'u-tu-bees nim-ra kam?
ما هو رقم الاوتوبيس؟

Can I go on foot?

mum-kin am-shee-ha?
هل استطيع الذهاب سيراً؟

Is it far from here? *da bi-^ceed ^can hi-na?* هل هو بعيد؟

How much
will it cost?

hay-kal-lif kam? كم ستكلف؟

Do you have
a meter?

^can-dak ^cad-dehd? هل عندك عداد؟

How much do you
charge per day?

bi-teh-khud kam fil-yohm?
كم الاجرة اليومية؟

I want to go and come back.	*ᶜa-wiz [ᶜaw-za] a-rooH war-gaᶜ*.	اريد الذهاب والعودة
Will you wait for me there?	*mum-kin tis-tan-neh-nee hi-nehk?*	هل ستنتظرني هناك؟
Slow down!	*ᶜa-la **mah-lak!***	قلل السرعة!
Please wait here a moment.	*is-**tan**-na hi-na shway-ya.*	من فضلك انتظر هنا لحظة
I'll be right back.	*har-gaᶜ Heh-lan.*	ساعود حالاً
Turn left here.	*Haw-wid shi-mehl hi-na*	الى اليسار هنا
■ right	■ *yi-meen*	الى اليمين
Straight on.	*dugh-ree.*	الى الامام
Stop here.	*'u-"af hi-na.*	قف هنا
I'll get out here.	*han-zil hi-na.*	سانزل هنا.
How much do I owe you?	*ᶜa-wiz kam?*	كم تريد؟
Thanks. That's for you.	*shuk-ran. da ᶜa-la-sheh-nak.*	شكراً. هذا لك
Please tell me where to get off.	*min faD-lak "ul-lee an-zil feyn.*	ارجوك قل لي اين انزل

SIGHTSEEING

Because the Arabic speaking countries span such a vast area, each offers different attractions to the traveler. In North Africa, Morocco and Tunisia have the most developed tourist industries. A holiday there can combine relaxing on superb beaches with visits to medieval walled cities and to ancient Greek and Roman sites, or trips into the dramatic Atlas mountains.

At the eastern end of the Mediterranean, in Syria, Jordan, and Lebanon, you will find some of the most spectacular monuments of the ancient world and of Islamic civilization, as well as marvelous swimming off the Mediterranean and Red Sea coasts. Though political turmoil in the area has discouraged foreign visitors, the intrepid traveler will be well rewarded. Not only will people be delighted to see you and want to show you the best of their country, you will be blissfully free of the hype and hassle that popular tourist centers tend to attract.

Egypt is understandably the Arab country best known to the foreign tourist. It has literally hundreds of miles of unspoiled beaches on its Mediterranean and Red Sea coasts; the coral reefs of the Red Sea and Sinai peninsula offer some of the best snorkeling and scuba diving in the world.

Most visitors with limited time to spend will want to concentrate on the great temples, pyramids, and tombs of the Nile valley. The daily flights from Cairo to Luxor and Aswan, and comfortable trains make it easy to stop off at lesser-known sites on route. Or you can travel one way by Nile steamer, the best of which retain an old-world elegance and charm.

Travel facilities in Egypt are being improved all the time, so that it is now possible to combine visits to the major Pharaonic monuments with trips to the chain of oases in the Western Desert and to Sinai in the east, where the famous Coptic monastery of St. Catherine stands at the foot of Mount Sinai. This *can* all be done in a couple of weeks, but it is much more rewarding to take a little longer, to rest up in a quiet corner, absorb your impressions of the country, and get to know the people.

The main tourist centers offer accommodations ranging from the absolutely basic to international five-star standard. In the oases and smaller coastal resorts accommodations will be inexpensive and simple, if not Spartan.

Where is the Tourist Office?	***mak**-tab is-si-**yeh**-Ha feyn?*	أين مكتب السياحة ؟
Do you have tourist information?	*^can-**du**-kum is-ti^c-la-**meht** si-yeh-**Hee**-ya?*	هل عندكم معلومات سياحية؟
Do you have a guidebook?	*^can-**du**-kum da-**leel** si-yeh-Hee?*	هل عندكم دليل سياحي؟
Are there tours of the city?	*fee riH-**leht** si-ya-**Hee**-ya fil-**ba**-lad?*	هل هناك جولات في المدينة ؟
When does the bus leave?	*bi-**yiT**-la^c 'im-ta il-'u-tu-**bees**?*	متى سيرحل الاوتوبيس؟
Where does it leave from?	*il-ma-**HaT**-Ta feyn?*	من أين سيرحل الاوتوبيس؟
How much does it cost?	*bee-**kal**-lif kam?*	كم تكلف؟
How long does it take?	*ha-**yeh**-khud kam seh-^ca?*	ما مدة الجولة؟
What are the main attractions?	*'eyh 'a-**hamm** il-'a-**meh**-kin is-si-yeh-**Hee**-ya?*	ما هي أهم الأماكن السياحية؟

I have only <u>one day.</u>	*^can-dee <u>yohm</u> bass*
	لم يبق لي إلا يوماً واحداً
■ two days	■ *yoh-meyn* يومين
■ three days	■ *ta-lat tee-yehm* ثلاثة أيام
■ one week	■ *'is-boo^c* أسبوع

I need a guide with good English.

^ca-wiz [^caw-za] da-leel bi-yit-kal-lim in-gi-lee-zee kway-yis.

احتاج لمرشد يتكلم الانجليزية بطلاقة

How much does he charge <u>per hour</u>?

hi-yeh khud kam fis-seh-^ca?

كم يطلب في الساعة؟

■ per day	■ *fil-yohm* في اليوم

I want to go to the <u>Islamic Museum.</u>

^ca-wiz [^caw-za] a-rooH il-mat-Haf il-is-leh-mee.

أريد أن أذهب الى المتحف الاسلامي

■ The Egyptian Museum	■ *il-mat-Haf il-maS-ree* المتحف المصري
■ Khan ElKhalili bazaar	■ *khan il-kha-lee-lee* خان الخليلي
■ the Azhar mosque	■ *geh-mi^c il-'az-har* جامع الأزهر
■ the Sultan Hasan mosque	■ *geh-mi^c is-sul-Taan Ha-san* جامع السلطان حسن
■ the Citadel	■ *il-"al-^ca* القلعة
■ the pyramids	■ *il-ha-ram* الهرم

■ the zoo	■ *gi-**ney**-nit il-Ha-ya-wa-**neht***	حديقة الحيوان
■ the market, bazaar	■ *is-**soo**"*	السوق
■ the old city	■ *il-ma-**dee**-na*	المدينة القديمة
■ Sakkara	■ *saq-**qaa**-ra*	سقارة
■ Fayyoum	■ *il-fay-**yoom***	الفيوم
■ the Valley of the Kings	■ ***weh**-di l-mu-**look***	وادي الملوك
■ the Temple of Luxor	■ ***ma**^c-bad **lu**"-Sur*	معبد الاقصر
■ the Temple of Hatshepsut	■ ***ma**^c-bad Hat-ship-**soot***	معبد الملكة حتشبسوت
■ Abu Simbel	■ *'a-boo **sim**-bil*	ابو سمبل
mosque	***geh**-mi^c*	جامع
monuments, antiquities	*il-'a-**saar***	الاثار
temple	***ma**^c-bad*	معبد
tomb	*maq-**ba**-ra*	مقبرة
Can I enter?	***mum**-kin **ad**-khul?*	هل يمكن ان ادخل؟
At what time does it open?	*bi-**yif**-taH is-**seh**-^ca kam?*	متى يفتح؟
When does it close?	*bi-**yi**"-fil is-**seh**-^ca kam?*	متى يغلق؟

Is it open every day?	*bi-**yif**-taH **kul**-li yohm?*	هل يفتح كل يوم؟
What is the admission price?	*'eyh si^cr id-du-**khool**?*	كم رسم الدخول؟
How much for children?	*bi kam lil-'aT-**faal**?*	كم رسم الدخول للاطفال؟
Do you know a good restaurant near here?	*ti^c-raf **maT**-^cam **kway**-yis "u-**ray**-yib min **hi**-na?*	هل تعرف مطعما جيدا قريبا من هنا؟
Is photography allowed?	*it-taS-**weer** mas-**mooH**?*	هل التصوير مسموح ؟
Do I need a permit?	***leh**-zim taS-**reeH**?*	هل احتاج لتصريح؟
I have a permit from the Ministry.	*ma-^c**eh**-ya taS-**reeH** min il-wi-**zaa**-ra*	معي تصريح من الوزارة
Let's rest and have a drink.	*nis-ta-**ray**-yaH wi **nish**-rab Ha-ga.*	فلنستريح ونشرب شيئا
Can you pick us up here in <u>one hour</u> exactly?	***mum**-kin tir-ga^c-**li**-na ba^cd **seh**-^ca biZ-**ZabT**?*	هل تستطيع ان ترجع لنا هنا بعد ساعة بالضبط ؟
▪ two hours	*sa^c-**teyn***	بعد ساعتين

MOSQUES

Some of the most beautiful and historic buildings to be found in the Middle East are mosques; you will certainly want to visit a number on your trip.

Attitudes toward non-Muslim visitors vary a good deal. Many famous mosques, such as Ibn Tulun and AlAzhar in Cairo, are recognized as national monuments as well as places of worship, and it is easy to visit them as long as you are suitably dressed. Often, however, visitors are not admitted to some parts of the mosque while prayers are in progress. Check whether photography is permitted (you may have to leave your camera at the door).

The mosque is the social as well as the religious center of the community; in the early days of Islam especially all important public announcements were made from the pulpit (**min**-bar). Schools (mad-**ra**-sas) have always been associated with mosques, primarily to teach the Koran but also reading, writing, and arithmetic. A feature of the **geh**-mi^c, or congregational mosque, is the large inner courtyard, where prayer or teaching may take place; this is usually absent from the smaller **mas**-gids, less monumental but often gems of Islamic architecture.

At the entrance to most mosques is a place to leave your shoes. Ask there whether it is all right to go in. Apart from removing your shoes, be sure you are properly dressed: shorts and halter tops are not acceptable. A skirt should cover the knee, and arms should be covered to the elbow. It is appreciated if women wear a headscarf.

Don't disturb anyone who is praying, and avoid walking between them and the **mih**-rab (niche) indicating the direction of Mecca. On leaving, you may want to put a contribution in the offerings box, which will go toward the upkeep of the mosque.

PLANNING A TRIP

TRAVEL BY AIR

When is there a flight <u>to Aswan</u>?	*Tay **yaa** rit '**aS waan** 'im-ta?*	متى تكون الرحلة إلى اسوان؟
◼ to Luxor	◼ *lu"-Sur*	إلى الاقصر
◼ to Sinai	◼ *see-na*	إلى سيناء
I'd like a single (one-way) ticket.	*ᶜa-wiz [ᶜaw-za] taz-ka-ra reh-yiH bass.*	اريد تذكرة ذهاب
◼ a return ticket	◼ *taz-ka-ra reh-yiH gayy*	تذكرة ذهاب وعودة
I want to <u>cancel</u> my reservation.	*ᶜa-wiz [ᶜaw-za] al-ghee il-Hagz*	اريد إلغاء الحجز
◼ confirm	◼ *a-'ak-kid*	تاكيد الحجز
When should I be at the airport?	*leh-zim a-koon fil-ma-Taar 'im-ta?*	متى يجب ان اكون بالمطار؟
I'd like a seat — .	*ᶜa-wiz [ᶜaw-za] kur-see — .*	اريد مقعدا —
◼ by the window	◼ *gamb ish-shib-behk*	بجانب الشباك
◼ on the aisle	◼ *ᶜal-ma-marr*	على الممر
◼ in the smoking (nonsmoking) section	◼ *fi man-Ti-"it il-mu-dakh-khi-neen (gheyr il-mu-dakh-khi-neen)*	في الجزء المخصص للمدخنين (لغير المدخنين)

Tourist class	*da*-ra-ga si-yeh-**Hee**-ya	درجة سياحية
First class	*da*-ra-ga '**oo**-la	درجة اولى
What is the fare?	bi **kam** it-taz-**ka**-ra?	بكم التذكرة؟
Can I pay by credit card?	**mum**-kin **ad**-fa^c bi **kri**-dit kard?	هل استطيع الدفع ببطاقة إعتماد؟
Is there an <u>earlier</u> flight?	fee ma-^cehd **bad**-ree shway-ya?	هل هناك رحلة قبل هذا الموعد؟
■ later	■ mit-'**akh**-khar	بعد هذا الموعد ■
Is there a daily flight?	fee Tay-**yaa**-ra **kul**-li yohm?	هل هناك رحلة يومية؟
When does it arrive?	bi-**tiw**-Sal '**im**-ta?	متى تصل؟
Where do I check my bags?	a-**sag**-gil ish-**shu**-naT feyn?	اين اسجل حقائبي؟
I have only hand luggage.	ma-^c**eh**-ya **shu**-naT yad bass.	ليس معي سوى حقائب يد
What gate do we leave from?	bi-**nu**-khrug min '**an**-hee behb?	من اي بوابة سنرحل؟

TRAVEL BY TRAIN AND BUS

Where is the ticket office?	shib-**behk** it-ta-**zeh**-kir feyn?	أين مكتب بيع التذاكر؟
May I see a schedule?	**mum**-kin a-**shoof gad**-wal il-ma-wa-^c**eed**?	هل استطيع ان ارى جدول المواعيد؟

When does the bus to Alexandria leave?	il-'u-tu-**bees** lis-kin-di-**ree**-ya bi-**yiT**-la^c '**im**-ta?	متى يرحل الاوتوبيس إلى الاسكندرية؟
▇ the train	▇ il-"**aTr**	القطار
Is there a student rate?	fee takh-**feeD** liT-**Ta**-la-ba?	هل يوجد تخفيض للطلبة؟
I have a student card.	ma-^c**eh**-ya kar-**ney** Taa-lib.	معي بطاقة طالب
Does it take the desert road?	bi-**yeh**-khud iT-**Ta**-ree" iS-SaH-**reh**-wee?	هل ياخذ الطريق الصحراوي؟
Does it stop en route?	bi-**yu**-"af fis-**sik**-ka?	هل يقف على الطريق؟
I'd like a seat at the front.	^c**u**-wiz [^c**aw**-za] **kur**-see "ud **dchm**.	اريد مقعدا في المقدمة
Are the seats numbered?	ik-ka-**reh**-see ^ca-**ley**-ha **ni**-mar?	هل المقاعد مرقمة؟
A first class ticket, please.	taz-**ka**-ra **da**-ra-ga-'**oo**-la, min **faD**-lak.	اريد تذكرة درجة اولى من فضلك
▇ second class	**da**-ra-ga **tan**-ya	درجة ثانية
Two tickets please.	taz-kar-**teyn**, min **faD**-lak.	تذكرتين من فضلك
Which platform?	ra-**Seef** nim-ra kam?	ما هو رقم الرصيف؟
I'd like a berth (couchette) to Luxor.	^c**a**-wiz [^c**aw**-za] ma-**kehn** fi ^ca-ra-**bee**-yit in-**nohm** li lu"-Sur.	اريد مكانا بعربة النوم إلى الاقصر

■ two berths (couchettes)	■ *ma-ka-**neyn***	مكانين
Is it air-conditioned?	*fee tak-**yeef**?*	هل هو مكيف الهواء؟
Where is the checked luggage office?	*feyn **mak**-tab il-'a-ma-**neht**?*	اين مكتب الامانات؟
Is this the train for Asyut?	*da"aTr 'as-**yooT**?*	هل هذا قطار اسيوط؟
■ the bus	■ *'u-tu-**bees***	أوتوبيس
Is there a dining car on the train?	*fee ᶜa-ra-**bee**-yit 'akl fil-"**aTr**?*	هل هناك عربة طعام في القطار؟
■ a buffet car	■ *bu-**feyh***	بفيه
What do you have to eat?	*ᶜan-dak 'ak-li 'eyh?*	ما هى أنواع الأكل عندكم؟
■ to drink	■ *mash-roo-**beht***	المشروبات
Is this seat taken?	*fee Hadd **hi**-na?*	هل هذا المقعد محجوز؟
Can I change to first class?	***mum**-kin a-ghay-**yar**-ha li **da**-ra-ga 'oo-la?*	هل استطيع أن اغير للدرجة الاولى؟
Where are we now?	***iH**-na **feyn** dil-**wa**"-tee?*	اين نحن الآن؟
What's the next stop?	*'eyh il-ma-**HaT**-Ta g-**gay**-ya?*	ما هي المحطة القادمة؟

TRAVEL BY BOAT

I'd like to
take a boat —.

ᶜa-wiz [ᶜaw-za] اريد ان آخذ سفينة
'eh-khud *mar*-kib — .

■ from Cairo
to Luxor

■ *min maSr li lu"-Sur*

من القاهرة للاقصر

■ from Luxor
to Aswan

■ *min lu"-Sur
li-'aS-waan*

من الاقصر لأسوان

I want to return
by air.

ᶜa-wiz [ᶜaw-za] اريد العودة بالطائرة
ar-gaᶜ biT-Tay-yaa-ra.

How long does
the cruise take?

ir-riH-la bi-teh-khud kam yohm?

ما مدة الرحلة؟

I'd like a cabin
<u>for one.</u>

ᶜa-wiz [ᶜaw-za] ka-bee-na اريد
li waH dee. حجرة/كابينة لشخص واحد.

■ for two people

■ *lit-neyn*

لشخصين

Does it have a
private bathroom?

fee-ha Ham-mehm khaSS?

هل لها حمام خاص؟

Where does it stop?

bi-tu-"af feyn?

اين تتوقف؟

Is there a <u>ferry</u>?

fee mi-ᶜad-dee-ya?

هل هناك عبارة/معدية ؟

■ hydrofoil

■ *hay-dro-feel*

هيدروفيل

What time do
we have to
be back on board?

leh-zim nir-gaᶜ lil-mar-kib متى يجب
is-seh-ᶜa kam? أن نعود إلى السفينة؟

I'd like to take a sailboat ride —.	^{c}a-wiz [^{c}aw-za] 'eh-khud fa-loo-ka — .	أريد أن اذهب في نزهة على مركب شراعي
■ around the island	■ Ha-wa-leyn ig-gi-zee-ra	■ حول الجزيرة
■ across the river	■ lin-naH-ya t-tan-ya	■ عبر النهر
■ for a couple of hours	■ li mud-dit sa^c-teyn	■ لمدة ساعتين
When will we get back?	ha-nir-ga^c 'im-ta?	متى سنعود؟
Is the wind right?	ir-reeH mu-nas-ba?	هل الرياح مناسبة؟

OTHER MODES OF TRANSPORT

Where does the river bus leave from?	feyn ma-HaT-Tit il-'u-tu-bees in-nah-ree?	أين محطة الاوتوبيس النهري؟
Can I take a streetcar/tram?	mum-kin 'eh-khud tur-maay?	هل استطيع أن آخذ الترام ؟
Can I take a microbus?	mum-kin 'eh-khud mee-kro-bus?	هل استطيع أن آخذ ميكروبس ؟
Can I hitchhike from here?	mum-kin ar-kab oh-toh-stop min hi-na?	هل استطيع ركوب سيارة مارة من على الطريق ؟

Could you give me a lift to —?	***mum***-kin ti-waS-***Sal***-nee li —?	هل تستطيع توصيلي إلى —؟
Where can I get a shared taxi to —?	mi-***neyn*** '***eh***-khud ***tak***-see mush-***ta***-rak li — ?	أين آخذ تاكسي مشترك (تاكسي بالنفر) إلى — ؟
I'd like to hire —.	ᶜ***a***-wiz [ᶜ***aw***-za] a-'***ag***-gar —.	أريد إستئجار —
▓ a motorbike/ scooter	▓ mo-to-***sikl***	دراجة بخارية
▓ a bicycle	▓ ᶜ***a***-ga-la	دراجة
▓ a horsedrawn carriage	▓ Han-***Toor***	حنطور
▓ a donkey	▓ Hu-***maar***	حمار
▓ a camel	▓ ***ga***-mal	جمل

ENTERTAINMENT AND DIVERSIONS

BEACH AND POOL

I love swimming.	*ba-**Hibb** il-ᶜohm.*	أحب السباحة
It's very hot.	*id-**dun**-ya Harr **gid**-dan.*	الجو حار جداً
Is there a swimming pool?	*fee Ham-**mehm** si-beh-Ha?*	هل يوجد حمام سباحة ؟
Is there a sandy beach?	*fee plehj raml?*	هل يوجد شاطىء رملي؟
The water's beautiful.	*il-**may**-ya **Hil**-wa **gid**-dan.*	المياه جميلة
Is it safe to swim?	*il-ᶜohm hi-na 'a-mehn?*	هل السباحة مأمونة هنا؟
Is it deep?	*il-**baHr** hi-na ᶜa-mee"?*	هل المياه عميقة هنا ؟
Are there sharks?	*fee "u-**roosh**?*	هل توجد أسماك القرش؟
I'd like to go scuba diving.	*ᶜa-wiz [ᶜaw-za] agh-Tas.*	أريد الغطس
Do they give diving lessons?	*fee du-**roos** ghaTs?*	هل هناك دروس غطس؟
I want to buy a mask.	*ᶜa-wiz [ᶜaw-za] ash-ti-ree naD-**Daa**-rit baHr.*	أريد شراء قناع

■ a snorkel	■ *payp*	انبوبة للتنفس تحت الماء
■ flippers	■ *za-ᶜeh-nif*	زعانف
■ suntan lotion	■ *kreym li Hi-meh-yit il-bash-ra*	
		كريم لحماية البشرة
■ sunglasses	■ *naD-Daa-rit shams*	نظارات شمس
■ a sunhat	■ *bur-ney-Tit shams*	قبعة شمس
■ a swimsuit	■ *ma-yoh*	لباس بحر/ مايوه
■ a beach towel	■ *foo-Tit baHr*	منشفة شاطئ
■ an inflatable mattress	■ *mar-ta-bit baHr*	مرتبة بحر

I want to go <u>waterskiing.</u>	*ᶜa-wiz [ᶜaw-za] at-zaH-laᵐᶜal-may-ya.*	
		اريد التزحلق على الماء
■ windsurfing	■ *aᶜ-mil wind-surf*	ركوب الامواج
How much is it an hour?	*bi kam fis-seh-ᶜa?*	كم في الساعة؟
I'd like to hire <u>an umbrella.</u>	*ᶜa-wiz [ᶜaw-za] a-'ag-gar sham see-ya.*	اريد إستئجار شمسية
■ a deck chair	■ *kur-see baHr*	كرسي شاطئ
■ a surfboard	■ *lohH ru-koob il-'am-wehg*	
		لوح ركوب الامواج
■ skin diving equipment	■ *'a-da-weht ghaTs*	أدوات الغوص

Is there a diving club?	*fee **neh**-dee ghaTs?*	هل يوجد نادي غوص ؟
shells	***Sa**-daf*	أصداف
coral	*mur-**gehn***	مرجان
coral reefs	***shu**-ʿab mur-ga-**nee**-ya*	شعب مرجانية
crabs	*a-boo ga-**lam**-boo, ka-**boor**-ya*	أبو جلمبو، سرطان البحر
sponges	*sa-**fing***	إسفنج
Is swimming forbidden?	*is-si-**beh**-Ha mam-**noo**-ʿa?*	هل السباحة ممنوعة؟
Will you keep an eye on my things?	***mum**-kin ti-**khal**-li **beh**-lak min il-Ha-**geht dee**?*	هل ترعى أشيائي؟
Is there a lifeguard?	*fee ghaT-**Taas**?*	هل هناك عامل إنقاذ / غطاس؟

SAILING AND FISHING

I'd like to hire a sailboat.	*ʿa-wiz [ʿaw-za] a-'ag-gar <u>mar-kib</u> <u>shi-raa-ʿee</u>.*	أريد إستئجار مركب شراعي
◼ a motorboat	◼ *lansh*	قارب بخاري
◼ a yacht	◼ *yakht*	يخت
I want to spend the whole day on the water.	*ʿa-wiz [ʿaw-za] a-"aD-Dee yohm keh-mil fil-baHr*	أريد قضاء يوماً كاملاً في البحر

Let's take a picnic.	**neh**-khud il-'**akl** ma-**ᶜeh**-na.	
		دعنا نقوم بنزهة
the Mediterranean	il-**baHr** il-'**ab**-yaD	
		البحر الأبيض المتوسط
the Red Sea	il-**baHr** il-'**aH**-mar	البحر الأحمر
the Atlantic	il-'**aT**-**lan**-Tee	المحيط الاطلنطي
the sea is very rough.	il-**baHr** **heh**-yig **gid**-dan.	
		البحر هائج جداً
▦ calm	▦ **heh**-dee	هادىء
I don't feel very well.	a-na **Heh**-sis [**Has**-sa] **in**-nee taᶜ-**behn** [taᶜ **boh**-na]	انا متعب
Let's head back to shore.	**nir**-gaᶜ lil-**barr**.	فلنرجع الى الشاطىء
Is there a boat race?	fee si-**beh**" ma-reh-kib?	هل هناك سباق مراكب؟
I'd like to go fishing — .	ᶜa-wiz [ᶜaw-za] aS-**Taad** — .	أريد الذهاب لصيد الأسماك — .
▦ with rod and line	▦ biS-Sin-**naa**-ra	بصنارة صيد
▦ with nets	▦ bish-**sha**-ba-ka	بالشباك
Can I come with you?	**mum**-kin a-**rooH** ma-ᶜeh-kum?	
		هل أستطيع الذهاب معكم ؟
What bait should I use?	as-**taᶜ**-mil Taᶜm 'eyh?	ما الطعم الذي ساستعمله؟

Did you have a good catch?	*iS-**Tad**-too **kway**-yis?*	هل وفقت في الصيد؟
What's the name of this fish?	*is-**sa**-mak da '**is**-moo 'eyh?*	ما اسم هذه السمكة؟

HUNTING

What do you hunt in this area?	*bi-tiS-**Taa**-doo 'eyh fil-man-**Ti**-"a dee?*	ماذا تصطادون في هذه المنطقة؟
I'd like to go hunting in the desert.	*ᶜa-wiz [ᶜaw-za] aS-**Taad** fiS-**SaH**-ra.*	أريد أن أصطاد في الصحراء
Can I rent <u>a shotgun</u>?	*mum-kin a-'**ag**-gar <u>bun-du-"ee-yit rashsh?</u>*	هل استطيع إستئجار <u>بندقية رش؟</u>
▪ a rifle	▪ *bun-du-"ee-yit Seed*	▪ بندقية صيد
Do I need a permit?	*leh-zim taS-reeH?*	هل أحتاج لتصريح؟
Are there <u>rabbits</u>?	*fee '**a-reh**-nib?*	هل هناك <u>ارانب</u> ؟
▪ partridges	▪ *Ha-gal*	▪ حجل
▪ pigeons	▪ *Ha-mehm*	▪ حمام
▪ deer	▪ *gha-zehl*	▪ غزال
▪ foxes	▪ *ta-ᶜeh-lib*	▪ ثعالب
Do you go hunting with hawks?	*bi-tiS-**Taa**-doo biS-Su-"oor?*	هل تصطاد بالصقور؟

Can you give me some cartridges?	***mum**-kin tid-**dee**-nee kha-ra-**Teesh**?*	هل يمكنك أن تعطني بعض الخراطيش؟

RIDING AND RACING

I'd like to hire a horse.	*^ca-wiz [^caw-za] a-'**ag**-gar Hu-**Saan**.*	أريد إستئجار حصاناً
■ a camel	■ *ga-mal*	جمل
Let's go riding in the desert.	*yal-la **nir**-kab kheyl fiS-**SaH**-ra.*	فلنركب الخيل في الصحراء
I need some riding lessons.	*^ca-wiz [^caw-za] du-**roos** ru-**koob** il-**kheyl**.*	أحتاج لبعض الدروس في الفروسية
How much is a lesson?	*id-**dars** bi kam?*	بكم الدرس؟
■ a series of lessons	■ *mag-**moo**-^cit du-**roos***	مجموعة دروس
This horse is lazy.	*il-Hu-**Saan** da kas-**lehn**.*	هذا الحصان كسول
■ bad-tempered	■ *shi-ris*	شرس
I want a quiet horse.	*^ca-wiz [^caw-za] Hu-**Saan** heh-**dee**.*	أريد حصانا هادئا
■ lively	■ *na-**sheeT***	نشيط
Is there a racecourse near Cairo?	*fee mal-^cab si-beh" gamb il-qaa-**hi**-ra?*	هل هناك ميدان سباق قريب من القاهرة؟

When are the races?	*fee si-beh" 'im-ta?*	متى تجرى السباقات؟
Are there camel races?	*fee si-beh" lig-gi-mehl?*	هل هناك سباق للجمال؟
Is betting allowed?	*ir-ri-hehn mas-mooH?*	هل الرهان مسموح؟

TENNIS AND SQUASH

Is there <u>a tennis court</u> here?	*fee **mal-^cab ti-nis hi-na?***	هل يوجد ملعب تنس هنا؟
■ a squash court	■ ***mal-^cab skwash*** ملعب إسكواش
Is it a private club?	*da neh-dee khaaS?*	هل هذا نادي خاص؟
Do I have to be a member?	***leh**-zim a-koon ^c**uDw**?*	هل يجب ان اكون عضواً؟
Can I rent a racket and balls?	***mum**-kin a-'**ag**-gar **maD**-rab wi **ko**-war?*	هل يمكن ان استأجر مضرب وكور؟
Would you like a game?	*^ca-wiz [^caw-za] til-^cab [til-^ca-bee]?*	هل تريد ان تلعب معي؟

CAMPING

| Is there a camp site near here? | *fee mu-**khay**-yam si-**yeh**-Hee "u-**ray**-yib?* | هل يوجد مخيم سياحي قريباً؟ |

Can we spend the night here?	**mum**-kin ni-**beht** hi-na?	هل يمكن ان نبيت هنا ؟
Is there <u>drinking water</u>?	fee **may**-yit shurb?	هل توجد مياه للشرب ؟
■ a grocery store	■ ba"-"**ehl**	محل بقالة
■ gasoline	■ ban-**zeen**	بنزين
Are there <u>showers</u>?	fee du-**sheht**?	هل توجد دشات ؟
■ toilets	■ twa-**litt**	تواليت
Can we do some washing here?	**mum**-kin **nigh**-sil hi-na?	هل يمكن ان نغسل هنا ؟

SOCCER

I'd like to see a soccer match.	^c**a**-wiz [^c**aw**-za] a-**shoof matsh koh**-ra.	اريد ان ارى مباراة كرة القدم
Where is the match?	il-**matsh** feyn?	اين ستجري المباراة ؟
When does it begin?	bi-yib-**ti**-dee ' **im**-ta?	متى تبدا ؟
Can you get tickets?	**mum**-kin ti-**gib**-lee ta-**zeh**-kir?	هل تستطيع ان تشتري تذاكر لي ؟
Is it an international match?	da matsh **daw**-lee?	هل هي مباراة دولية ؟
Who is playing?	**meen** il-lee bi-**yil**-^cab?	من يلعب ؟

When is the Cup Final?	*ni-**heh**-'ee il-**kehs** 'im-ta?*	متى يكون نهائي الكاس ؟
Who won (the Cup)?	***meen keh**-sib (il-**kehs**)?*	من كسب (الكاس) ؟
Who do you support?	*bit-**shag**-ga^c [bit-shag-**ga**-^cee] meen?*	أي فريق تشجع ؟
What is the score?	*in-na-**tee**-ga kam?*	ما هى النتيجة؟
It was a draw.	*kehn ta-^c**eh**-dul.*	كانت تعادل
Foul!	*fawl!*	خطا !
Goal!	*gohn!*	هدف!
Will it be shown on television?	*hay-**gee**-boo fit-til-li-viz-**yohn**?*	هل ستذاع فى التليفزيون؟
Are they a famous team?	*dee **fir**-"a mash-**hoo**-ra?*	هل هذا الفريق مشهور؟

INDOOR ENTERTAINMENT

Do you play <u>chess</u>?	*til-^cab [til-^c**a**-bee] <u>sha-Ta-**rang**</u>?*	هل تلعب الشطرنج؟
■ backgammon	■ ***Taw**-la*	الطاولة
■ roulette	■ *ru-**litt***	الروليت
■ poker	■ ***poh**-kar*	البوكر

■ blackjack	■ *blak*-jak	البلاك جاك
■ pool	■ bil-**yar**-du	البلياردو

Is gambling
allowed?

il-"u-**maar** mas-**mooH**?

هل القمار مسموح؟

Do you have <u>videos</u>? ᶜ**an**-dak vi-dyo-**heht**?

هل عندك افلام فيديو؟

■ video games	■ 'al-ᶜ**ehb** vid-yo	العاب فيديو
■ a home computer	■ kom-**byoo**-tar man-**zi**-lee	

كمبيوتر منزلي

How many TV
channels are there?

fee kam qa-**naat** ti-li-viz-**yohn**?

كم قناة تليفزيونية عندكم؟

Is this an
<u>Egyptian</u> serial?

da mu-**sal**-sal <u>**maS**-ree</u>?

هل هذا مسلسل مصري؟

■ American/English ■ am-ri-**keh**-nee/in-gi-**lee**-zee

امريكي / انجليزي

What's on at
the movies?

fee 'af-**lehm** 'eyh fis-**si**-ni-ma?

ماذا يعرض في السينما؟

Is there an
<u>open air</u> cinema?

foa si-ni-ma **Sey**-fee?

هل توجد دار عرض صيفية؟

■ air-conditioned ■ mu-**kay**-ya-fa

مكيفة

Is it an <u>Egyptian</u>
film?

da film <u>**maS**-ree</u>? هل هذا فلم مصري؟

■ American/English ■ *am-ri-**keh**-nee/in-gi-**lee**-zee*

امريكي / انجليزي

Is it dubbed
in <u>English</u>?

*da mu-**da**-blaj bi-lin-gi-**lee**-zee?*

هل هو مترجم إلى الانجليزية؟

■ in Arabic ■ *bil-ᶜ**a**-ra-bee* الى العربية

■ Is it subtitled
in English?

*da mu-**tar**-gam bi-lin-gi-**lee**-zee?*

هل عليه ترجمة انجليزية؟

What time does the
show <u>begin</u>?

*il-ᶜ**arD** bi-yib-**ti**-dee 'im-ta?*

متى يبدا العرض؟

■ end ■ *bi-yin-**ti**-hee* ينتهي

Can I book
seats (now)?

***mum**-kin **aH**-giz
ka-**reh**-see (dil-**wa**"-tee)?*

هل استطيع

حجز الاماكن (الآن) ؟

We would like to
go to <u>the theater</u>.

*ᶜaw-**zeen** ni-**rooH** il-**mas**-raH.*

نريد الذهاب للمسرح

■ the opera ■ *il-'**o**-bi-ra* للاوبرا

■ the ballet ■ *il-ba-**ley*** للباليه

■ the folk dancing ■ *ir-**ra**"S ish-**sha**ᶜ-bee* لرقص شعبي

■ a concert ■ ***Haf**-la mu-si-**qee**-ya* لحفل موسيقي

Is it western or
oriental music?

*il-mu-si-**qee**-ya ghar-**bee**-ya **wal**-la
shar-"**ee**-ya?*

هل هي موسيقى غربية أم شرقية؟

That singer is very famous isn't he (she)?	*il-mu-**ghan**-nee da [il-mu-ghan-**nee**-ya dee] mash-**hoor** [mash-**hoo**-ra] **gid**-dan, mish **ki**-da?*	هذا المغني (المغنية) مشهور(ة) جداً. اليس كذلك؟
What's his (her) name?	*'**is**-moo ['is-**ma**-ha] 'eyh?*	ما اسمه (اسمها)؟
I'd like to go to a nightclub.	*ᶜa-wiz [ᶜaw-za] a-**rooH** **mal**-ha **lay**-lee.*	أريد الذهاب الى ملهى ليلي
Which <u>club</u> has good belly dancing?	*an-hee **mal**-ha fee ra"S ba-la-dee **kway**-yis?*	في أي ملهى يوجد رقص شرقي جيد؟
▣ restaurant	▣ ***maT**-ᶜam*	مطعم
Is there an <u>oriental</u> cabaret?	*fee ka-ba-**rey** <u>shar-"ee</u>?*	هل هناك كباريه شرقي؟
▣ western-style	▣ ***ghar**-bee*	غربي
Can you get us a table near the dance floor?	*mum kin ti-leh-"ee-lee Ta-ra-**bey**-za gamb il-**beest**?*	هل تستطيع أن تجد لنا طاولة قريبة من حلبة الرقص؟
When does the floor show start?	*il-ᶜ**arD** bi-yib-**ti**-dee 'im-ta?*	متى يبدا العرض؟
Is there a disco- theque in the hotel?	*fee **dis**-ko fil-'u-**teel**?*	هل يوجد ديسكو في الفندق؟
It's very crowded.	*da **zaH**-ma **gid**-dan.*	إنه مزدحم جداً

I'd like to go home.	^c**a**-wiz [^c**aw**-za] a-**raw**-waH. اريد العودة الى المنزل
I'd like to go back to the hotel.	^c**a**-wiz [^c**aw**-za] اريد العودة الى الفندق a-**raw**-waH lil-'u-**teel**.

EATING OUT

Part of the fun of your trip will be experimenting with Middle East cuisine — one of the most subtle and varied in the world. The dishes mentioned here are to be found in most Arab countries, though each has its own regional specialties.

In North Africa couscous (*kus*-ku-see), fine grains of semolina, steamed, forms the basis for many dishes, whereas further east rice and beans are the staple food. Meat is served either charcoal-grilled or braised slowly in the oven. Because most Arab countries border an ocean, seafood is abundant.

Lunchtime is from about one o'clock till three, dinner from eight till eleven. This means you can — in theory! — sleep off your lunch in the hottest part of the day, and make the most of the cool of the evening.

lunch	il-**gha**-da
dinner	il-ᶜ**a**-sha

Big hotels serve Western as well as local dishes, and French and Italian restaurants are to be found in most major cities. Cairo offers an incredible range, from Hungarian to Japanese, whereas in the Gulf you will have the chance to try excellent Indian food. American style chicken and hamburger restaurants and take-outs are becoming increasingly popular throughout the region.

Good guidebooks, a helpful receptionist, or a tourist information office will direct you to the restaurants where local people go for a really good meal. These will often specialize in grilled meat, fish, or chicken and pigeon. Lower-priced restaurants specialize in a range of meatless dishes, served at tiny tables on tin plates; they are inexpensive and friendly places where you are likely to be engaged in conversation by your neighbors.

Do you know a good restaurant?	*ti*^c*-raf* **maT**-*c*-*am* **kway**-*yis?*	هل تعرف مطعماً جيداً؟
I want to eat <u>local</u> food.	^c*a-wiz* [^c*aw-za*] '*eh-kul* '*akl ma-***Hal***-lee.*	أريد أن آكل أكلاً محلياً.
■ oriental	■ *shar-"ee*	شرقي
■ western-style	■ *ghar-bee*	غربي
I am looking for a <u>French</u> restaurant.	*ba-***daw***-war* ^c*a-la* **maT**-^c*am* *fa-ran-***seh***-wee*	أبحث عن مطعم فرنسي
■ Italian	■ *ee-Tal-***yeh***-nee*	إيطالي
■ Indian	■ *hin-dee*	هندي
I want to have lunch at — .	^c*a-wiz* [^c*aw-za*] *at-***ghad***-da fi* — .	أريد الغداء في —
I want to dine at — .	^c*a-wiz* [^c*aw-za*] *at-*^c***ash***-sha fi* — .	أريد العشاء في — .
Is it expensive?	*da* **gheh***-lee?*	هل هو غال ؟
How much (roughly) for two people?	"*ad-di* '*eyh (ta*"-*ree-ban*) *li shakh-***Seyn***?*	بكم تقريبا لشخصين ؟

AT THE RESTAURANT

My name is — .	'*is-mee* — .	اسمي —
I have (haven't) a reservation.	^c***an***-dee (ma-*^c*an-***deesh***) Hagz.*	(ليس) لي حجز
I'd like a table <u>for four</u> please.	^c*a-wiz* [^c*aw-za*] *Ta-ra-***bey***-za li* '*ar-ba-*^c*a min* **faD***-lak.*	أريد طاولة لأربعة من فضلك

■ for two	■ *li-'it-**neyn***	لشخصين
Waiter!	*mitr!*	! جرسون
Could I have the menu, please.	*id-**dee**-nee il-**min**-yu min **faD**-lak.*	أعطني قائمة الطعام من فضلك
What do you recommend?	*'eyh '**aH**-san 'aT-**baa**" ᶜan-**du**-kum?*	ماذا تقترح؟
I'd like something light.	*ᶜa-wiz [ᶜaw-za] Ha-ga kha-fee-fa.*	أريد شيئاً خفيفاً.
Is it fresh?	*da **Taa**-za?*	هل هو طازج ؟
Is it very hot? (i.e., spicy)	*da **Heh**-mee?*	هل هو متبل (حار) ؟

SOMETHING TO DRINK

In Saudi Arabia and some of the countries in the Gulf, alcohol is prohibited; in others the sale of alcohol is strictly limited in Ramadan. But in most countries in the Middle East, beer, wine, and spirits are available. In North Africa, Egypt, and Lebanon, wine is produced locally, the best-known labels being Gianaclis in Egypt and Ksara in Lebanon. Local beers tend to be light lagers.

International hotels will have a wide range of alcoholic drinks, and open-air *casinos* or cafés catering to a middle-class clientele will probably serve beer. Many neighborhood restaurants will, however, be "dry."

Do you have — ?	*ᶜan-**du**-kum — ?*	هل عندكم — ؟
■ beer	■ *bee-ra*	بيرة
■ wine	■ *ni-beet*	نبيذ

■ whiskey	■ *wis*-kee	ويسكي
■ arak (an anise-flavored spirit, excellent with *mezza*)	■ ^{c}***a***-ra"	عرق
■ soft drinks	■ ***Ha***-ga sa"-^{c}a	مشروبات غير روحية
■ fruit juice	■ ^{c}a-**Seer**	عصير
■ mineral water	■ ***may***-ya ma^c-da-*nee*-ya	مياه معدنية

Do you have any (fresh) <u>fruit juice</u>?	^{c}an-***du***-kum ^{c}<u>a-**seer**</u> (***Taa***-za)? هل عندكم عصير طازج ؟
■ orange juice	■ ^{c}a-**Seer** bur-tu-"***aan*** عصير برتقال
We'd like some red/white wine.	^{c}aw-**zeen** ni-**beet** '***aH***-mar/'***ab***-yaD. نريد نبيذاً احمر / ابيض
What is the best local wine?	'eyh '***aH***-san ni-**beet** ma-***Hal***-lee? ما هو افضل نبيذ محلي؟
a bottle (two bottles) <u>of wine</u>	"i-***zeh***-zit ("i-***zehz***-teyn) ni-**beet**. زجاجة (زجاجتين) نبيذ

■ of beer	■ ***bee***-ra	بيرة
cold beer	***bee***-ra sa"-^{c}a	بيرة مثلجة
a glass	kub-***bay***-ya	كأس
a glass of wine	kub-***bay***-yit ni-**beet**	كأس نبيذ
with ice	bi ***talg***	بثلج
without ice	min ***gheyr*** talg	بدون ثلج

TRAVEL TIP

Mineral water is inexpensive and easily obtainable throughout the Middle East. It is better not to risk the tap water, though tempting glasses of iced water will be served automatically with almost any order in a café or restaurant. Remember, the ice will be made from tap water, even in many international hotels.

Tea — especially mint tea — is both safe and more thirst-quenching than sweet carbonated drinks.

GENERAL REQUESTS

Please bring some <u>bread</u>.	*min* **faD**-*lak* **gib**-*lee* ^c*eysh/khubz*.	ارجوك احضر لي خبزا
■ oriental bread	■ *khubz* **ba**-*la-dee*	خبز عربي
■ a napkin	■ *man-***deel**	منديل
■ a glass	■ *kub-***bay**-*ya*	كاس
■ butter	■ **zib**-*da*	زبدة
■ a plate	■ **Ta**-*ba"*	طبق
■ a spoon	■ *ma*^c-**la**-*"a*	ملعقة
■ a knife	■ *sik-***kee**-*na*	سكينة
■ a fork	■ **shoh**-*ka*	شوكة
■ toothpicks	■ *sal-la-***keht** اعواد لتنظيف الاسنان	
■ salt and pepper	■ *malH wi* **fil**-*fil*	ملح وفلفل
We'd like more —.	^c*aw-***zeen** — *ka-***mehn**.	نريد — اكثر

| Please bring —. | min **faD**-lak
gib-lee —. | ارجوك احضر لي — |
| What desserts
do you have? | ^can-**du**-kum Hal-la-**wee**-yeht 'eyh? | ماهي انواع الحلوى عندكم ؟ |

If you're not satisfied try these phrases:

I didn't order this	ma Ta-lab-**toosh**.	لم اطلب هذا
This isn't properly cooked.	da **mish** mis-ti-**wee**.	هذا ليس ناضجاً
This is overdone (dry).	da **neh**-shif.	هذا زائد النضج
This is cold.	da **beh**-rid.	هذا بارد
I want to speak to <u>the headwaiter</u>.	^c**a**-wiz [^c**aw**-za] a-**kal**-lim il-**mitr**. اريد أن اكلم مدير غرفة الطعام	
■ the manager	■ il-mu-**deer**	المدير
Do you have any appetizers?	^can-**du**-kum **maz**-za?	هل عندكم مزة؟

UNDERSTANDING THE MENU

Appetizers

The Middle East is famous for the variety of its *mezza*, snacks such as dips, pickles, cheese, and olives served either as appetizers to the main course or with drinks.

The best known creamy dips, a specialty of Middle East cuisine are:

dips (in general)	sa-la-**Taat**	سلطات
tahina (pureed chick-peas and sesame seed paste)	Ta-**Hee**-na	طحينة
hummus (pureed chick-peas)	**Hum**-mu*S*	حمص
baba rannouj (roast eggplant (aubergine) with tahina)	**ba**-ba ghan-**noog**	بابا غنوج
foul (broad beans, pureed and seasoned)	fool	فول
yogurt and cucumber dip with garlic	**la**-ban za-**beh**-dee bil-khi-**yaar**	لبن زبادي بالخيار

The best way of eating these is with oriental bread (khubz **ba**-la-dee).

Other appetizers include:

stuffed vine leaves	**wa**-ra″ ᶜ**i**-nab	ورق عنب
fish roe	ba-**Taa**-rikh	بطارخ
olives	zey-**toon**	زيتون
herring	**rin**-ga	رنجة

cracked wheat with with parsley, onion, and tomato	*tab-**boo**-la*	تبولة
pickles	***Tur**-shee, ma-**khal**-lil*	طرشي/مخلل

Soups

soup	***shur**-ba*	شربة
vegetable soup	***shur**-bit khu-**Daar***	شربة خضار
onion soup	***shur**-bit ba-Sal*	شربة بصل
lentil soup	***shur**-bit ᶜads*	شربة عدس
fish soup	***shur**-bit **sa**-mak*	شربة سمك
consommé with noodles	***shur**-bit shiᶜ-**ree**-ya*	شربة شعرية
mulukhiyya (spinach- (like vegetable soup served with rice and meat)	*mu-lu-**khee**-ya*	ملوخية

Salads

salad	***sa**-la-Ta*	سلطة
mixed salad	***sa**-la-Ta **khaD**-ra*	سلطة خضراء
tomato salad	***sa**-la-Tit Ta-**maa**-Tim*	سلطة طماطم
potato salad	***sa**-la-Tit ba-**Taa**-Tis*	سلطة بطاطس
beet salad	***sa**-la-Tit **ban**-gar*	سلطة بنجر

Meat Dishes

meat	*laH*-ma	لحم
kebab (grilled marinated meat)	ka-*behb*	كباب
kibba (baked minced meat with cracked wheat and spices)	*kib*-ba	كبة
kufta (minced grilled meat)	*kuf*-ta	كفتة
meat and vegetable casserole	*Taa*-gin	طاجن
(roast) lamb	*Daa*-nee (*rus*-too)	ضاني (رستو)
veal	bi-*til*-loo	بتلو
veal cutlets	is-ka-*loop* bi-*til*-loo	اسكالوب بتلو
lamb cutlets	kus-ta-*ley*-ta	شرائح ضاني/كستلية
beefsteak	fi-*ley*, steyk	بفتيك
▦ well done	▦ mis-*ti*-wee	▦ مستوي/تام النضج
▦ medium	▦ nuS-Si *si*-wa	▦ نصف ناضج
▦ rare (unusual in the Middle East)	▦ ya *doh*-bak maH-*TooT* ᶜan-*naar*	▦ قليل النضج
liver	*kib*-da	كبدة
kidneys	ka-*leh*-wee	كلاوي
brains	mukh	مخ

spiced grilled meat, served in fine slices	*sha-**wir**-ma*	شاورمة
fatta (mutton stewed in broth with bread and rice)	***fat**-ta*	فتة

Poultry and Game

(grilled) chicken	*fi-**rehkh**/da-**jehj** (**mash**-wee)*	دجاج (مشوي)
(stuffed) pigeon	*Ha-**mehm** (**maH**-shee)*	حمام (محشي)
duck	*baTT*	بط
rabbit	*'**ar**-nab*	ارنب
quail	*sim-**mehn***	سمان
turkey	*deek **roo**-mee*	ديك رومي

Because pork is forbidden to Muslims it is found only (occasionally) in international hotels and tourist restaurants:

ham, pork	*khan-**zeer***	خنزير

You may want to know how the dish is prepared:

roast	***rus**-too*	رستو
fried	***ma**"-lee*	مقلي
grilled	***mash**-wee*	مشوي
boiled	*mas-**loo**"*	مسلوق
stuffed	***maH**-shee*	محشي
baked	*fil-**furn***	في الفرن
minced (ground)	*maf-**room***	مفروم

Fish Dishes

What kind of fish do you have?	ⁿan-**du**-kum 'as-**mehk** 'eyh?	ما هي انواع السمك عندكم؟
fish	**sa**-mak	سمك
prawns	gam-**ba**-ree	جمبري
squid	ka-la-**mar**-ya	ام الحبر، حبار
octopus	okh-Tu-**booT**	اخطبوط
swordfish	**a**-boo-**seyf**	ابو سيف
crab	**a**-boo ga-**lam**-boo, ka-**boor**-ya	كابوريا، ابو جلمبو
lobster	is-ta-**koh**-za	سرطان بحري ، استاكوزا
tuna	**too**-na	تونة
sardines	sar-**deen**	سردين
sole	**sa**-mak **moo**-sa	سمك موسى

Vegetables

What vegetables do you have?	ⁿan-**du**-kum khu-**Daar** 'eyh?	ما هي انواع الخضروات عندكم؟
artichokes	khar-**shoof**	خرشوف
beans	fa-**Sul**-ya	فاصوليا
carrots	**ga**-zar	جزر
cauliflower	"ar-na-**beeT**	قرنبيط
cucumber	khi-**yaar**	خيار

lettuce	*khass*	خس
mixed vegetables	*khu-**Daar** mi-**shak**-kil*	خضروات مشكلة
okra ("ladies' fingers")	***bam**-ya*	بامية
onions	***ba**-Sal*	بصل
(fried) potatoes	*ba-**Taa**-Tis (ma"-**lee**-ya)*	بطاطس (مقلية)
peas	*bi-**sil**-la*	بسلة
radishes	*figl*	فجل
rice	*ruzz*	أرز
spinach	*sa-**beh**-nikh*	سبانخ
sweet potatoes	*ba-**Taa**-Ta*	بطاطا
tomatoes	*Ta-**maa**-Tim*	طماطم

The following vegetables are often served stuffed (***maH**-shee*) with rice and herbs and sometimes minced meat:

aubergines, eggplants	*bi-din-**gehn***	باذنجان
cabbage	*ku-**rumb***	كرنب
zucchini, squash	***koh**-sa*	كوسة
green peppers	***fil**-fil '**akh**-Dar*	فلفل اخضر

Dishes may be served or cooked with:

garlic	*bit-**toom***	بالثوم

mint	*bi ni^c-**neh**^c*	بالنعناع
lemon	*bi la-**moon***	بالليمون
olive oil	*bi zeyt zey-**toon***	بزيت الزيتون

Side Dishes

macaroni (and pasta generally)	*ma-ka-**roh**-na*	مكرونة
(fried) eggs	*beyD (**ma**"-lee)*	بيض (مقلي)
lentils	*^cads*	عدس
(cheese) omelette	*om-**leet** (big-**gib**-na)*	اومليت (بالجبنة)
eggs baked with onions, tomatoes, and green peppers	*^c**ig**-ga*	عجة
spiced sausages	*su-**gu**" "*	سجق
pastrami	*bas-**Tir**-ma*	بسطرمة
hard, mild cheese	***gib**-na **roo**-mee*	جبنة رومي
soft white salty cheese	***gib**-na **bey**-Da*	جبنة بيضاء
yogurt	***la**-ban za-**beh**-dee*	لبن زبادي

Some North African Dishes

couscous	***kus**-ku-see*	كسكسي
peppery fish soup	***mar**-qa*	مرقة

| paper-thin pancakes filled with egg and deep fried | *breek* | بريك |
| spiced sausages | *mer-**gez*** | مرجاز |

Desserts

Though Western style restaurants will offer a range of desserts, it is not customary to end a meal with an elaborate sweet course, and many local restaurants may list only ice cream, crème caramel, or fruit.

ice cream	*ays-**kreem***	ايس كريم
■ chocolate	■ *sho-ko-**laa**-Ta*	شكولاتة
■ vanilla	■ *va-**nil**-ya*	فانيلا
mixed ice cream	*ays-**kreem** mi-**shak**-kil*	ايس كريم مشكل
crème caramel	*kreym ka-ra-**mel***	كريم كرامل
rice pudding	*ruzz bi **la**-ban*	ارز بلبن
vanilla blancmange	*ma-hal-la-**bee**-ya*	مهلبية
Umm Ali (pastry and milk pudding with raisins)	*'umm ᶜeh-lee*	ام علي
qamar eldin (apricot jelly, sometimes served as a drink)	*"a-mar id-**deen**, mish-mi-**shee**-ya*	قمر الدين، مشمشية
fatir (large baked pancakes often served with jam or honey)	*fi-**Teer** Hilw*	فطير

Fruit

fruit	*fak-ha*	فاكهة
apples	*tuf-fehH*	تفاح
apricots	*mish-mish*	مشمش
bananas	*mohz*	موز
dates	*ba-laH*	بلح
figs	*teen*	تين
grapefruit	*greyp froot*	جريبفروت
grapes	*ci-nab*	عنب
guava	*ga-weh-ʃu*	جوافة
lemon	*la-moon*	ليمون
mangoes	*man-ga*	مانجو
melon	*sham-mehm*	شمام
oranges	*bur-tu-"aan*	برتقال
peaches	*khohkh*	خوخ
pears	*kom-mit-ra*	كمثرى
plums	*bar-"oo"*	برقوق
pomegranates	*rom-maan*	رومان
strawberries	*fa-raw-la*	فراولة
tangerines	*yu-sa-fan-dee*	يوسف افندي
watermelon	*baT-Teekh*	بطيخ

Oriental Pastries

Every visitor must experience the delights of the oriental pastry shop (*il-Ha-la-weh-nee*). Pastries are rich and very sweet, made with clarified butter and steeped in syrup, often stuffed with different kinds of nuts. A dollop of chilled cream ("*ish-Ta*) is an optional extra. You can eat your pastry on the spot, usually at a marble-topped bar, or buy a selection to take away with you (they are generally sold by weight). Give a small tip to the person who deftly ties up your package with ribbon tape.

basbousa (semolina baked in the oven, often with nuts, and steeped in syrup)	*bas-**boo**-sa*	بسبوسة
baclava (layers of paper-thin pastry and crushed nuts, with syrup)	*ba"-**leh**-wa*	بقلاوة
kunafa (fine-spun pastry stuffed with nuts)	*ku-**neh**-fa*	كنافة
qatayif (tiny pancakes, layered with nuts, syrup, and cream)	*"a-**Taa**-yif*	قطايف
with cream	*bil-"**ish**-Ta*	بالقشطة
Turkish delight	***mal**-ban/lu-**koom***	ملبن، حلقوم

AFTER THE MEAL

The bill (check), please.	*il-Hi-sehb, min faD-lak.*
	الحساب، من فضلك
Can I pay by credit card?	***mum**-kin **ad-fa**ᶜ bi kri-dit kard?*
	هل استطيع أن ادفع ببطاقة اعتماد؟
Is service included?	*da bil-**khid**-ma?* هل هذا يشمل الخدمة؟
That's for you.	*da ᶜa-la-**sheh**-nak.* تفضل، هذا لك
The food was excellent.	*il-'**akl** kehn mum-**tehz**.* كان الاكل ممتازاً
We will come again.	*ha-**nee** gee **teh**-nee.* سناتي مرة ثانية

AT THE CAFÉ

Street cafés usually serve only tea, Turkish coffee, and soft drinks. They are excellent places to sit and rest and watch the world go by. Traditionally, men go there to chat and smoke a water pipe (*shee-sha*) or play backgammon. Tourists are welcome, though a woman on her own might feel uncomfortable.

If you order a coffee you will automatically be given a small black Turkish coffee and a glass of water. Tea is usually served black, sometimes already sweetened.

In the big cities elegant tearooms or tea gardens, such as the famous Groppi's in Cairo, also serve light meals and pastries. Service may be leisurely, because most people go there to spend an hour or two.

coffee	_"ah-wa_	قهوة
tea	_shayy_	شاي
fruit juice	_ᶜa-Seer_	عصير
soda	_Soh-da_	صودا
soft drinks	_Ha-ga sa"-ᶜa_	مشروبات غير روحية

Do you have French (i.e., filter) coffee?	_ᶜan-du-kum "ah-wa fa-ran-seh-wee?_	هل عندكم قهوة فرنسية؟
■ instant coffee	■ _nes-ka-fey_	نسكافيه

I'd like a Turkish coffee without sugar.	_ᶜa-wiz [ᶜaw-za] "ah-wa seh-da._	أريد قهوة سادة
■ medium sweet	■ _maZ-booT_	مضبوط
■ very sweet	■ _suk-kar zee-yeh-da_	سكر زيادة

Do you have mineral water?	_fee may-ya maᶜ-da-nee-ya?_	هل عندكم مياه معدنية؟

tea with lemon	_shayy bi la-moon._	شاي بالليمون
■ with milk	■ _bi la-ban_	باللبن
■ with mint	■ _bi niᶜ-nehᶜ_	بالنعناع
■ without sugar	■ _min gheyr suk-kar_	بدون سكر

Some sugar, please.	_suk-kar, min faD-lak._	سكر من فضلك

sahlab (a hot milky drink topped with chopped nuts and shredded coconut)	*saH-lab*	سحلب
hot chocolate	*sho-ko-**luu**-Ta, ka-**kaw***	شكولاتة، كاكاو
Do you have anything to eat?	*ᶜan-**du**-kum 'akl?*	هل عندكم اكل؟
Do you have sandwiches?	*ᶜan-**du**-kum sand-wit-**sheht**?*	هل عندكم سندويتشات؟

Some cafés and fruit juice bars sell chilled Middle Eastern drinks:

tamarind juice	***ta**-mar **hin**-dee*	تمر هندي
karkaday (refreshing hisbicus drink)	*kar-ka-dey*	كركدية

SNACKS IN THE STREET

The Middle East is famous for the variety of its "street food": fried and grilled snacks sold from tiny kiosks and brightly decorated mobile stalls to be found on every street corner in cities such as Cairo. The flat "oriental" bread *(khubz ba-la-dee)* is stuffed with fried bean cakes, grilled meat, or cheese. Fruit juice bars will squeeze oranges or puree bananas while you wait.

bean purée	*fool*	فول
ta'miyya (fried balls of ground beans or chick-peas mixed with herbs and spices)	*Taᶜ **maa**-ya, fa-**leh**-fil*	طعمية، فلافل

kushary (macaroni or rice with noodles, lentils, fried onion, and a hot tomato sauce)	*ku-sha-ree*	كشري
shawirma, doner kebab (spiced lamb or veal grilled on a vertical spit)	*sha-**wir**-ma*	شاورمة
sandwiches	*sand-wit-**sheht***	سندويتشات
a <u>cheese</u> sandwich	*sand-**witsh** **gib**-na.*	سندويتش جبنة
■ liver	■ **kib**-da	كبدة
■ ta'miyya	■ *Taᶜ-**mee**-ya*	طعمية
peanuts	*fool su-**deh**-nee*	فول سوداني
popcorn	*fi-**shaar***	فشار

TRAVEL TIP

The visitor should naturally be cautious of what and where he or she eats; anything freshly fried or grilled is likely to be safe, whereas the usual rules about avoiding salads — even garnishes on sandwiches — and fruit that cannot be peeled, should be strictly observed.

GETTING TO KNOW PEOPLE

GREETINGS

It is customary to shake hands when you are formally introduced to someone. When close friends or relations — men or women — haven't met for some time, they usually exchange kisses on both cheeks.

At Any Time of Day

Hello!	*is-sa-**leh**-mu ^ca-**ley**-kum!*	السلام عليكم!
(reply)	*^ca-**ley**-kum is-sa-**lehm***	عليكم السلام
Hi!/Welcome!	*ah-lan wa sah-lan!*	أهلا وسهلا
	ah-lan!	أهلا
(reply)	*ah-lan beek [bee-kee]*	أهلا بك
… to two or more	*ah-lan bee-kum*	أهلا بكم
Welcome!	*mar-**Ha**-ba!*	مرحباً
(reply)	*mar-Hab beek [bee-kee]*	مرحباً بك
… to two or more	*mar-Hab bee-kum*	مرحباً بكم
Goodbye!	*ma-^ca s-sa-**leh**-ma!*	مع السلامة
Remember me to —.	*sal-**lim**-lee ^ca-la —.*	سلم لي على —.
Nice to have met you.	*fur-Sa sa-^cee-da **gid**-dan.*	فرصة سعيدة جداً
(reply) I am (even) happier.	*a-na 'as-^cad.*	انا اسعد

In the Morning

Good morning.	*Sa-baH il-**kheyr**.*	صباح الخير
(reply)	*Sa-**baH** in-**noor***	صباح النور

In the Afternoon/Evening

Good evening.	*mi-seh' il-**kheyr**.*	مساء الخير
(reply)	*mi-seh' in-**noor***	مساء النور

At Night

Good night.	***tiS**-baH [tiS-ba-Hee] ⁽a-la-**kheyr**.*	

تصبح [تصبحي] على خير

. . . to two or more *tiS-**ba**-Hoo ⁽a-la **kheyr***

تصبحون على خير

How are you?	*iz-**zay**-yak? [iz-**zay**-yik?]*	ازيك ؟
or	*keyf **Heh**-lak? [keyf **Heh**-lik?]*	
		كيف حالك ؟
or	*keyf il-**Hehl**?*	كيف الحال؟
. . . to two or more	*iz-zay-**yu**-kum?*	ازيكم ؟
or	*keyf **Hehl**-kum?*	كيف حالكم ؟
or	*keyf il-**Hehl**?*	كيف الحال ؟
I'm fine, thanks.	*bi **kheyr**, il-**Ham**-du lil-**leh**.*	

بخير، الحمد لله

or	***kway**-yis [kway-**yi**-sa], il-**Ham**-du lil-**leh**.*	كويس [كويسة], الحمد لله
or	*il-**Ham**-du lil-**leh***	الحمد لله
	("praise be to God")	
	may be used	
	by itself	

CONSERVATIVE ETIQUETTE

In Saudi Arabia and some of the countries of the Gulf very conservative traditions are maintained. Women are still secluded and rarely appear at social gatherings, though this is changing gradually. It is impolite to ask after someone's wife, although a general inquiry about the family is acceptable. Presenting the soles of one's feet to someone is considered ill-mannered. If you are being entertained in traditional style, seated on carpets and cushions, leave your shoes at the door and sit cross-legged or with your feet tucked under you. Showing a lot of arm or leg, whether you are a man or a woman, is to be avoided. During a meal interest is focussed on the food, and conversation drops to a minimum level.

Show deference to someone by insisting that they pass through a door in front of you. Always offer a drink or a snack to a visitor, however casual the visit. In other countries there are fewer social constraints, but when in doubt it is always safest to err on the side of conservatism.

NAMES AND POLITE
FORMS OF ADDRESS

When talking to someone directly, the word *ya* is usually put in front of the name or title.

How are you, Ahmad?	*iz-**zay**-yak, ya '**aH**-mad?*
	ازيك، يا أحمد ؟
Good morning, madam.	*Sa-**baH** il-**kheyr**, ya ma-**dehm**.*
	صباح الخير، يا مدام

When talking to an elderly person whose name you
don't know, it's polite to address them as

ya Hagg   يا حاج [يا حاجة]

or (to a woman) *ya **Hag**-ga*

which is the title given to anyone who has been on the
pilgrimage to Mecca.

In Egypt especially, you will find yourself being
addressed as

	ya beyh	يا بيه
	*ya **fan**-dim*	يا افندم
	*ya **beh**-sha*	يا باشا

— all honorific titles of Turkish origin, used mostly to
men.

INTRODUCTIONS

May I introduce to you —.	***mum**-kin a-"ad-**dim**-lak [a-"ad-**dim**-lik]* —.	هل يمكن ان اقدم لك — .
■ Mr. —	■ *is-**say**-yid* —	■ السيد —
■ Mrs. —	■ *ma-**dehm**/is-say-**yi**-da* —	■ مدام، السيدة —
■ Miss —	■ *il-'eh-**ni**-sa* —	■ الآنسة —
■ Dr. —	■ *id-duk-**toor** [id-duk-**too**-ra]* —	■ الدكتور [الدكتورة] —
■ Professor —	■ *il-'us-**tehz** [il-'us-**teh**-za]* —	■ الاستاذ [الاستاذة] —

My name is — .	'is-mee — .	. — إسمي
This is <u>my husband</u>.	da **goh**-zee.	هذا زوجي
■ my father	■ 'a-**boo**-ya	ابي
■ my brother	■ 'a-**khoo**-ya	اخي
■ my son	■ '**ib**-nee	ابني
■ my fiancé	■ kha-**Tee**-bee	خطيبي
■ my friend	■ **SaH**-bee	صديقي
This is <u>my wife</u>.	dee mi-**raa**-tee.	هذه زوجتي
■ my mother	■ '**um**-mee, wal-di-**tee**	امي
■ my sister	■ '**ukh**-tee	اختي
■ my daughter	■ **bin**-tee	بنتي
■ my fiancée	■ kha-**Tib**-tee	خطيبتي
■ my friend (fem)	■ SaH-**bi**-tee	صديقتي
These are my children.	dohl 'aw-**leh**-dee.	هؤلاء اولادي
This is my family.	dee ᶜ**eyl**-tee/'us-ri-tee.	هذه اسرتي

MAKING FRIENDS

People will want to know all about you — and it's quite polite to ask them questions about their family and their work in return. Family are very important, so why not take a couple of snapshots with you — of your family and home.

Where are you from?	*in*-ta [*in*-tee] mi-**neyn**?	من أين انت؟
I am from —.	*a*-na min —.	انا من —
■ America	■ am-**ree**-ka	امريكا
■ Britain	■ bri-**Taan**-ya	بريطانيا
■ Canada	■ **ka**-na-da	كندا
■ Australia	■ os-**tral**-ya	استراليا
What is your name?	'*is*-mak ['*is*-mik] '*eyh*?	ما اسمك؟
Pleased to meet you. (lit., "a happy occasion")	**fur**-Sa sa-ᶜ**ee**-da.	فرصة سعيدة
The pleasure's mine.	*a*-na '*as*-ᶜad	انا اسعد
What's your job?	bi-tish-**ta**-ghal [bi-tish-**ta**-gha-lee] '*eyh*?	ماذا تعمل؟
Are you married?	*in*-ta mit-**gaw**-wiz? [*in*-tee mit-gaw-**wi**-za?]	هل انت متزوج [متزوجة]؟
Do you have any children?	ᶜ*an*-dak [ᶜ*an*-dik] '*aw*-lehd?	هل عندك اطفال؟
Are you here on holiday?	*in*-ta [*in*-tee] fee '*a*-**geh**-za?	هل انت هنا في عطلة؟
Where are you staying?	*in*-ta **neh**-zil [*in*-tee **naz**-la] feyn?	أين تقيم؟
I'm staying at —.	*a*-na **neh**-zil [**naz**-la] fee —.	انا اقيم في —
Yes, I'm married.	'*ay*-wa, *a*-na mit-**gaw**-wiz [mit-gaw-**wi**-za].	نعم، انا متزوج [متزوجة].

| No, I'm not married. | *la'*, *a-na* **mish** *mit-gaw-wiz* [*mit-gaw-wi-za*]. | لست
متزوجا [متزوجة] |

OCCUPATIONS

I am a <u>businessman</u>.	*a-na* <u>**raa**-gil *'a^c*-**mehl**</u> / **teh**-gir.	انا رجل اعمال، تاجر
■ a businesswoman	■ *say*-**yi**-dit *'a^c*-**mehl**	سيدة اعمال
■ a student	■ **Taa**-lib [**Taa**-li-ba]	طالب [طالبة]
■ a teacher	■ *mu*-**dar**-ris [*mu dar*-**ri**-sa]	مدرس [مدرسة]، معلم [معلمة]
■ a doctor	■ *duk*-**toor** [*duk*-**too**-ra]	دكتور [دكتورة]، طبيب [طبيبة]
■ a farmer	■ *mu*-**zeh**-ri^c	مزارع
■ an engineer	■ *mu*-**han**-dis [*mu-han*-**di**-sa]	مهندس [مهندسة]
■ a secretary	■ *si*-kir-**teer** [*si-kir*-**tee**-ra]	سكرتير [سكرتيرة]
■ a company director	■ *mu*-**deer** [*mu*-**dee**-rit] **shir**-ka	مدير [مديرة] شركة
■ a consultant	■ *mus-ta*-**shaar** [*mus-ta*-**shaa**-ra], *kha*-**beer** [*kha*-**bee**-ra]	مستشار [مستشارة]
■ a housewife	■ **sit**-ti beyt	ربة منزل

■ a journalist	■ **Sa**-Ha-fee [Sa-Ha-**fee**-ya]	صحفي [صحفية]
■ a lawyer	■ mu-**Heh**-mee [mu-Heh-**mee**-ya]	محامي [محامية]
I'm in <u>import/export.</u>	**a**-na <u>fil-'is-ti-**raad**</u> wit-taS-**Deer**.	أعمل بالاستيراد والتصدير
■ manufacturing	■ fiS-Si-**naa**-ᶜa	في الصناعة
■ banking	■ fi bank	في بنك
■ publishing	■ fi daar nashr	بالنشر
He is (is he?) — .	**huw**-wa — (?)	(هل) هو —
She is (is she?) —.	**hee**-ya — (?)	(هل) هي —

GENERAL CONVERSATION

Whenever you meet and talk with people, for example, when discussing a purchase or making a routine business call, you are likely to be presented with coffee or tea or a soft drink.

I'm here for <u>a few days.</u>	**ha**"-ᶜud **ka**-za yohm.	سأبقى هنا عدة ايام
■ a week	■ 'is-**booᶜ**	اسبوع
■ two weeks	■ 'is-boo-ᶜ**eyn**	اسبوعين
■ (about) a month	■ (Ha-**weh**-lee) shahr	مدة شهر (تقريبا)
■ a few months	■ **ka**-za shahr	عدة أشهر

It's the first time I've been to Egypt.	dee '**aw**-wil **mar**-ra '**eh**-gee maSr.
	إنها المرة الاولى لي في مصر
I hope to visit — .	ⁱ**a**-wiz [ⁱ**aw**-za] a-**zoor** —.
	اريد ان ازور —
I'm traveling by myself.	a-na mi-**seh**-fir [mi-**saf**-ra] li **waH**-dee.
	انا مسافر [مسافرة] وحدي
I am with friends.	a-na ma-ⁱa 'aS-**Haab**. انا مع اصدقاء
I'm waiting for someone.	a-na mis-**tan**-nee [mis-tan-**nee**-ya] Hadd.
	انا منتظر [منتظرة] واحداً
I love the country.	ba-**Hibb** il-**ba**-lad. احب البلد
I love the people here.	ba-**Hibb** in-**nehs** hi-na. احب الناس هنا
The people are very kind.	in-**nehs** Tay-yi-**been** gid-**dan**.
	الناس طيبون جداً
■ generous	■ ku-ra-ma كرماء
I've had no problems.	ma-ⁱan-**deesh** ma-**sheh**-kil **khua**-liS.
	ليس عندي مشاكل
It is rather hot.	ig-**gaww** Harr shway-ya.
	الطقس حار الى حد ما
It is very humid.	fee ru-**Too**-ba ki-**teer**. الطقس رطب جداً
Do you speak English?	bi-tit-**kal**-lim [bi-tit-kal-**li**-mee] in-gi-**lee**-zee? هل تتكلم الانجليزية؟
You speak English very well!	bi-tit-**kal**-lim [bi-tit-kal-**li**-mee] in-gi-**lee**-zee **kway**-yis gid-**dan**!
	تتكلم الانجليزية بطلاقة '

I have learned a little <u>Arabic</u>.	*da-rast °a-ra-bee shway-ya.* انا تعلمت قليلا من العربية
■ Egyptian Arabic	■ *°a-ra-bee maS-ree* اللهجة المصرية
It's very difficult!	*da Sa°b gid-dan!* هذه اللغة صعبة جداً
Please join us.	*it-faD-Dal [it-faD-Da-lee].* تفضل [تفضلي]
. . . to two or more	*it-faD-Da-loo* تفضلوا

(*it-faD-Dal* can also mean "please take this," "do come in," "have a seat," etc.)

What will you have to drink?	*tish-rab [tish-ra-bee] 'eyh?* ماذا تريد ان تشرب ؟
. . . to two or more	*tish-ra-boo 'eyh?* ماذا تشربون؟
May I take a picture of you?	*mum-kin a-Saw-wa-rak?* هل يمكن *[a-Saw-wa-rik]?* ان اصورك؟
Would you take a picture of me (us)?	*mum-kin ti-Saw-war-nee* هل يمكن *(ti-Saw-war-na)?* ان تصورني؟
Many thanks!	*'al-fi shukr!* شكراً جزيلا!
I will send you the photos.	*hab-°at-lak iS-So-war.* سارسل لك الصور

ARRANGING TO SEE SOMEONE AGAIN

When will I see you?	*a-**shoo**-fak [a-**shoo**-fik] '**im**-ta?*	متى أراك ثانية؟
Can I see you tomorrow?	*a-**shoo**-fak [a-**shoo**-fik] **buk**-ra?*	هل ساراك غداً؟
I'll see you <u>here</u>.	*a-**shoo**-fak [a-**shoo**-fik] **hi**-na.*	ساراك هنا
■ at the hotel	■ *fil-**fun**-du", fil-'u-**teel***	في الفندق
■ at the office	■ *fil-**mak**-tab*	في المكتب
At what time?	*is-**seh**-ᶜa kam?*	متى؟
Do join us for lunch.	*it-**faD**-Dal [it-faD-**Da**-lee]* *tit-**ghad**-da [tit-**ghad**-dee]* *ma-ᶜ**eh**-na.*	تفضل للغذاء معنا
Do join us for dinner.	*it-**faD**-Dal [it-faD-**Da**-lee]* *tit-ᶜ**ash**-sha [tit-ᶜ**ash**-shee]* *ma-ᶜ**eh**-na.*	تفضل للعشاء معنا
May I call you?	***mum**-kin a-kal-**li**-mak [a-kal-**li**-mik] bit-ti-li-**fohn**?*	هل استطيع الاتصال بك؟
What is your telephone number?	***nim**-rit ti-li-**foh**-nak [ti-li-**foh**-nik] '**eyh**?*	ما هو رقم تليفونك؟
This is my telephone number.	*dee **nim**-rit ti-li-**foh**-nee.*	هذا هو رقم تليفوني

This is my address (in Egypt).	da ʿin-**weh**-nee (fi maSr).	هذا عنواني (في مصر)
Be seeing you!	i-la li-**qaa**'!	إلى اللقاء!

When making any plans for the future it's usual to add:

God willing (i.e., I hope).	'in **shaa**' al-**laah**.	إن شاء الله
See you tomorrow, I hope.	a-**shoo**-fak **buk**-ra, 'in **shaa**' al-**laah**.	أراك غداً إن شاء الله

VISITING SOMEONE'S HOME

If you are lucky enough to be invited to someone's home for a meal, there are only a few points of etiquette to remember. No gifts are expected, but a box of candy for the children or a small souvenir typical of your home country would be a thoughtful gesture. The host will probably choose the best pieces of meat and add these to your plate whenever it looks as though it needs replenishing. Protest politely *before* you are full, because you will definitely be urged to eat more! It is good manners to allow yourself to be persuaded to eat with a certain show of reluctance.

In many country areas it is still customary to eat some dishes with the fingers. In this case use the right hand only.

To indicate you have finished, sit back with a satisfied 'il-**Ham**-du lil-**leh**!' ("praise be to God!").

In a village, a large bowl and jug of water will be brought after a meal so that you can wash your hands and rinse your mouth. A bottle of cologne may be passed round, so that guests may refresh themselves (cologne, scent, and aftershave are always welcome gifts).

Tea or coffee will be served, and, if it is lunchtime, you may be invited to have a rest. More usually, it is polite to leave when the tea or coffee cups have been removed.

If you come upon people eating a meal, they will, out of politeness, invite you to join them; but if you were not expected, you should refuse unless they absolutely insist.

It was a lovely party.	*keh*-nit *Haf*-la mum-*teh*-za.	كان الحفل ممتازاً
The food was delicious.	il-'*akl* kehn la-*zeez* gid-dan.	كان الأكل لذيذاً جداً
(lit.) Blessings on your hands (to the hostess).	*tis*-lam 'ee-*dey*-kee.	تسلم يديك
Thank-you so much	'*al*-fi shukr, mu-ta-*shak*-kir *gid*-dan.	متشكر جداً
It's been lovely meeting you.	it-shar-*raf*-na.	تشرفت بلقائك
Can I give you a lift?	*mum*-kin a-waS-*Sa*-lak [a-waS-*Sa*-lik]?	هل اوصلك ؟
. . . to two or more	*mum*-kin a-waS-*Sal*-kum?	هل اوصلكم؟

SHOPPING

Opening times of shops, offices, and banks vary from country to country and season to season; in summer, business may start and end early to avoid the heat of the day. Many shops close in the middle of the day and reopen in the late afternoon. In Saudi Arabia and some Gulf countries business comes to a halt briefly with the call to prayer; shops are either closed or simply left unattended while the shopkeeper goes to the local mosque or prays in a quiet back room.

In some countries businesses and institutions tend to close on Fridays, whereas in others the Western custom of Sunday closing has been retained.

The traditional *souk* (market or bazaar) — a maze of streets and tiny alleyways where you can buy everything from a frying pan to a silk carpet — is a fascinating place to visit, even if you don't want to buy. Because goods of a particular kind — jewelry, spices, hardware, clothing, and so on — are sold in one area of the souk, it's easy to compare prices when you are buying a major item. This incidentally is considered the sensible way to shop, so there will be no hard feelings if you decide to "come back later." The most famous souks are perhaps the Hamidiyya in Damascus and the Khan ElKhalili in Cairo. Because these are both at the heart of the old cities, you can explore some of the early mosques and palaces at the same time.

GENERAL EXPRESSIONS

| I'd like to go shopping. | ᶜ*a-wiz* [ᶜ*aw-za*] *ash-ti-ree Ha-geht*. | اريد الذهاب للتسوق |

Can I see that?	**mum**-kin a-**shoof** da?	هل يمكن أن أرى هذا؟
I prefer this one.	ba-**faD**-Dal da.	أفضل هذا
How much is it?	bi **kam**?	بكم؟
That's (a bit) expensive.	da **gheh**-lee (**shway**-ya).	هذا غال الى حد ما
Do you have anything cheaper?	ʿan-dak **Ha**-ga 'ar-khaS?	هل عندك شيء أرخص؟
Do you have anything better?	ʿan-dak **Ha**-ga 'aH-san?	هل عندك شيء افضل؟
I owe you —.	ʿan-dee — lak[lik]	— لك علي
You owe me —.	ʿan-dak [ʿan-dik] — lee-ya	— لي عليك
Where can I find a —?	a-leh-"ee — feyn?	— اين اجد

- bakery
- bank
- barber
- beauty parlor
- bookshop
- butcher
- pharmacy (chemist)

- **furn**, **makh**-baz
- bank
- Hal-leh"
- Sa-**lohn** tag-meel
- mak-ta-ba
- gaz-**zaar**
- 'ag-za-**kheh**-na, Say-Da-**lee**-ya

مخبز
بنك
حلاق
صالون تجميل
مكتبة
جزار
اجزخانة، صيدلية

■ clothing store —	■ ma-**Hall** ma-leh-bis —	
		محل ملابس —
for men's clothes	lir-rig-**geh**-la	للرجال
for women's clothes	li s-sit-**teht**	للسيدات
for children's clothes	li l-'aT-**faal**	للاطفال
■ confectioner	■ Ha-la-**weh**-nee	حلواني
■ department store	■ ma-**Hall** ki-**beer**	محل كبير
■ dressmaker	■ khay-**yaa**-Ta	خياطة
■ drugstore	■ 'ag-za-**kheh**-na, Say-Da-**lee**-ya	اجزخانة، صيدلية
■ dry cleaner	■ ma-**Hall** tan-**Deef**	
		محل تنظيف جاف
■ flower shop	■ ma-**Hall** zu-**hoor**	محل زهور
■ greengrocer	■ **khu**-Da-ree	محل خضروات
■ grocery store	■ ba"-"**ehl**	محل بقالة
■ hairdresser	■ kwa-**feer**	كوافير، مصفف الشعر
■ hardware store	■ ma-**Hall** 'a-da-**weht** man-zi-**lee**-ya	محل ادوات منزلية
■ jewelry store	■ ga-wa-**hir**-gee	جواهرجي
■ laundry	■ magh-**sa**-la	مغسلة
■ newsstand	■ kushk ga-**reh**-yid	كشك جرائد
■ optician	■ naD-Da-**raa**-tee	محل نظارات
■ pastry shop	■ Ha-la-**weh**-nee	حلواني

- shoemaker
- shoe store
- shops
- stationer
- tailor

- *gaz-**ma**-gee*   محل تصليح احذية
- *ma-**Hall** gi-zam*   محل احذية
- *da-ka-**keen**, ma-Hal-**leht***   محلات
- *muk-**ta**-ba*   مكتبة
- *tar-**zee**, khay-**yaaT***   خياط

BOOKS

Where can I buy English-language books?	*ash-**ti**-ree **ku**-tub in-gi-**lee**-zee feyn?* أين استطيع شراء كتب بالانجليزية؟

I would like — .   *ᶜa-wiz [ᶜaw-za]* —.   اريد —

- a guidebook
- a map
- a map of the city

- *da-**leel** si-**yeh**-Hee*   دليل سياحي
- *kha-**ree**-Ta*   خريطة
- *kha-**ree**-Ta lil-**ba**-lad*   خريطة للمدينة

Do you have any books in English?   *ᶜan-**du**-kum **ku**-tub bi-lin-gi-**lee**-zee?* هل عندكم كتب بالانجليزية؟

Do you have books about Egypt?   *ᶜan-**du**-kum **ku** tub ᶜan maSr?* هل عندكم كتب عن مصر ؟

- about the Middle East

- *ᶜan ish-**sharq** il-'**aw**-SaT?*   عن الشرق الاوسط

Do you have any novels?   *ᶜan-**du**-kum ri-wa-**yeht**?* هل عندكم روايات؟

■ detective stories   ■ *qi-SaS boo-li-See-ya*

قصص بوليسية

■ short stories   ■ *qi-SaS qa-See-ra* قصص قصيرة

■ dictionary   ■ *qa-moos* قاموس

■ English-Arabic   ■ *qa-moos in-gi-lee-zee-ᶜa-ra-bee*
dictionary

قاموس إنجليزي – عربي

■ a pocket dictionary ■ *qa-moos geyb* قاموس جيب

I'll take these books. ***heh*-khud ik-*ku*-tub dee.**

سآخذ هذه الكتب

CLOTHING

I'm looking for — . *ba-daw-war ᶜa-la —.* — أريد

■ a belt   ■ *Hi-zehm* حزام

■ a blouse   ■ *bloo-za* بلوزة

■ a bra   ■ *soot-yehn* حملة صدر

■ briefs (men)   ■ *kee-lott* سروال داخلي

■ a cardigan   ■ *ja-kitt tree-koh* جاكيت (تريكو)

■ a coat   ■ *bal-Too* معطف

■ a dress   ■ *fus-tehn* فستان

■ handkerchiefs   ■ *ma-na-deel* مناديل

■ a hat   ■ *bur-ney-Ta* قبعة

■ a jacket   ■ *ja-kit-ta* جاكيت، سترة

jeans	jeenz	بنطلون جينز
a necktie	ka-ra-**vat**-ta	ربطة عنق
a nightgown	"a-**meeS** nohm	قميص نوم
panties	kee-**lott**	سروال داخلي نسائي
pantyhose, tights	koo-**lohn**	جوارب طويلة
a robe, dressing gown	rohb	ثوب، روب
sandals	**san**-dal	صندل
a scarf	'i-**sharb**, ku-**fee**-ya	كوفية
a shawl	shehl	شال
a shirt	"a-**meeS**	قميص
shoes	**gaz**-ma	حذاء
a skirt	gu-**nil**-la	جيبة، جونلة
a slip	kom-bi-ney **zohn**	قميص داخلي
slippers	**shib**-shib	شبشب
socks, stockings	sha-**raab**	جوارب
a suit (man's)	**bad**-la	بدلة
a suit (woman's)	tay-**yeer**	طاقم حريمي
a sweater	bu-**loh** var	بلوفر، كنزة صوفية
a swimsuit	ma-**yoh**	مايو، لباس بحر
a T-shirt	fa-**nil**-la	فانلة، قميص نصف كم
a tracksuit	libs tad-**reeb**	بدلة تدريب

■ trousers, pants	■ *ban-Ta-lohn*	بنطلون، سروال
■ an undershirt, vest	■ *fa-nil-la*	فانلة، قميص داخلي
■ underwear	■ *ma-leh-bis dakh-lee-ya*	ملابس داخلية

You may find it comfortable to wear the long loose robe (usually made of cotton) which is still traditional dress in many parts of the Middle East — the galabiyya (*gal-la-bee-ya*) (known in the Arab countries further east as the *thawb* or the *dish-da-sha*) — or the more widely cut version, with broad sleeves — the *kaftan* — ("*uf-Taan*). A long cloak, the *abaya* — *ᶜa-beh-ya* — may be worn over these; or, in North Africa especially, the woollen *burnous* — (*bur-noos*).

Colors, Styles, Fabrics

I want something in —.	*ᶜa-wiz [ᶜaw-za] lohn* —.	اريد لون —
■ black	■ '*is-wid*	اسود
■ blue	■ '*az-ra*"	ازرق
■ red	■ '*aH-mar*	احمر
■ green	■ '*akh-Dar*	اخضر
■ yellow	■ '*aS-far*	اصفر
■ white	■ '*ab-yaD*	ابيض
■ brown	■ *bun-nee*	بني
■ gray	■ *ra-maa-dee*	رمادي
■ beige	■ *beyj*	بني فاتح

■ pink	■ **war**-dee	وردي
■ purple	■ ba-naf-**si**-gee	بنفسجي
I don't like this color.	ma-ba-**Hib**-bish il-**lohn** da.	لا أحب هذا اللون
I prefer this one.	ba-**faD**-Dal da.	أفضل هذا
I'd like something <u>lighter</u> (in color).	ʿa-wiz **Ha**-ga 'af-**taH**.	أريد لوناً افتح
■ darker	■ 'agh-ma"	أغمق
■ plain	■ **seh**-da	سادة
■ patterned	■ mu-shag-ga-ra, man-"**oo**-sha	منقوش
■ striped	■ mu-khaT-**Ta**-Ta	مخطط
■ (hand) embroidered	■ mash-**ghool** (bil-**yadd**)	مطرز (شغل يد)
Do you have anything <u>else</u>?	ʿan-**du** kum **Ha**-ga tan-ya?	هل يوجد شيء آخر؟
■ better	■ 'aH-san	أفضل
■ cheaper	■ 'ar-khaS	أرخص
■ larger	■ 'ak-bar	أكبر
■ fuller	■ 'aw-saʿ	أوسع
■ smaller	■ 'aS-ghar	أصغر
■ longer	■ 'aT-wal	أطول
■ shorter	■ 'a"-Sar	أقصر

Do you have anything in (pure) — ?	*ᶜan-**du**-kum **Ha**-ga — (**Saa**-fee)?* هل عندكم شيء — خالص ؟

■ cotton	■ *"uTn*	قطن
■ wool	■ *Soof*	صوف
■ silk	■ *Ha-**reer***	حرير
■ polyester	■ *pul-**yis**-tir*	الياف صناعية
■ leather	■ *gild*	جلد

I'd like something heavier (i.e., warmer)	*ᶜa-wiz [ᶜaw-za] **Ha**-ga '**at**-"al.* اريد شيئاً اثقل

■ lighter (i.e., cooler)	■ *'a-**khaff***	اخف
■ for the evening	■ *swa-**reyh***	لحفلة ساهرة

Is this handmade?	*da shughl **yadd**?* هل هذا صنع يد ؟

Trying It On

Can I try this on?	***mum**-kin al-**bi**-soo?* هـل استطيـع لبـس هـذا؟
I take size —	*ma-"**eh**-see — .* مقاسي — .
Could you measure me?	***mum**-kin ti-"**ees**-nee?* خذ مقاسي من فضلك
This is too — .	*da — ᶜa-**leh**-ya.* هذا — جداً

■ long	■ *Ta-**weel***	طويل
■ short	■ *"u-**Say**-yar*	قصير

| loose | **weh**-si^c | واسع |
| tight | **day**-ya" | ضيق |

Can you alter this for me?	**mum**-kin tuZ-buT-**heh**-lee?	هل يمكنك تغيير هذا لي ؟
When will it be ready?	hat-**koon** gah-za '**im**-ta?	متى ستكون جاهزة ؟
The zipper doesn't work.	is-**sus**-ta mak-**soo**-ra.	السوستة مكسورة

ELECTRICAL APPLIANCES

Most countries in the Middle East use 220 volts, but there are exceptions; so check before you go, or take an adapter with you.

| I want to buy — . | ^{c}**a**-wiz [^{c}**aw**-za] ash-**ti**-ree — . | أريد شراء — . |

an adapter	mu-**Haw**-wil	محول
a battery	baT-Ta-**ree**-ya	بطارية
a blender	khal-**laaT**	خلاط
a calculator	'eh-la **Has**-ba	آلة حاسبة
a cassette player	gi-**hehz** ka-**sitt**	جهاز كاسيت
a cassette recorder	gi-**hehz** ka-**sitt** mu-**sag**-gil	مسجل كاسيت
a shaver	**ma**-ka-nit Hi-**leh**-"a	آلة حلاقة

■ a hair dryer	■ sish-**waar**, mu-**gaf**-fif li sh-**sha**ᶜr مجفف للشعر
■ a microcasette player	■ **wok**-man, gi-**hehz** ka-**sitt** Su-**ghay**-yar ووكمان، جهاز كاسيت صغير
■ a plug	■ **fee**-sha فيشة
■ a (portable) radio	■ **rad**-yo (Su-**ghay**-yar) راديو (صغير)
■ a television	■ ti-li-viz-**yohn** تليفزيون
■ a video- recorder	■ gi-**hehz** **vid**-yo جهاز فيديو

What voltage does this take?	kam il-**volt**? ما هو الفولت الذي تستخدمه ؟
Could you demonstrate it for me?	**mum**-kin ti-**shagh**-ghal-**hoo**-lee? هل يمكن ان تشغله لي ؟
It doesn't work.	mab-yish-ta-**ghalsh**. لا يعمل

FOOD AND HOUSEHOLD ITEMS

(See p. 79-88 for food words.)

I'd like — .	ᶜa-wiz [ᶜaw-za] — .	. — اريد
■ a bar of soap	■ Sa-**boo**-na	صابونة
■ breakfast cereal	■ korn fleyks	كورن فلاكس
■ a can of sardines	■ ᶜil-bit sar-**deen**	علبة سردين
■ chocolate (candy)	■ sho-ko-**laa**-ta	شكولاتة

▪ cocoa (hot chocolate)	▪ *ka-kaw*	كاكاو
▪ (ground) coffee	▪ *bunn*	بن
▪ cookies (biscuits)	▪ *bas-ka-weet*	بسكويت
▪ cooking oil	▪ *zeyt Ta-beekh*	زيت للطهي
▪ a loaf	▪ *ri-gheef*	رغيف خبز
▪ matches	▪ *ka-breet*	كبريت
▪ milk	▪ *la-ban, Ha-leeb*	حليب
▪ paper tissues	▪ *ma-na-deel wa-ra"*	مناديل ورق
▪ salt	▪ *malH*	ملح
▪ soap powder	▪ *Sa-boon bud-ra*	صابون بودرة
▪ sugar	▪ *suk-kar*	سكر
▪ tea	▪ *shayy*	شاي
▪ toilet paper	▪ *wa-ra" twa-litt*	ورق تواليت
▪ vinegar	▪ *khall*	خل
▪ liquid detergent	▪ *Sa-boon seh-yil*	صابون سائل
▪ yogurt	▪ *la-ban za-beh-dee*	لبن زبادي

Containers

a bottle	*"i-zeh-za*	زجاجة
a bottle of —	*"i-zeh-zit —*	زجاجة —
a packet	*beh-koo*	كيس
a tin, a can, a carton	*ᶜil-ba*	علبة

a can of —   ‛il-bit —   علبة —

a jar   bar-Ta-maan   برطمان

THE SPICE MARKET

Oriental spices are increasingly popular in the West. A selection bought from the great sacksful on display in the spice section of the bazaar makes an unusual gift for adventurous cooks back home. (Label them at once so that you know which is which!) The most common are:

■ cardamom (*Hab-ba-hehn* حبهان) Small pods of highly aromatic seeds, used in both sweet and savory dishes and to flavor Turkish coffee.

■ cumin (*kam-moon* كمّون) sold as whole seeds or in powdered form, adds interest to simple foods like lentils and beans. It is often used in combination with coriander.

■ coriander (*kuz-ba-ra* كسبرة), either its ground seeds or leaves, which look like flat-leaved parsley and can also be used as a garnish.

■ saffron (*za‛-fraan* زعفران) gives rice a subtle, slightly earthy flavor and delicate yellow color. (Turmeric is a cheaper substitute.)

■ harissa (*ha-ree-sa* شطة), or ground red chilies, also sold as a paste, is an important ingredient in many North African dishes.

Nutmeg, cinnamon, and cloves — used for centuries in the West as an ingredient in desserts, punches, and milk drinks — are also used in savory dishes in the Middle East, and can be bought there for a fraction of the price.

Every region has its own preferred mixture of ground spices. In North Africa the mixture known as *raas il-ha-noot* usually includes red pepper, coriander, and cumin.

Unless you are buying a readymade mixture, buy the whole seeds, to be freshly ground when needed. In the spice bazaar you also find dried fruit and nuts, again great bargains compared with the cost in Europe or the States.

Quantities

The metric system is generally used, that is, kilos, grams and liters. These words don't change in the plural in Arabic:

a kilo	(X) *kee-loo* —	كيلو —
(X kilos of) — .		
a gram	(X) *grehm* —	جرام —
(X grams) of —		
a liter	(X) *litr* —	لتر —
(X liters) of —		
half a kilo	nuSS *kee-loo*	نصف كيلو
a quarter of a kilo	rub^c *kee-loo*	ربع كيلو

The traditional measure of one pound — about half a kilo — is still widely used:

a pound (of —)	*raTl* (—)	رطل
That's enough.	ki-*feh-ya* **ki**-da.	هذا يكفي
A little more.	ka-*mehn* shway-ya.	أكثر قليلاً
A little less.	'a-"all shway ya.	أقل قليلاً
Can I see that, please?	**mum**-kin a-**shoof** da, min **faD**-lak?	هل يمكن أن أرى هذا من فضلك ؟
Is it fresh?	da **Taa**-za?	هل هو طازج ؟

AT THE JEWELER'S

I'd like to see — .	*ᶜa-wiz [ᶜaw-za] a-shoof* — .	. — أريد أن أرى
■ a bracelet	■ *ghi-wey-sha*	سوار
■ a brooch	■ *brohsh*	دبوس
■ a chain	■ *sil-si-la*	سلسلة
■ a charm, medallion	■ *ᶜul-li-"a*	مدالية، تعليقة
■ some earrings	■ *Ha-la"*	حلق
■ a necklace	■ *ᶜu"d*	عقد
■ prayer beads	■ *sib-Ha*	سبحة
■ a ring	■ *kheh-tim*	خاتم
■ a wristwatch	■ *seh-ᶜit yadd*	ساعة يد
■ an alarm clock	■ *mi-nab-bih*	منبه
■ a watch with an alarm	■ *seh-ᶜit yadd bi mi-nab-bih*	ساعة يد بها منبه
Is this — ?	*da* — ?	هل هذا — ؟
■ gold	■ *da-hab*	ذهب
■ platinum	■ *bleh-teen*	بلاتين
■ silver	■ *faD-Da*	فضة
■ stainless steel	■ *steyn-lis steel*	صلب لا يصدا
■ solid gold	■ *da-hab Saa-fee*	ذهب صافي

■ gold plated　　■ **maT**-lee **da**-hab　　مطلي ذهب

Gold jewelry is often sold by weight, with a sum added for the workmanship involved. The price of gold is published daily in the newspapers.

How many carats is it?	da kam "i-**raaT**?	كم قيراط هذا ؟
How much is it per carat?	il-"i-**raaT** bi kam?	بكم القيراط ؟
Is this new or antique?	da gi-**deed** wal-la "a-**deem**?	هل هذا جديد أم قديم ؟
What is this stone?	'eyh il-**Ha**-gar da?	ما هذا الحجر ؟

Precious and Semiprecious Stones

amethyst	ga-**masht**	جمشت
aquamarine	za-**bar**-gad	زبرجد
coral	mur-**gehn**	مرجان
diamond	al-**maaz**	ماس
emerald	zu-**mur**-rud	زمرد
ivory	ᶜehg, sinn il-**feel**	عاج
jade	jehd	يشب
onyx	ᶜa-"**ee**"	عقيق
pearls	**lu**'-lu'	لؤلؤ
ruby	ya-"**oot**	ياقوت
sapphire	ya-"**oot** 'az-ra"	زفير ، ياقوت ازرق

| topaz | to-**behz** | توباز |
| turquoise | fey-**rooz** | فيروز |

MUSIC, RECORDS, AND TAPES

Is there a record shop around here?	fee ma-**Hall** is-Ti-wa-**naat** "u-**ray**-yib?	هل هناك محل اسطوانات قريب ؟
Do you have — ?	ʿan-**du**-kum — ?	هل عندكم — ؟
■ cassettes	■ ka-sit-**teht**	شرائط كاسيت
■ compact discs	■ is-Ti-wa-**naat** ley-zar	اسطوانات ليزر
■ needles	■ 'i-bar	إبر
■ records	■ is-Ti-wa-**naat**	اسطوانات
■ tapes	■ sha-**raa**-yiT	شرائط
I'd like — .	ʿa-wiz [ʿaw-za] — .	اريد —
■ Western music	■ mu-**see**-qa ghar-**bee**-ya	موسيقى غربية
■ classical music	■ mu-**see**-qa kla-see-**kee**-ya	موسيقى كلاسيكية
■ folk music	■ mu-**see**-qa shaʿ-**bee**-ya	موسيقى شعبية
■ jazz	■ jazz	جـاز
■ light music	■ mu-**see**-qa kha-**fee**-fa	موسيقى خفيفة

| ■ opera | ■ *'u-bi-ra* | أوبرا |
| ■ oriental music | ■ *mu-see-qa shar-"ee-ya* | موسيقى شرقية |

Can I listen to this?   ***mum*-kin *as*-ma^c *da?***

هل يمكن أن أسمع هذا ؟

NEWSPAPERS AND MAGAZINES

Do you have an English language newspaper?	^c*an*-dak ga-**ree**-da in-gi-**lee**-zee?	هل عندكم جريدة بالإنجليزية ؟
■ magazine	■ *ma-***gal**-la	مجلة
Do you have stamps?	^c*an*-dak Ta-**waa**-bi^c?	هل عندك طوابع ؟
■ postcards	■ ku-**root** bus-**tehl**	بطاقات بريدية
■ a map of the town	■ kha-**ree**-Ta lil-**ba**-lad	خريطة للمدينة
■ a guidebook	■ da-**leel** si-yeh-**Hee**	دليل سياحي

PHOTOGRAPHIC SUPPLIES

Is there a camera shop near here?	fee ma-**Hall** ka-me-reht "u-**ray**-yib?	هل يوجد محل آلات تصوير قريب ؟
I'd like a good camera.	^c*a*-wiz [^c*aw*-za] ka-me-ra kway-**yi**-sa.	أريد آلة تصوير جيدة
■ inexpensive	■ ri-**khee**-Sa	رخيصة

Do you have <u>color</u> film?	ʿan-**du**-kum film mu-**law**-win?	
		هل عندكم أفلام ملونة ؟
■ black and white	■ 'ab-yaD **wis**-wid	أبيض وأسود
I'd like <u>20</u> . exposures.	ʿa-wiz [ʿaw-za] <u>ʿish-**reen**</u> **Soo**-ra.	
		أريد فلم ٢٠ صورة
■ 36	■ **sit**-ta wa-ta-la-**teen**	٣٦ صورة
What is the expiration date?	'eyh ta-**reekh** il-'in-ti-**heh**'?	
		ما هو تاريخ إنتهاء الصلاحية؟
Do you develop film?	bit-Ham-**ma**-Doo 'af-**lehm**?	
		هل تحمض الأفلام ؟
I'd like a roll of film for slides.	ʿa-wiz [ʿaw-za] film slaydz.	
		أريد فلم شرائح
A print with <u>glossy</u> finish.	**Soo**-ra lam-**mee**-ʿa.	
		أريد طباعة لامعة
■ mat	■ maT, maT-**fee**-ya	مطفية
I want an <u>enlargement</u> of this one.	ʿa-wiz [ʿaw-za] a-**kab**-bar dee.	
		أريد تكبير هذه
■ another print	■ **nus**-kha **tan**-ya min dee	
		نسخة أخرى من هذه
When will they be ready?	hat-**koon** gah-za 'im-ta?	
		متى ستكون جاهزة ؟
Do you have flashbulbs?	ʿan-dak lam-**beht** flash?	
		هل عندكم لمبات فلاش ؟

SOUVENIRS

The Middle East is famous for ceramics, carpets, jewelry, copper and brassware, leather goods, and fine inlay work in metal and wood. There is no problem in having goods shipped or air-freighted home, though there are likely to be restrictions on the export of antiques. If you are considering buying an antique, make sure you get a government guarantee of authenticity.

Bargaining is a normal practice in traditional markets and bazaars, though not in modern shops or supermarkets. The basic technique is to express mild shock and disbelief at the price suggested, propose a sum well below that, then gradually work up to a compromise between the two. Often the shopkeeper will make you a "final offer" as you are about to leave the shop. It is quite all right to shop around and compare prices, then return to a shop where you have already bargained strenuously. You will always be welcome!

Arabic has many elaborate phrases for use on such occasions. Some of the most useful are:

Be generous!	*khal-**leek** ka-**reem**!*	! كن كريما
You're putting me off (with the price)!	*khaD-**Deyt**-nee!*	! افزعتني
Come down a bit.	***naz**-zil **shway** ya.*	اخفض لي السعر
Let's split the difference.	***ni"**-sim il-**ba**-lad nuS-**Seyn**.*	نقسم البلد نصفين
Here's the money.	*it-**faD**-Dal.*	تفضل

When you do buy something, the shopkeeper — and friends, too — will congratulate you with:

| Congratulations! | *mab-rook!* | مبروك ! |

To which the reply is: *al-laah yi-beh-rik feek [fee-kee]*

الله يبارك فيك

| Do you have leather goods? | *ʿan-du-kum maS-nu-ʿaat gil-dee-ya?* | هل عندكم مصنوعات جلدية ؟ |

■ jewelry	■ *mu-gaw-ha-raat*	مجوهرات
■ pottery, ceramics	■ *fukh-khaar*	فخار ، خزف
■ carpets	■ *sa-ga-geed*	سجاجيد
■ (long narrow) rugs	■ *mash-sha-yeht*	مشايات
■ woven rugs	■ *'ak-li-ma*	اكلمة
■ caftans	■ *"a-fa-Teen*	قفاطين
■ galabiyyas (Arab robe)	■ *gal-la-bee-yeht*	جلاليب
■ brassware	■ *muS-nu-ʿaat ni-Hehs*	مصنوعات نحاس أصفر
■ copperware	■ *maS-nu-ʿaat ni-Hehs 'aH-mar*	مصنوعات نحاس احمر
■ glassware	■ *maS-nu-ʿaat "i-zehz*	مصنوعات زجاجية

| I am looking for a brass tray. | *ʿa-wiz [ʿaw-za] Sa-nee-ya ni-Hehs.* | اريد صينية نحاس |

■ a tray with inlay	■ Sa-**nee**-ya mu-Ta^c-^{c}a-ma	صينية مطعمة
■ a tray with a stand	■ Sa-**nee**-ya bi **kur**-see	صينية بكرسي
■ a box with inlay	■ san-**doo**" mu-Ta^c-^{c}am	صندوق مطعم
■ a coffee set	■ Ta"m lil-"**ah**-wa	طاقم للقهوة
■ a chess set	■ sha-Ta-**rang**	طاقم شطرنج
■ a coffeepot	■ 'ab-**ree**" "**ah**-wa	إبريق قهوة
■ an ashtray	■ Ta"-**Too**-"a	طفاية
■ slippers	■ **shib** shib	شبشب
■ sandals	■ **san**-dal	صندل
■ a leather bag	■ **shan**-Ta gild	حقيبة جلدية
■ a leather cushion (pouffe)	■ boof gild	حشية جلدية
■ a water (hubble bubble) pipe	■ **shee**-sha	نارجيلة . شيشة
■ a vase	■ zuh-**ree**-ya	زهرية
■ prayer beads	■ **sib**-Ha	سبحة

Do you sell oriental perfumes?	^{c}an-**du**-kum ^{c}u-**Toor** shar-"**ee**-ya?	هل عندكم عطور شرقية ؟
■ jasmine	■ yas-**meen**	ياسمين

■ rose	■ *ward*	ورد
■ sandalwood	■ *san-dal*	صندل

Is this handmade?	*da shughl* **yadd**?	هل هذا شغل يد ؟
Please wrap these for me.	*lif-fu-**hum**-lee, min* **faD**-lak.	أرجو ان تلف هذا لي
Will you air freight this for me?	**mum**-kin tib-*ᶜat*-**hoo**-lee bil-ba-**reed** il-gaw-wee?	
		هل ترسل لي هذا بالبريد الجوي ؟
Please send it by surface mail.	*ib-ᶜat*-**hoo**-lee bil-ba-**reed** il-ᶜeh-dee.	أرجو ان ترسل لي هذا بالبريد العادي

STATIONERY ITEMS

I want —	*ᶜa-wiz [ᶜaw-za]* — .	اريد — .
■ a ball-point pen	■ "*a-lam* **gaff**	قلم جاف
■ envelopes	■ *Zu-**roof***	ظروف
■ an eraser	■ *as-**tee**-ka*	ممسحة
■ glue	■ *Samgh*	صمغ
■ a notebook	■ **noh**-ta	دفتر جيب
■ a pencil	■ "*a-lam* ru-**SaaS**	قلم رصاص
■ a pencil sharpener	■ *bar-**reh**-ya*	مبراة
■ a ruler	■ *mas-**Ta**-ra*	مسطرة
■ Scotch tape	■ ***wa**-ra" laz-**zeh**"*	شريط لاصق

■ string	■ *du-**baa**-ra*	حبل دوبارة
■ typing paper	■ *wa-ra" li l-'eh-la l-**kat**-ba*	
		ورق آلة كاتبة
■ wrapping paper	■ *wa-ra" gal-**lehd***	ورق لف طرود
■ a writing pad	■ *blok noht*	دفتر

TOBACCO

Do you have (American) cigarettes?	*^can-**du**-kum sa **geh**-yir (am-ree-**keh**-nee)?*	هل عندكم سجائر (أمريكية) ؟
I'd like a pack of <u>filter</u> cigarettes.	*^ca-wiz [^caw-za] ^cil-bit sa-**geh**-yir fil-tar.*	أريد علبة سجائر بالفلتر
■ unfiltered	■ *bi-**doon** fil-tar*	بدون فلتر
■ menthol	■ *min-**tool***	بالمنتول
■ king size	■ *king sayz*	كنج سايز
■ mild	■ *kha-**fee** fa*	خفيفة
What brands do you have?	*^can-dak 'aS-**naaf** 'eyh?*	ما هي الأنواع عندكم ؟
Do you have — ?	*^can-**du**-kum — ?*	هل عندكم ـ ؟
■ cigars	■ *see-**gaar***	سيجار
■ pipe tobacco	■ *dukh-**khehn** bee-ba*	دخان غليون
■ a lighter	■ *wal-**leh**-^ca*	ولاعة

■ lighter fluid	■ *ban-zeen/ghehz wal-leh-ᶜa*	بنزين / غاز ولاعة
■ matches	■ *kab-reet*	كبريت

TOILETRIES

Is there a pharmacy (chemist) near here?   *fee 'ag-za-kheh-na "u-ray-yi-ba min hi-na?*   هل توجد اجزخانة قريبة ؟

Do you have — ?   *ᶜan-du-kum — ?*   هل عندكم — ؟

■ aftershave	■ *los-yohn baᶜd il-Hi-leh-"a*	سائل بعد الحلاقة
■ bobby pins	■ *bi-nas*	دبابيس للشعر
■ a brush	■ *fur-sha*	فرشاة
■ cleansing cream (makeup remover)	■ *kreym li-'i-zeh-lit il-mak-yaj*	كريم لازالة المكياج
■ cologne	■ *ko-lon-ya*	كولونيا
■ a comb	■ *mishT*	مشط
■ depilatory cream	■ *kreym li-'i-zeh-lit ish-shaᶜr*	كريم لازالة الشعر
■ a deodorant	■ *mu-zeel lil-ᶜa-ra"*	مزيل لرائحة العرق
■ diapers	■ *ka-wa-feel*	احفضة للاطفال
■ emery boards	■ *mab-rad wa-ra" liD-Da-waa-fir*	مبرد ورق للاظافر

■ eyebrow pencil	■ *"a-lam Ha-***weh**-*gib*	قلم حواجب
■ eye liner	■ ***ay**-lay-nar, kuHl*	قلم كحل
■ eye shadow	■ *Dill lil-ᶜu-***yoon**	ظل جفون
■ wash cloth (face flannel)	■ *foo-Ta lil-***wishsh**	فوطة /منشفة وجه
■ gargle	■ *ghar-***gha**-*ra*	غرغرة
■ hairspray	■ *is-***brey** *lish-***sha**ᶜr	مثبت للشعر
■ lipstick	■ *rooj*	احمر شفاه
■ makeup	■ *mak-***yaj**	مكياج
■ mascara	■ *mas-***ka**-*ra*	ماسكره
■ mirror	■ *mi-***reh**-*ya*	مرآة
■ mouthwash	■ *gha-***seel** *lil-***famm**	غسيل للفم
■ nail clippers	■ *"aS-***Saa**-*fa liD-Da-***waa**-*fir*	قصافة للأظافر
■ a nail file	■ ***mab**-*rad Da-***waa**-*fir*	مبرد للأظافر
■ nail polish	■ *ma-nee-***keer**	طلاء اظافر
■ nail polish remover	■ *a-see-***tohn**	مزيل طلاء الأظافر
■ nail scissors	■ *ma-"***aSS** *liD-Da-***waa**-*fir*	مقص اظافر
■ night cream	■ *kreym lil-***leyl**	كريم لليل
■ razor blades	■ *'am-***wehs** *Hi-***leh**-*"a*	أمواس حلاقة
■ sanitary napkins	■ *fo-waT SiH-***Hee**-*ya*	فوط صحية

■ shampoo	■ *sham-**poo***	شامبو
■ shaving soap	■ *Sa-**boon** Hi-**leh**-"a*	صابون حلاقة
■ soap	■ *Sa-**boon***	صابون
■ a sponge	■ *sa-**fin**-ga*	إسفنجة
■ suntan lotion	■ *los-**yohn** li Hi-**meh**-yit il-**bash**-ra*	سائل حماية البشرة
■ suntan oil	■ *zeyt li Hi-**meh**-yit il-**bash**-ra*	زيت حماية البشرة
■ talcum powder	■ ***bud**-rit talk*	بودرة تلك
■ tampons	■ ***tam**-paks*	صمامات قطنية ، تامبونات
■ tissues	■ *ma-na-**deel** wa-ra"*	مناديل ورق
■ toilet paper	■ ***wa**-ra" twa-**litt***	ورق تواليت
■ a toothbrush	■ *fur-**shit** 'as-**nehn***	فرشاة للأسنان
■ toothpaste	■ *ma^c-**goon** lil-'as-**nehn***	معجون اسنان
■ tweezers	■ *mul-"**aaT***	ملقاط

PERSONAL CARE AND SERVICES

AT THE BARBER

Does the hotel have a barber shop?	*fee Hal-leh" fil-fun-du"?* هل يوجد حلاق بالفندق ؟
Where is there a good barber shop?	*feyn a-leh-"ee Hal-leh" kway-yis?* اين اجد حلاقاً جيداً ؟
Do I have to wait long?	*leh-zim as-tan-na ki-teer?* هل يجب ان انتظر فترة طويلة ؟
I want a shave.	*^caw-zak tiH-la"-lee id-da"n.* اريد ان احلق ذقني
■ a haircut	■ *ti-"uS-Si-lee sha^c-ree* اقص شعري
■ just a trim	■ *ti-"aS-Sar-hoo-lee shway-ya* مجرد تهذيب
Trim it at the front.	*khif-fu-hoo-lee min"ud-dehm.* قصه قليلاً من الأمام
■ at the back	■ *min wa-ra* من الخلف
■ at the sides	■ *min ig-gi-nehb* على الجوانب
Leave it long.	*khal-lee Ta-weel shway-ya.* اتركه طويل
I'd like it very short.	*"aS-Sar-hoo-lee khaa-liS.* اريده قصير جداً

I'd like a razor cut.	**"uS**-Soo bil-**moos**.	قصه بالموسى
Please trim my — .	min **faD**-lak u**Z**-**buT**-lee — .	من فضلك قص قليلاً — .
■ beard	■ id-**da**"n	ذقني
■ mustache	■ ish-**sha**-nab	شاربي ، شنبي
■ sideburns	■ is-sa-**weh**-lif	سوالفي
I want to have <u>my beard</u> shaved off.	*c*a-wiz a**H**-la" **da**"-nee.	اريد ان احلق ذقني
■ my mustache	■ **sha**-na-bee	شاربي ، شنبي
I part my hair <u>on the left.</u>	af-ri" sha*c*-ree *c*ash-shi-**mehl**.	افرق شعري من اليسار
■ on the right	■ *c*al-yi-**meen**	من اليمين
■ in the middle	■ fil-**wuST**	من الوسط
A little more here.	'**ak**-tar shway-ya **hi**-na.	اكثر قليلاً من هنا
That's enough.	ki-**feh**-ya **ki**-da.	هذا يكفي
That's fine.	**kway**-yis **ki**-da.	هذا حسن
I (don't) want — .	(mish) *c***a**-wiz — .	(لا) اريد —
■ shampoo	■ sham-**poo**	شامبو
■ tonic	■ ko-**lon**-ya	كولونيا
■ hair oil	■ zeyt sha*c*r	زيت شعر
■ hairspray	■ is-**brey**	مثبت الشعر

| Can I see it in the mirror? | ***mum*-kin a-*shoo*-foo fil-mi-*reh*-ya?** | أريد أن انظر في المرآة |
| How much do I owe you? | ***ᶜa*-wiz kam?** | كم الحساب ؟ |

AT THE BEAUTY PARLOR

[For cutting and trimming terms, see "At the Barber"]

Is there a beauty parlor near here?	***fee* Sa-*lohn* tag-*meel* "u *ray*-yib?**	هل يوجد صالون تجميل قريب ؟
■ hairdresser	■ kwa-*feer*	مصفف شعر ، كوافير
Can I make an appointment — ?	***mum*-kin a*H*-giz ma-ᶜ*ehd* — ?**	أريد حجز موعد
■ this afternoon	■ baᶜd iD-**Duhr**	بعد الظهر
■ tomorrow	■ **buk**-ra	غداً
Can you give me — ?	***mum*-kin tiᶜ-*mil*-lee — ?**	أريد — ؟
■ a color rinse	■ sham-*poo* bil-*lohn*	شامبو تلوين
■ a facial massage	■ tad-*leek*	تدليك وجه
■ a steam massage	■ tad-*leek* bil-bu-*khaar*	تدليك بالبخار
■ a manicure	■ ma-*nee heer*	مانيكير
■ a pedicure	■ pi-di-*keer*	باديكير
■ a permanent	■ ber-ma-*nant*	برماننت
■ a shampoo	■ sham-*poo*	شامبو

■ a tint	■ **Sab**-gha	صبغة
■ a touch up	■ **Sab**-gha lig-gu-**zoor**	صبغة الجزور
■ a wash and set	■ **mee**-zam plee	غسيل وتصفيف
■ a wash and blow dry.	■ gha-**seel** wi sish-**war** bass	غسيل وتجفيف
I (don't) want hairspray.	(mish) ^c**aw**-za is-**brey**.	(لا) اريد مثبت للشعر
Just a little.	**shway**-ya bass.	قليل فقط
I'd like to see a color chart.	^c**aw**-za a-**shoof** da-**leel** 'al-**wehn**.	اريد ان ارى دليل الالوان
I want <u>this color</u>.	^c **aw**-za il-**lohn** da.	اريد هذا اللون
■ the same color	■ nafs il-**lohn**	نفس اللون
■ a darker color	■ lohn ' **agh**-ma"	لون اغمق
■ a lighter color	■ lohn ' **af**-taH	لون افتح

THE HAMMAM

Known in the West as the "Turkish bath," the *Ham-mehm* is in fact a general Middle East development of the Roman communal bath house — a social as well as a hygienic institution. Gossip, intrigue, and sometimes serious debate were as important to the clientele as the steaming, bathing, and massage that took place.

Many hammams still function; if you decide to use their services establish first what you want and how much it will cost. The price quoted may well not include tips to whoever hands out the towels, minds the clothes, and so on.

LAUNDRY AND DRY CLEANING

You may see the *mak-wa-gee* working in a tiny shop open to the street. He will press clothing and bed linens and have them delivered to your door within 24 hours if you are staying in the neighborhood. Note that the quality of dry cleaning services is highly variable. It is safest to take clothes with you that can be washed.

Is there a <u>laundry service</u> in the hotel?	*fee gha-seel wi **mak**-wa fil-**fun**-du"?*	هل يوجد غسيل ومكواة في الفندق ؟
▣ a dry cleaning service	▣ *tan-**Deef** neh-shif*	تنظيف جاف
Is there a <u>laundry</u> near here?	*fee magh-sa-la"u-ray-yi-ba?*	هل توجد مغسلة قريبة
▣ an ironer	▣ *mak-**wa**-gee*	مكوجي ، محل للكي
I want to have these — .	*dee — .*	هذه — .
▣ washed	▣ *lil-gha-seel*	للغسيل
▣ dry cleaned	▣ *lit-tan-**Deef** in-neh-shif*	للتنظيف الجاف
▣ mended	▣ *lit-taS-**leeH***	للتصليح
▣ ironed	▣ *lil-**mak**-wa*	للكي
Here's the list.	*it-**faD**-Dal il-"**ay**-ma.*	هذه هي القائمة

[See Shopping section for clothes words.]

When will it/they be ready?

*Hat-**koon** gah-za '**im**-ta?*

متى ستكون جاهزة؟

I need them <u>for tonight.</u>

*a-na miH-**tehg**-ha [miH-ta-**geh**-ha] bil-**leyl***

أريدهم الليلة

■ tomorrow

■ *buk-ra*

غداً

■ the day after tomorrow

■ *ba^c-di **buk**-ra*

بعد غد

I am leaving <u>soon</u>.

*a-na mi-**seh**-fir [mi-**saf**-ra] "u-**ray**-yib.*

سأسافر قريبا

■ tomorrow

■ *buk-ra*

غداً

Is my laundry ready?

*il-gha-**seel** bi-**teh**-^cee **geh**-hiz?*

هل غسيلي جاهز ؟

This isn't my laundry.

*dee mish bi-**ta**^c-tee.*

هذه ليست لي

There's something missing.

*fee **Ha**-ga na"-Sa.*

ينقص شيء ما

There's a button missing.

*fee zu-**raar** naa-"iS.*

ينقص زر

This is silk.

*da Ha-**reer**.*

هذا حرير

SHOE REPAIRS

Can you repair these shoes for me?

*.**mum**-kin ti-Sal-**laH**-lee ig-**gaz**-ma dee?*

هل يمكن ان تصلح هذه الاحذية لي ؟

They need new <u>heels</u>.	**leh**-zim <u>ka^cb</u> gi-**deed**.	تحتاج لكعب جديد
■ soles	■ na^cl	لنعل
Can you fix it while I wait?	**mum**-kin ti-Sal-**laH**-ha **Heh**-lan?	هل يمكن تصليحها حالا ؟
Would you polish them too?	**mum**-kin ti-lam-ma^c-**heh**-lee ka-**mehn**?	هل يمكن ان تلمعها ايضاً؟
I need them tomorrow.	**a**-na miH-**tehg**-ha [miH ta-**geh**-ha] buk-ra.	احتاجها غداً

WATCH REPAIRS

Can you fix <u>this</u> watch for me?	**mum**-kin ti-Sal-**laH**-lee <u>is-**seh**-^ca dee</u>?	هل تستطيع إصلاح هذه الساعة لي ؟
■ this alarm clock	■ il-mi-**nab**-bih da?	هذا المنبه
It needs a new <u>strap</u>.	^c**aw**-za '<u>us-**teek**</u> gi-**deed**	تحتاج لاوستيك جديد
■ crystal (glass)	■ "₁-**zehz**	لزجاج
■ hour hand	■ ^c**a**"-rab sa-^c**eht**	لعقرب ساعات
■ minute hand	■ ^c**a**"-rab da-"**eh**-yi"	لعقرب دقائق
■ second hand	■ ^c**a**"-rab sa-**weh**-nee	لعقرب ثواني
■ battery	■ baT-Ta-**ree**-ya	لبطارية
It's stopped.	**wi**"-fit.	توقفت

It's fast.	bit-"**ad**-dim.	تقدم
It's slow.	bit-'**akh**-khar.	تؤخر
It needs cleaning.	ͨ**aw**-za tan-**Deef**.	تحتاج لتنظيف
When will it be ready?	hat-**koon** gah-za 'im-ta?	متى ستكون جاهزة ؟
May I have a receipt?	**mum**-kin tid-**dee**-nee waSl?	أرجوك أعطني إيصالاً

CAMERA REPAIRS

| Can you fix this camera? | **mum**-kin ti-Sal-**laH**-lee ik-**ka**-me-ra dee? | هل يمكن تصليح آلة التصوير هذه ؟ |
| There's a problem with — . | fee mush-**ki**-la ma-ͨa — . | هناك مشكلة في — . |

- the exposure counter
  - ͨad-**dehd** iS-**So**-war
  - عداد الصور
- the film winder
  - di-**reh**ͨ it-tagh-**yeer**
  - ذراع التغيير
- the light meter
  - gi-**hehz** it-taͨ-**reeD**/ miq-**yehs** iD-**Doh'**   مقياس الضوء
- the range finder
  - **Daa**-bit il-ma-**seh**-fa
  - ضابط المسافة
- the shutter
  - il-**gheh**-li", ish-**sha**-tar   الغالق

How much will
it cost to fix it?

*it-taS-**leeH** hay-**kal**-lif kam?*

كم يكلف تصليحها ؟

When can I
come and get it?

*as-ti-**lim**-ha '**im**-ta?*

متى احضر لاستلامها ؟

I need it as
soon as possible.

*^ca-**wiz**-ha [^caw-**zeh**-ha]
fi ' **a**"-rab wa"t **mum**-kin.*

احتاجها في
أقرب وقت ممكن

MEDICAL CARE

AT THE PHARMACY

Where is the nearest <u>pharmacy</u>?	*feyn 'a"-rab 'ag-za-**kheh**-na/ Say-Da-**lee**-ya?*	اين اقرب اجزاخانة/ صيدلية؟
■ all-night pharmacy	■ *'ag-za-**kheh**-na ley-**lee**-ya*	■ اجزاخانة ليلية
At what times does it open (close)?	*bi-**yif**-taH (bi-**yi**"-fil) is-**seh**-ʿa kam?*	متى تفتح (تغلق) ؟
I need something for — .	*ʿa-wiz [ʿaw-za] **Ha**-ga li — .*	اريد دواء —
■ asthma	■ *ir-**rabw***	■ للربو
■ a cold	■ *zu-**kehm**, il-**bard***	■ للبرد
■ constipation	■ *il-'im-**sehk***	■ للامساك
■ a cough	■ ***kuH**-Ha*	■ للسعال
■ diarrhea	■ *il-'is-**hehl***	■ للاسهال
■ a fever	■ *su-khu-**nee**-ya*	■ للحمى
■ hay fever	■ *Ha-seh-**see**-ya ra-bee-ʿ**ee**-ya*	■ للحساسية الربيعية
■ headache	■ *Su-**daa**ʿ*	■ للصداع
■ indigestion	■ *soo'il-**haDm***	■ لسوء الهضم
■ insomnia	■ *ʿa-dam in-**nohm***	■ للارق
■ nausea	■ *gham-ma-**mehn***	■ لغثيان النفس

■ sunburn	■ *Hu-roo"* ish-**shams**	حروق الشمس
■ toothache	■ *wa-ga^c* fiD-**Dirs**	لألم الأسنان
■ an upset stomach	■ *ta-^{c}ab* fil *mi^c*-da	لاضطراب المعدة

Do I need a prescription for this medicine?	*leh*-zim ru-**shit**-ta lid-**da**-wa da? هل احتاج لروشتة لهذا الدواء؟
Can you fill this prescription for me now?	*mum*-kin tiS-**rif**-lee ir-ru-**shit**-ta dee dil-**wa**"-tee? هل يمكنك ان تصرف الروشتة لي الآن؟
Do you stock this medicine?	^{c}an-**du**-kum id-**da**-wu da? هل عندكم هذا الدواء؟
It's an emergency.	da Ta-**waa**-ri'. هذه طوارىء
Can I wait for it?	as-tan-**neh**-ha? هل انتظره؟
How long will it take?	ha-**yeh**-khud "**ad**-di 'eyh? كم من الوقت يحتاج ؟

I would like —.	^{c}a-wiz [^{c}aw-za] —. أريد — —.
■ adhesive tape	■ mu-**sham**-ma^c laa-Siq شريط لاصق
■ antacid	■ **da**-wa **Didd** il-Hu-**moo**-Da دواء ضد الحموضة
■ an antiseptic	■ mu-**Tah**-hir مطهر
■ aspirins	■ as-bi-**reen** اسبرين

▪ bandages	▪ *ru-**baaT***	رباط
▪ Band-Aids	▪ ***blaas**-tir*	ضمادات لاصقة
▪ corn plasters	▪ ***blaas**-tir ^ca-**shehn** il-**kal**-loo*	ضمادات لاصقة للمسامير
▪ (absorbent) cotton	▪ *"uTn **Tib**-bee*	قطن طبي
▪ cough drops	▪ *bas-**til**-ya liz-**zohr***	باستيليا طبية
▪ cough syrup	▪ *da-wa **kuH**-Ha*	دواء للسعال
▪ ear (nose) drops	▪ *nu-"aT lil-**widn** (lil-ma-na-**kheer**)*	نقط للأذن (للأنف)
▪ eye drops	▪ *"aT-ra lil-^c**eyn***	نقط للعين
▪ an inhaler	▪ *bakh-**kheh**-kha*	جهاز للاستنشاق
▪ insect repellent	▪ *kreym **Taa**-rid lil-Ha-sha-**raat***	كريم طارد للحشرات
▪ iodine	▪ ***Sab**-ghit **yood***	يود
▪ a (mild) laxative	▪ *mu-**lay**-yin*	مسهل
▪ milk of magnesia	▪ *maH-**lool** il-magh-**nee**-sya*	محلول المغنيزيا
▪ painkillers	▪ *mu-sak-ki-**neht***	مسكنات
▪ potassium permanganate	▪ *ber-min-ga-**neht** il-bu-tas-**yoom***	برمنجنات البوتاسيوم
▪ sanitary napkins	▪ *fo-waT SiH-**Hee**-ya*	فوط صحية

■ sleeping pills	■ *Hu-**boob** mu-naw-**wi**-ma*
	حبوب منومة
■ suppositories	■ *lu-**boos**, mu-**sah**-hil*
	لبوس
■ tampons	■ ***tam**-paks*
	تامبونات طبية
■ a thermometer	■ *tir-mo-**mitr**, mi zehn*
	*Ha-**raa**-ra* ثرمومتر
■ tranquilizers	■ *mu-had-di-'**eht***
	مهدئات
■ vitamins	■ *vi-ta-mi-**neht***
	فيتامينات

Do you have   *ᶜan-**du**-kum maH-**lool***
care products for   <u>*lil-ᶜa-da-**seht** il-**laS**-qa?*</u>
<u>contact lenses</u>?

هل عندكم محلول عدسات لاصقة ؟

■ hard lenses	■ *li l-ᶜa-da-**seht** in-**nash**-fa*
	عدسات صلبة
■ soft lenses	■ *li l-ᶜa-da-**seht** iT-Ta-**ree**-ya*
	عدسات لينة

FINDING A DOCTOR

Most doctors you will come across in the Middle East are likely to have a good working knowledge of English, because English is used in the teaching of medicine in many Arab countries.

I need a doctor.   ***a**-na miH-**tehg** [miH-**teh**-ga]*
*Ta-**beeb**.*   انا محتاج لطبيب

Do you know a doctor who speaks English?	*ti^c-raf Ta-beeb bi-yit-kal-lim in-gi-lee-zee kway-yis?*	هل تعرف طبيبا يتكلم الانجليزية بطلاقة ؟
Where is his office (his clinic)?	*mak-ta-boo (^cee-yat-too) feyn?*	اين مكتبه (عيادته) ؟
Where is the hospital?	*il-mus-tash-fa feyn?*	اين المستشفى ؟

TALKING TO THE DOCTOR

I don't feel well.	*a-na ta^c-behn [ta^c-beh-na]* .	أشعر بتعب
I feel sick.	*nif-see gham-ma^ca-leh-ya.*	أشعر بغثيان النفس
I feel dizzy.	*a-na deh-yikh [day-kha].*	أشعر بدوخة
It hurts me here.	*bi-yiw-ga^c-nee hi-na.*	الألم هنا
<u>My ear</u> hurts.	<u>*wid-nee*</u> *bi-tiw-ga^c-nee.*	اذني تؤلمني
▪ eye	▪ *^cey-nee*	عيني
▪ foot	▪ *rig-lee*	قدمي
▪ hand	▪ *'ee-dee*	يدي
▪ head	▪ *raa-see*	راسي
▪ neck	▪ *ra-"ab-tee*	عنقي
▪ knee	▪ *ruk-bi-tee*	ركبتي
▪ leg	▪ *rig-lee*	رجلي

■ wrist	■ *khun-"it 'ee-dee*	رسغي
<u>My arm</u> hurts.	<u>di-**reh**-ᶜee</u> *bi-yiw-**ga**ᶜ-nee.*	ذراعي يؤلمني
■ ankle	■ *kaᶜ-bee*	كعب القدم
■ back	■ *Dah-ree*	ظهري
■ chest	■ *Sid-ree*	صدري
■ elbow	■ *koo-ᶜee*	كوعي
■ finger	■ *Su-baa-ᶜee*	أصبعي
■ heart	■ *"al-bee*	قلبي
■ hip	■ *ra-da-fee*	ردفي
■ mouth	■ *bu"-"ee*	فمي
■ shoulder	■ *kit-fee*	كتفي
■ tooth	■ *Dir-see*	ضرسي
■ throat	■ *zoh-ree*	حنجرتي
I've broken my —.	*ka-sart* —.	— مكسور
My whole body aches.	*kul-li gis-mee bi-yiw-**ga**ᶜ-nee.*	كل جسمي يؤلمني
I feel feverish.	*ᶜan-dee su-khu-nee-ya.*	أشعر بحمى
I'm constipated.	*ᶜan-dee 'im-sehk.*	عندي إمساك
I have <u>a cold</u>.	*ᶜan-dee <u>zu-kehm</u>.*	عندي برد
■ an abcess	■ *khur-raag*	خراج

something in my eye	*Ha*-ga fi *ʿey-nee*	شيء في عيني
an infection	*'il-ti-hehb*	إلتهاب
diabetes	*ma-raD is-suk-kar*	مرض السكر
diarrhea	*'is-hehl*	إسهال
dysentery	*du-sin-tar-ya*	دوسنتاريا
hepatitis	*'il-ti-hehb ka-bi-dee*	إلتهاب كبدي
a stomach ache	*taʿ-ab fil-miʿ-da*	ألم في المعدة

I am pregnant. *a-na Heh-mil.* انا حامل

I'm (not) allergic to — . *ʿan-dee (ma-ʿan-deesh) Ha-sa-see-ya min — .* (ليس) عندي حساسية من — .

| antibiotics | *mu-Da-Daat ha-ya-wee-ya* | للمضادات الحيوية |
| penicillin | *bi-ni-sil-leen* | للبنسلين |

I had a heart attack — years ago. *gat-lee 'az-ma qal-bee-ya min — si-neen.* أصبت بأزمة قلبية من — سنة

I have high (low) blood pressure. *ʿan-dee Daght ʿeh-lee (waa-Tee).* عندي ضغط دم مرتفع (منخفض)

Do I have <u>appendicitis</u>? *ʿan-dee 'il-ti-hehb iz-zay-da?* هل عندي إلتهاب الزائدة ؟

| tonsillitis | *'il-ti-hehb il-li-waz* | إلتهاب اللوز |
| flu | *in-floo-in-za* | إنفلونزا |

Do I have to go to hospital? *leh-zim ad-khul il-mus-tash-fa?* هل يجب أن اذهب للمستشفى ؟

What can I eat and drink?	*mum*-kin '*eh*-kul *wash*-rab '*eyh?*	ماذا استطيع ان آكل واشرب ؟

Doctor's Instructions

Open your mouth.	*if*-taH *bu''-''ak*/*fum*-mak.	إفتح فمك
Stick out your tongue.	*Tal*-la^c li-*seh*-nak.	أخرج لسانك
Cough.	*kuHH.*	إسعل
Breathe deeply.	khud *na*-fas Ta-*weel*	خذ نفساً طويلاً
Take off your clothes (to the waist).	i''-la^c hu-*doo*-mak (*il-lee foh''*).	إخلع ملابسك (حتى الوسط)
Lie down on your back.	nehm ^{c}a-la *Dah*-rak.	ارقد على ظهرك
■ on your stomach	■ ^{c}a-la *baT*-nak	على بطنك
Get dressed.	*il*-bis [il-*bi*-see].	إلبس

Patient

Are you going to give me a prescription?	hu-tid-*dee*-nee ru-*shit*-ta?	هل ستعطني روشتة ؟
How often should I take this?	a-*khud*-ha *kul*-li ''ad-di '*eyh?*	كم مرة في اليوم سآخذ من هذا ؟
(How long) do I have to stay in bed?	leh-zim a''-^{c}ud fis-si-*reer* (''*ad*-di '*eyh*)?	(حتى متى) سابقى بالسرير؟
Do you need a blood sample?	in-ta ^{c}a-wiz ^{c}ay-*yi*-nit damm?	هل تحتاج لعينة دم ؟
■ a urine sample	■ ^{c}ay-*yi*-nit *bool*	عينة بول

Will you test my blood pressure?	hat-**shoof** DakhT id-**damm**?	هل ستقيس ضغط الدم ؟
Should I have X-rays taken?	ha-ti^c-**mil**-lee 'a-**shi**^{c}-^{c}a?	هل أقوم بعمل أشعة ؟
What is your fee?	**kam** 'at-^{c}**eh**-bak?	كم اتعابك ؟
I have medical insurance.	^{c}**an**-dee ta'-**meen** SiH-Hee.	عندي تأمين صحي
Thank-you very much.	'al-fi shukr.	شكراً جزيلاً

ACCIDENTS AND EMERGENCIES

Help!	il-Ha-"**oo**-nee!	النجدة !
Quickly, get a doctor!	u**T**-lub Ta-**beeb** Heh-lan!	أطلب الطبيب بسرعة
Call an ambulance!	heht il-'is-^{c}**ehf**	أطلب سيارة الاسعاف
We must go to the hospital.	**leh**-zim ni-**rooH** il-mus-**tash**-fa.	يجب أن نذهب للمستشفى
I've (he's) lost a lot of blood.	na-**zaft** (**na**-zaf) damm ki-**teer**.	فقدت (فقد) دماً كثيراً
I've (he's) had a heart attack.	**gat**-lee (**gat**-loo) 'az-ma qal-**bee**-ya.	أصبت (أصيب) بأزمة قلبية
I think the bone is broken.	a-**Zunn** inn il-^{c} aDm in-ka-sar.	أعتقد أن العظم مكسور

I cut myself.	*in-ga-**raHt**.*	جرحت نفسي
I burned myself.	*it-Ha-**ra**"t.*	حرقت نفسي
I was (he was) knocked down.	*kha-ba-**Tit**-nee (kha-ba-**Ti**-too) ᶜa-ra-**bee**-ya.*	صدمتني (صدمته) سيارة
I was (he was) bitten by a dog.	*kalb ᶜaD-**Di**-nee (ᶜ**aD**-Doo).*	عضني (عضه) كلب
rabies	***ma**-raD il-**kalb***	مرض الكلب

AT THE DENTIST

Can you recommend a dentist?	***mum**-kin ti-"**ul**-lee ᶜa-la Ta-**beeb** 'as-**nehn** kway-yis?*	هل تستطيع ان تقترح طبيب اسنان ؟
I'd like to make an appointment.	*ᶜ**a**-wiz [ᶜ**aw**-za] **aH**-giz ma-ᶜ**ehd**.*	اريد ان احجز موعداً
I must see him as soon as possible.	*leh-zim a **shoo**-foo fi 'a"-rab wa"t mum-kin.*	يجب ان اراه في اقرب وقت ممكن
I have an awful toothache.	*'as-**neh**-nee bi-tiw-**gu**ᶜ-noo gid-dan.*	عندي الم اسنان رهيب
I've lost a filling	*il-**Hashw** **wi**-"iᶜ.*	وقع الحشو
I've lost a crown.	*iT-Tar-**boosh** **wi**-"iᶜ.*	وقع الطربوش
I've broken a tooth.	*fee **sin**-na in-**ka**-sa-rit.*	عندي سن مكسور
My gums hurt me.	*il-**li**-sa bi-tiw-**ga**ᶜ-nee.*	لثتي تؤلمني

Is there an infection? *fee "il-ti-**hehb**?* هل هناك إلتهاب ؟

Will it have to
be extracted? **leh**-zim tit-**khi**-li^c^?

هل يجب ان تخلع السن ؟

Will you fill it — ? *ha-tiH-**shee**-ha — ?* هل ستحشوه — ؟

- temporarily
  - *mu-'aq-**qa**-tan* مؤقتاً
- with amalgam
  - *bi Hashw ^c^**eh**-dee* بحشو عادي
- with gold
  - *bi Hashw **da**-hab* بذهب
- with silver
  - *bi Hashw **faD**-Da* بفضة
- with platinum
  - *bi Hashw bla-**teen*** ببلاتين

I need a painkiller. *^c^**a**-wiz [^c^**aw**-za] mu-**sak**-kin.*

احتاج لمسكن

Can you fix? **mum**-kin ti-**Sal**-laH — ?

هل تستطيع إصلاح — ؟

- this bridge
  - *ik-**kub**-ree da* هذا الكوبري
- this crown
  - *iT-Tar-**boosh** da* هذا الطربوش
- this denture
  - *iT-**Ta"**-mi da* هذا الطاقم

When should I
come back? **ar**-ga^c^ '**im**-ta? متى اعود ؟

What is your fee? '*ug-**ri**-tak kam?* كم اتعابك ؟

WITH THE OPTICIAN

Is there an optician near here?	*fee na-Da-Da-**raa**-tee "u-**ray**-yib min **hi**-na?*	هل يوجد محل للنظارات قريب ؟
Can you repair these glasses for me?	***mum**-kin ti-Sal-**laH**-lee in-naD-**Daa**-ra dee?*	هل يمكنك إصلاح هذه النظارة لي ؟
Can you put in a new lens?	***mum**-kin ti-**rak**-kib **Ha**-gar gi-**deed**?*	هل تستطيع تركيب عدسة جديدة ؟
Can you repair the frame?	***mum**-kin ti-Sal-**laH**-lee ish-**sham**-bar?*	هل يمكنك أن تصلح الاطار ؟
I (don't) have the prescription.	*^c**an**-dee (ma-^can-**deesh**) il-ma-"ehs.*	(ليس) معي قياس النظر
Can you do an eye test now?	***mum**-kin ti^c-**mil**-lee ma-"ehs na-Zar dil-wa" tee?*	هل يمكنك عمل قياس النظر الآن ؟
Do you sell contact lenses?	*^can-**du**-kum ^ca-da-**seht laS**-qa?*	هل تبيع عدسات لاصقة ؟
■ hard	■ ***nash**-fa*	صلبة
■ soft	■ *Tu-**ree**-ya*	لينة
I've lost a lens.	***Daa**-^cit ^ca-da-sa*	فقدت عدسة
Can you replace it right away?	***mum**-kin tid-**dee**-nee **waH**-da dil-wa"-tee?*	هل تستطيع إستبدالها حالاً ؟

Do you sell
sunglasses?

*ᶜan-**du**-kum naD-**Daa**-rit shams?*

هل عندك نظارات الشمس ؟

COMMUNICATIONS

POST OFFICE

Where's the nearest post office?	*feyn 'a''-rab **muk**-tab ba-**reed**?*	أين أقرب مكتب بريد ؟
Where's a mailbox?	*feyn san-**doo**'' il-**bus**-Ta?*	أين صندوق البريد ؟
What's the postage on — to America?	*'eyh '**ug**-rit il ba-**reed** li 'am-**ree**-ka ᶜa-**shehn** —?*	كم أجرة البريد لأمريكا — ؟
▓ this letter	▓ *ig-ga-**wehb** da*	▓ لهذا الخطاب
▓ an airmail letter	▓ *ga-**wehb** bil-ba-**reed** ig-**gaw**-wee*	▓ خطاب بالبريد الجوي
▓ a postcard	▓ *kart bus-**tehl***	▓ لبطاقة بريدية
▓ this package	▓ *iT-**Tar**-di da*	▓ لهذا الطرد
I'd like to send this — .	*ᶜa-**wiz** [ᶜaw-za] ab-ᶜat da — .*	أريد إرسال هذا —
▓ by surface mail	▓ *bil-ba-**reed** il-ᶜeh-dee*	▓ بالبريد العادي
▓ by registered post	▓ *bil-ba-**reed** il-mu-**sag**-gal*	▓ بالبريد المسجل
▓ by special delivery (express)	▓ *bil-ba-**reed** il-mis-taᶜ-gil*	▓ بالبريد المستعجل
▓ cash on delivery	▓ *id-**daf**ᶜᶜand it-tas-**leem***	▓ الدفع عند التسليم

Is a customs declaration form necessary?	**leh**-zim '**is**-ti-**maa**-rit ig-**gum**-ruk? هل تلزم استمارة الجمرك ؟
Could you give me a receipt?	**mum**-kin tid-**dee**-nee waSl? هل يمكنك أن تعطني إيصالاً ؟
When will it arrive?	ha-**yiw**-Sal '**im**-ta? متى ستصل ؟
Which is the window for — ?	min **an**-hee shib-**behk** ash-**ti**-ree — ? أين شباك — ؟

- ■ stamps
  - ■ Ta-**waa**-bi^c الطوابع
- ■ money orders
  - ■ Ho-wa-**leht** meh-**lee**-ya الحوالات المالية

Where is the general delivery (poste restante)?	feyn **mak**-tab tas-**leem** ig-ga-wa-**beht**? أين مكتب تسليم الخطابات ؟
My name is — .	'**is**-mee — . إسمي — .
Are there any letters for me?	fee ga-wa-**beht** ^{c}a-**sheh**-nee? هل هناك خطابات لي ؟

TELEGRAMS

Where is the telegram section?	feyn shib-**behk** it-til-ligh-ra-**feht**? أين شباك التلغراف ؟
I'd like to send a telegram to — .	^{c}a-wiz [^{c}aw-za] ab-^{c}at أريد إرسال til-li-**ghraaf** li — . تلغراف لـ —

How much is it per word?	*ik-**kil**-ma bi kam?*	كم سعر الكلمة ؟
May I have a form, please.	*id-**dee**-nee 'is-ti-**maa**-ra min **faD**-lak.*	اعطني إستمارة من فضلك
I want to send it collect.	*ᶜa-**wiz** [ᶜaw-za] inn il-mus-**ta**-lim **yid**-faᶜ.*	اريد ان يدفع المستلم

TELEPHONES

Where is —?	*feyn —?*	اين — ؟
▦ a public telephone	▦ *ti-li-**fohn** ᶜamm*	تليفون عام
▦ a telephone directory	▦ *da-**leel** ti-li foh-**neht***	دليل التليفون
I want to find this name.	*ᶜa-**wiz** [ᶜaw-za] a-**leh-"ee** il-'**is**-mi da.*	اريد ان اجد هذا الاسم
May I use your phone?	***mum**-kin as-**taᶜ**-mil it-ti-li-**fohn**?*	هل استطيع إستعمال هذا التليفون ؟
I want to make a —.	*ᶜa-**wiz** [ᶜaw-za] **aᶜ**-mil mu-**kal**-ma —.*	اريد عمل —
▦ local call	▦ *ma-**Hal**-lee-ya*	مكالمة محلية
▦ person-to-person call	▦ *shakh-**See**-ya*	مكالمة شخصية
Can I call direct?	*fee khaTT mu-**beh**-shir?*	هل استطيع الاتصال مباشرة ؟

I'd like to reverse the the charges.	*ᶜa-wiz [ᶜaw-za] inn ish-shakhS il-maT-loob yid-faᶜ.*	اريد ان يدفع الشخص المطلوب
I'd like to book a call to — .	*ᶜa-wiz [ᶜaw-za] aH-giz mu-kal-ma li — .*	اريد حجز مكالمة لـ ـ
How long will it take?	*ha-yeh-khud kam wa"t?*	هل يجب ان انتظر مدة طويلة ؟
I'd like to cancel the call.	*ᶜa-wiz [ᶜaw-za] al-ghee il-mu-kal-ma.*	اريد إلغاء المكالمة
How much does it cost — ?	*— bi kam?*	كم سعر ـ ؟
■ per minute	■ *id-da-"ee-"a*	الدقيقة
■ for three minutes	■ *ta-lat da-"eh-yi"*	الثلاث دقائق
Please give me Cairo 4810572.	*min faD-lak id-dee-nee il-qaa-hi-ra ar-ba-ᶜa ta-man-ya weh-Hid Sifr kham-sa sab-ᶜa it-neyn*	من فضلك اعطني القاهرة ٤٨١٠٥٧٢

(see p. 17 for numbers)

My number is — .	*nim-ri-tee — .*	رقمي ـ
May I speak to — ?	*mum-kin a-kal-lim — ?*	هل يمكن ان اتكلم مع ـ ؟
Is Mr. [Mrs.] — in?	*is-say-yid [ma-dehm/is-say-yi-da] — maw-good [maw-goo-da]?*	هل السيد ـ موجود [السيدة ـ موجودة] ؟
— isn't in.	*— mish maw-good.*	ـ ليس موجود

Hello.	*'a-**loh***.	آلو
This is — .	*a-na* — .	انا —
Who is calling?	*meen bi-yit-**kal**-lim?*	من يتكلم ؟
One moment.	*la**H**-Za.*	لحظة
I can't hear.	*mish **seh**-mi^c [**sam**-^ca]* .	لا أسمع
Speak louder.	*ir-fa^c **Soh**-tak [ir-fa-^cee **Soh**-tik].*	
		إرفع صوتك
Don't hang up.	*khal-**leek** [khal-**lee**-kee] ma-^c**eh**-ya.*	
		لا تغلق
It's a bad line.	*il-**khaTT** wi-Hish.*	الخط سيء
I'll try again.	*ha-**gar**-rab **khaT**-Ti teh-nee.*	
		ساحاول مرة ثانية
There's no reply.	*ma-**Had**-dish bee-**rudd**.*	لا إجابة
The line is busy.	*il-**khaTT** mash-**ghool**.*	الخط مشغول
Wrong number.	*nim-ra gha-la'l'.*	الرقم خطأ
I was cut off.	*il-**khaTT** in-"a-Ta^c*	قطع الخط
Please dial it again.	*u**T**-lub in-**nim** ra **teh**-nee min-**fuD**-luk.*	أرجوك حاول ثانية
I want to leave a message.	*^ca-wiz [^caw-za] a-seeb ri-**seh**-la.*	أريد أن أترك رسالة
How much was the call?	*keh-nit bi kam il-mu-**kal**-ma?*	كم كان سعر المكالمة ؟

DRIVING A CAR

SIGNS

No parking	mam-**noo**^{c} il-'in-ti-**Zaar**	ممنوع الانتظار
No stopping	mam-**noo**^{c} il-wu-"**oof**	ممنوع الوقوف
Caution	**iH**-dar	إحذر
Stop	qif	قف
Slow	hadd is-**sur**-^{c}a	هدىء السرعة
Danger	**kha**-Tar	خطر
Work in progress	man-**Ti**-qit ^{c}**a**-mal	منطقة عمل
School	mad-**ra**-sa	مدرسة
Hospital	mus-**tash**-fa	مستشفى
Motorway	Ta-**ree**" sa-**ree**^{c}	طريق سريع
One way	it-ti-**geh weh**-Hid	إتجاه واحد
No entry	mam-**noo**^{c} id-du-**khool**	ممنوع الدخول
Detour	taH-**wee**-la	تحويلة
Dangerous bends	mun-**Ha**-na kha-Tar	منحنى خطر
Keep right (left)	**il**-zim il-yi-**meen** (**ish**-shi-mehl)	الزم اليمين (اليسار)

CAR RENTALS

Where can I rent a car?	min feyn a-'**ag**-gar <u>c</u>a-ra-**bee**-ya/say-**yaa**-ra?	من أين استاجر سيارة ؟
■ a motorcycle	■ mo-to-**sikl**	دراجة بخارية
■ a bicycle	■ ^ca-ga-la	دراجة
■ a scooter	■ **skoo**-tar	دراجة صغيرة
I want a — car.	^ca-wiz [^c**aw**-za] ^ca-ra-**bee**-ya/ say-**yaa**-ra — .	أريد سيارة — .
■ small	■ Su-ghay-**ya**-ra	صغيرة
■ large	■ ki-**bee**-ra	كبيرة
■ sports	■ spoor	سبور
How much does it cost — ?	bi kam — ?	بكم — ؟
■ per day	■ fil-**yohm**	في اليوم
■ per week	■ fil-'us-**boo**^c	في الاسبوع
■ per kilometer	■ il-ki-lo-**mitr**	الكيلومتر
Does that include full insurance?	da bit ta'-**meen** ik-**keh**-mil?	هل هذا يشمل التامين الكامل ؟
Is the gas included?	da bil-ban-**zeen**?	هل هذا يشمل البنزين ؟
Do you accept credit cards?	bi-ti"-**ba**-loo **kri**-dit kard?	هل تقبلوا بطاقات إعتماد ؟

اِحترس نوجد جيوانات

Caution: Animal Crossing

طريق غير ممهد

Bumpy Road

كوبري متحرك

Draw Bridge

طريق ضيق

Narrow Road

منحني مزدوج
الأول للليسار

Double curves (S-curve)
(First one to the left)

منحدر خطر

Dangerous Incline

اِحترس

Caution

عبور المشاة

Pedestrian Crossing

مركز اسعاف

Ambulance Center

لافتة تشير إلى الاتجاهات

Sign indicating directions

علامة نهاية المدينة

Sign indicating city limits

منوع الانتظار في الأيام الفردية
No standing on odd days

ممنوع الوقوف قطعا
Absolutely no parking

Low clearance bridge

ممنوع الانتظار في الأيام الزوجية
No standing on even days

ممنوع الانتظار
No standing

Passage in both directions

مزلقان مفتوح
Open crossing

طريق غير ممهد
Bumpy road (potholes)

ممنوع الدخول
No entry

أقصى عرض ٢ متر
Maximum Width 2 meters

انتهاء منطقة تحديد الانتظار
End of no standing zone

Here's my driver's license.	*it-**faD**-Dal ir-**rukh**-Sa.*	تفضل ها هي الرخصة
Here's my passport.	*it-**faD**-Dal il-baS-**boor**/ga-**wehz** is-**sa**-far.*	تفضل ها هو جواز السفر
Do I have to leave a deposit?	***leh**-zim **ad**-fa^c ^{c}ar-**boon**?*	هل يجب ان اترك عربونا ؟
I want to rent the car here and leave it in — .	*^{c}a-**wiz** [^{c}**aw**-za] a-'**ag**-gar il-^{c}a-ra-**bee**-ya **hi**-na w a-**seeb**-ha fi — ..*	أريد إستئجار السيارة هنا وتسليمها في — ..
What kind of gas does it take?	*a-HuT-**Til**-ha ban-**zeen** 'eyh?*	ما نوع البنزين الذي تستخدمه السيارة ؟

Renting a car tends to be expensive, and facilities are usually rather limited; you may have little choice of drop-off points and if you break down it may take some time to repair or replace the car.

Driving techniques in the big cities can be hair-raising. You will encounter every kind of wheeled and four-legged transport, few of them respecting the highway code.

Bear in mind, too, that in the case of an accident, especially in Saudi Arabia and some of the Gulf countries, you could be involved in extremely lengthy legal proceedings, irrespective of who was at fault. You may well decide it is preferable to hire a driver for short periods of time or use public transport, which is generally both cheap and efficient.

ON THE ROAD

[For more directions see Getting Around.]

Excuse me . . .	*law sa-**maHt** . . .*	بعد إذنك . . .

| Can you tell me . . . ? | *tis-maH ti-"ul-lee . . . ?* |
| | ارجوك ان تقول لي . . . |

| Which way is it to — ? | *min feyn iT-Ta-ree" li — ?* |
| | ما هو الطريق إلى — ؟ |

| We're lost. | *tuh-na.* |
| | ضللنا الطريق ، تهنا |

| Is this the road to — ? | *da Ta-ree" — ?* |
| | هل هذا هو الطريق إلى — ؟ |

| Where does this road go? | *iT-Ta-ree"da bee-wad-dee ᶜa-la feyn?* |
| | إلى اين يؤدي هذا الطريق ؟ |

| How far is it to the next town? | *'a"-rab ba-lad ᶜa-la buᶜd "ad-di 'eyh?* |
| | كم نبعد عن البلدة القادمة ؟ |

| What's the next town called? | *'eyh 'ism il-ba-lad ig-gay-ya?* |
| | ما هو إسم البلدة القادمة ؟ |

| Can you show me on the map? | *mum-kin ti-war-ri-heh-lee ᶜal-kha-ree-Ta?* |
| | هل ممكن ان توضح لي الطريق على الخريطة ؟ |

| Is the road in good condition? | *is-sik-ka kway-yi-sa?* |
| | هل حالة الطريق جيدة ؟ |

| Is the road to — open? | *iT-Ta-ree" li — maf-tooH?* |
| | هل الطريق إلى — مفتوح ؟ |

| How far is the next filling station? | *feyn 'a"-rab ma-HaT-Tit ban-zeen?* |
| | اين اقرب محطة بنزين ؟ |

AT THE SERVICE STATION

I need gas.	*^ca-wiz [^caw-za] ban-zeen*.	أريد بنزينا
Fill her up with — .	*im-la l-khaz-zehn bi* — .	إملأها بِ —
■ diesel	■ *dee-zil*	ديزل
■ regular	■ *ban-zeen ^ceh-dee*	بنزين عادي
■ super	■ *soo-bar/mum-tehz*	سوبر / ممتاز
Give me — liters.	*HuT-Til-ha* — *litr.*	أعطني — لتر
Please check — .	*min faD-lak shoof-lee* — .	من فضلك إكشف على —
■ the battery	■ *il-baT-Ta-ree-ya*	البطارية
■ the brakes	■ *il-fa-raa-mil*	الفرامل
■ the carburetor	■ *ik-kar-bi-re-teer*	الكاربوراتير
■ the oil	■ *iz-zeyt*	الزيت
■ the spark plugs	■ *il-boo-jey-heht*	البوجيهات
■ the tires	■ *ik-ka-witsh*	الاطارات
■ the tire pressure	■ *DakhT ik-ka-witsh*	ضغط الاطارات
■ the water	■ *il-may-ya*	الماء
Change the oil.	*ghay-yar-lee iz-zeyt.*	غيّر الزيت
Grease the car.	*shaH-Ham-lee il-^ca-ra-bee-ya/ is-say-yaa-ra.*	شحّم السيارة

Charge the battery.	ish-**Hin**-lee il-baT-Ta-**ree**-ya.	إشحن البطارية
Change this tire.	ghay-**yar**-lee ik-ka-**witsh** da.	غيّر هذا الاطار
Wash the car.	igh-**sil**-lee il-ʿa-ra-**bee**-ya/ is-say-**yaa**-ra.	إغسل السيارة
Where are the rest rooms?	it-twa-**litt** feyn?	أين التواليت / دورة المياه ؟
Do you have a phone?	ʿan-**du**-kum ti-li-**fohn**?	هل عندكم تليفون ؟

ACCIDENTS, REPAIRS

My car has broken down.	il-ʿa-ra-**bee**-ya/is-say-**yaa**-ra ʿaT-**laa**-na.	سيارتي معطلة
It overheats.	bi-**tis**-khan.	هي تسخن
It doesn't start.	ma-bit-"**umsh**.	هي لا تقوم
I have a flat tire.	ik-ka-**witsh neh**-yim.	الاطار خال من الهواء
I have a puncture.	ik-ka-**witsh** makh-**room**.	الاطار مخروم
The radiator is leaking.	ir-rad-ya-**teer** bee-**khurr**.	الرادياتير يخر
The battery is dead.	il-baT-Ta-**ree**-ya **nay**-ma.	لا تعمل البطارية

The keys are locked inside the car.	*"a-**falt** il-ᶜa-ra-**bee**-ya* ᶜa-la l-ma-fa-**teeH**.	انا قفلت السيارة على المفاتيح
Is there a garage near here?	*fee **war**-sha "u-**ray**-yib min **hi**-na?*	هل توجد ورشة قريبة ؟
Do you know a good mechanic?	*ti ᶜ-raf mi-ka-**nee**-kee **kway**-yis?*	هل تعرف ميكانيكيا جيداً ؟
I need a mechanic (a tow truck).	*a-na miH-**tehg** [miH-**teh**-ga] mi-ka-**nee**-kee (wintsh yis-**Hab**-nee).*	احتاج ميكانيكي (شاحنة لسحب السيارة).
Do you have the spare part?	*ᶜan-dak **qiT**-ᶜit il-ghi-**yaar**?*	هل عندك قطعة الغيار ؟
Do you have distilled water?	*ᶜan-dak **may**-ya mi-"aT-**Ta**-ra?*	هل عندك ماء مقطر ؟
I (don't) have a spare wheel.	*ᶜan-dee (ma-ᶜan-**deesh**) is-**tab**-na/ ᶜa-ga-la stibn.*	ليس عندي إطار احتياطي
Can you — ?	***mum**-kin — ?*	هل من الممكن ان — ؟
▪ help me	▪ *ti-sa-ᶜ**id**-nee*	تساعدني
▪ push me	▪ *ti-zu"-"**i**-nee*	تدفعني
▪ tow me	▪ *ti-gur-**ri**-nee*	تجرني
I don't have any tools	*ma-ᶜan-**deesh** ᶜi-dad.*	ليس معي ادوات
Can you lend me — ?	***mum**-kin ti-sal-**lif**-lee — ?*	هل يمكن ان تسلفني — ؟
▪ a flashlight	▪ *kash-**shehf***	كشاف كهربائي

■ a hammer	■ *sha-koosh*	مطرقة ، شاكوش
■ a jack	■ *ku-reek, jehk*	جك ، مرفاع
■ a monkey wrench	■ *muf-tehH ki-beer/in-gi-lee-zee*	
		مفتاح ربط
■ a spanner	■ *muf-tehH Sa-moo-la*	
		مفتاح صواميل
■ pliers	■ *zar-ra-dee-ya*	زردية
■ a screwdriver	■ *mu-fakk ma-sa-meer*	مفك مسامير

There's something   *fee **Ha**-ga **bay**-Za fi —.*
wrong with the — .   هناك مشكلة في — .

■ directional signal	■ *il-fla-shar*	الاشارة
■ electrical system	■ *ni-Zaam ik-kah ra ba*	الكهرباء
■ exhaust	■ *ish-shak-mehn*	انبوبة العادم
■ fan	■ *il-mar-wa-Ha*	المروحة
■ fan belt	■ *seer il-mar-wu-Ha*	سير المروحة
■ fuel pump	■ *tu-rum-bit il-ban-zeen*	
		طلمبة البنزين
■ gas tank	■ *khaz-zehn il-ban-zeen*	
		خـزان البنزيـن
■ gears	■ *in-na"-leht, it-tu-roos*	التروس
■ gear shift	■ *ᶜa-Sa il-fee-tehs*	ناقل السرعة
■ horn	■ *ik-ka-laks, in-ni-feer*	
		البـوق ، الكلاكسـون

■ ignition	■ il-'ish-**c**ehl	الاشعال
■ radiator	■ ir-rad-ya-**teer**	الرادياتير
■ starter	■ il-kon-**takt**	مبدىء الحركة
■ steering wheel	■ id-di-rik-**syohn**/**c**a-ga-lit	
	is-si-**weh**-"a	عجلة القيادة
■ transmission	■ na"l il-**Ha**-ra-ka	نقل الحركة
■ water pump	■ tu-**rum**-bit il-**may**-ya	طلمبة الماء

EXTERNAL PARTS

bumper	il-'ak-Si-**daam**	الاكصدام
door	il-**behb**	الباب
door handle	il-'**uk**-ra	ممسكة الباب
fender, wing	ir-**raf**-raf	الرفرف
headlights	ik-kash-sha-**feht**	النور الأمامي
hood, bonnet	ik-kab-**boot**	الكبوت
tail light	il-fa-**noos**	النور الخلفي
trunk, boot	ish-shan-Ta	صندوق
wheel	il-**c**a-ga-la	عجلة
windshield	"iz-**zehz** ish-shib-**behk**	
		الحاجب الزجاجي
windshield wipers	il-mas-sa-**Heht**	المساحات

What's the matter?	*'eyh il-mush-**ki**-la?*	ما هي المشكلة ؟
Can you fix it today?	*mum-kin ti-S-al-laH-**heh**-lee in-na-**har**-da/il-**yohm**?*	
		هل يمكن ان تصلحها لي اليوم ؟
How long will it take?	*ha-**yeh**-khud "ad-di 'eyh?*	
		متى ستكون جاهزة ؟
Can you give me a lift to — ?	*mum-kin ti-waS-**Sal**-nee li — ?*	
		هل يمكن ان توصلني إلى — ؟
How much do I owe you?	*kam il-Hi-**sehb**?*	كم الحساب ؟

GENERAL INFORMATION

TELLING THE TIME

hour	*seh*-ᶜ*a*	ساعة
half an hour	*nuS-Si seh*-ᶜ*a*	نصف ساعة
a quarter of an hour	*rub*-ᶜ*i seh*-ᶜ*a*	ربع ساعة
twenty minutes	*til-ti seh*-ᶜ*a*	ثلث ساعة
What time is it?	*is-seh*-ᶜ*a kam?*	كم الساعة ؟
It is — .	*is-seh*-ᶜ*a* — .	الساعة — .
12:00	*it-naa-shar*	١٢
1:05	*waH-da wi kham-sa*	١٬٠٥
2:10	*it-neyn wi* ᶜ*a-sha-ra*	٢٬١٠
3:15	*ta-leh-ta wi rub*ᶜ	٣٬١٥
4:20	*ar-ba*-ᶜ*a wi tilt*	٤٬٢٠
5:25	*kham-sa wi kham-sa wi* ᶜ*ish-reen*	٥٬٢٥
6:30	*sit-ta wi nuSS*	٦٬٣٠
7:35	*sab*-ᶜ*a wi kham-sa wi ta-la-teen*	٧٬٣٥
7:40	*ta-man-ya il-la tilt*	٧٬٤٠
8:45	*tis*-ᶜ*a il-la rub*ᶜ	٨٬٤٥

9:50	*ᶜa-sha-ra il-la ᶜa-sha-ra*	٩,٥٠
10:55	*Hi-daa-shar il-la kham-sa*	١٠,٥٥
11:00	*Hi-daa-shar*	١١

EXPRESSIONS OF TIME

At what time (is —)?	— *is-seh-ᶜa kam?*	في اي وقت — ؟
When?	*'im-ta?*	متى ؟
at — o'clock	*is-seh-ᶜa* —	في الساعة —
at exactly five o'clock	*is-seh-ᶜa kham-sa biZ-ZabT*	في الساعة الخامسة بالضبط
in (i.e. after) 1 hour	*baᶜ-di seh-ᶜa*	بعد ساعة
in (i.e. within) 1 hour	*fi seh-ᶜa*	في خلال ساعة
in 2 hours	*baᶜd (or fi) saᶜ-teyn*	بعد (في خلال) ساعتين
(not) before 3 o'clock	*(mish) "abl is-seh-ᶜa ta-leh-ta*	(ليس) قبل الساعة الثالثة
(not) after 4:30	*(mish) baᶜd is-seh-ᶜa ar-ba-ᶜa wi nuSS*	(ليس) بعد الرابعة والنصف
at about 7 o'clock	*Ha-weh-lee is-seh-ᶜa sab-ᶜa*	في حوالي الساعة السابعة

between 8 and 9 o'clock	*beyn is-**seh**-ᶜa ta-**man**-ya wi tis-ᶜa*	بين الساعة الثامنة والتاسعة
until 6:30	*li **gheh**-yit is-**seh**-ᶜa sit-ta wi **nuSS***	حتى الساعة السادسة والنصف
I have been waiting — .	*a-na mis-**tan**-nee [mis-tan-**nee**-ya]* — .	انتظر — .
■ since 3 o'clock	■ *min is-**seh**-ᶜa ta-**leh**-ta*	■ من الساعة الثالثة
■ for half an hour	■ *ba-"**eh**-lee **nuS**-Si seh-ᶜa*	■ منذ نصف ساعة
■ for a quarter of an hour	■ *ba-"**eh**-lee **rub**-ᶜi seh-ᶜa*	■ منذ ربع ساعة
3 hours ago	*min **ta**-lat sa-ᶜeht*	منذ ثلاث ساعات
early	***bad**-ree*	مبكر
late	***wakh**-ree*	متأخر
late (in arriving)	*mut-'**akh**-khir*	متأخر
on time	*fil-ma-ᶜehd*	في الموعد
noon	*iD-**Duhr***	الظهر
midnight	*nuSS il-**leyl***	منتصف الليل
in the morning	*iS-**SubH***	في الصباح
in the afternoon	*baᶜd iD-**Duhr***	بعد الظهر
at night	*bil-**leyl***	بالليل

DAYS OF THE WEEK

What day is today?	*in-na-**har**-da '**eyh**?*	اي يوم اليوم ؟
Today is — .	*in-na-**har**-da/il-**yohm** —*	اليوم — .
Monday	*(yohm) lit-**neyn***	(يوم) الاثنين
Tuesday	*(yohm) it-ta-**leht***	(يوم) الثلاثاء
Wednesday	*(yohm) **lar**-ba^c*	(يوم) الاربعاء
Thursday	*(yohm) il-kha-**mees***	(يوم) الخميس
Friday	*(yohm) ig-**gum**-^ca*	(يوم) الجمعة
Saturday	*(yohm) is-**sabt***	(يوم) السبت
Sunday	*(yohm) il-**Hadd***	(يوم) الاحد
last Tuesday	*(yohm) it-ta-**leht** il-lee **feht***	
	(يوم) الثلاثاء الماضي	
yesterday	*im-**beh**-riH/'ams*	امس
the day before yesterday	*'**aw**-wil im-**beh**-riH/'ams*	اول امس
tomorrow	***buk**-ra*	غداً
the day after tomorrow	*ba^c-di **buk**-ra*	بعد غد
next Monday	*(yohm) lit-**neyn** ig-**gayy***	
	يوم الاثنين القادم	
the same day	***nafs** il-**yohm***	نفس اليوم

two days	yoh-**meyn**	يومان
three days	ta-lat ay-**yehm**	ثلاثة ايام
every day	**kul**-li **yohm**	كل يوم
day off	yohm 'a-**geh**-za	يوم إجازة / عطلة
holiday	'a-**geh**-za	إجازة / عطلة
birthday	^ceed mi-**lehd**	عيد ميلاد
from now on	min **hi**-na wi **reh**-yiH	في المستقبل
this week	il-'is-**boo**^c da	هذا الاسبوع
last week	il-'is-**boo**^c il-lee **feht**	الاسبوع الماضي
next week	il-'is-**boo**^c ig-**gayy**	الاسبوع القادم
month	**shahr**	شهر
two months	shah-**reyn**	شهران
three months	ta-lat shu-**hoor**	ثلاثة اشهر
this month	ish-**shah**-ri da	هذا الشهر
next month	ish-**shahr** ig-**gayy**	الشهر القادم
during the month of —	fi shahr —	في خلال شهر—
■ Ramadan	■ ra-ma-**Daan**	رمضان
since the month of —	min shahr —	منذ شهر—
every month	**kul**-li shahr	كل شهر
per month	fish-**shahr**	في الشهر

this year	*is-sa-**neh** dee*	هذه السنة
last year	*is-**sa**-na il-lee **feh**-tit*	السنة الماضية
next year	*is-**sa**-na g-**gay**-ya*	السنة القادمة
two years	*sa-na-**teyn***	سنتان
three years	***ta**-lat si-**neen***	ثلاث سنوات
per year	*fis-**sa**-na*	في السنة
all year	***Tohl** is-**sa**-na*	طوال السنة
every year	***kul**-li sa-na*	كل سنة
during the year	*fi khi-**lehl** is-**sa**-na*	في خلال السنة

MONTHS OF THE YEAR

Western calendar

January	*ya-**neh**-yir*	يناير
February	*fib-**reh**-yir*	فبراير
March	***meh**-ris*	مارس
April	*ab-**reel***	ابريل
May	***may**-yoo*	مايو
June	***yoon**-yoo*	يونيو
July	***yool**-yoo*	يوليو
August	*a-**ghus**-Tus*	اغسطس
September	*sib-**tam**-bir*	سبتمبر
October	*uk-**too**-bar*	اكتوبر

| November | *nu-**vim**-bir* | نوفمبر |
| December | *di-**sim**-bir* | ديسمبر |

Eastern calendar (used in Syria, Lebanon, Jordan, Iraq)

January	*ka-**noon** it-teh-nee*	كانون الثاني
February	*shu-**baaT***	شباط
March	*mart, 'a-**thaar***	مارت ، آذار
April	*ney-**sehn***	نيسان
May	*meh-yis, 'ay-**yaar***	مايس ، ايار
June	*Ha-zee-**raan***	حزيران
July	*Tam-**mooz***	تموز
August	*'ehb*	آب
September	*'ay-**lool***	ايلول
October	*tish-**reen** il-'**aw**-wal*	تشرين الاول
November	*tish-**reen** it-**teh**-nee*	تشرين الثاني
December	*ka-**noon** il-'**aw**-wal*	كانون الاول

THE FOUR SEASONS

spring	*ir-ra-**bee**ᶜ*	الربيع
summer	*iS-**Seyf***	الصيف
autumn	*il-kha-**reef***	الخريف
winter	*ish-**shi**-ta*	الشتاء

WEATHER

The weather is fine.	ig-**gaww** **kway**-yis	الطقس جيد
It's (very) hot.	id-**din**-ya Harr (**gid**-dan)	الطقس حـار (جـداً)
It's chilly.	id-**din**-ya bard	الطقس بارد
It's cloudy.	ig-**gaww** mi-**ghay**-yim	الطقس مغيّم
It's windy.	id-**din**-ya reeH	الهواء شديد
It's foggy.	fee Da-**baab**	يوجد ضباب
There's a sandstorm.	fee ᶜaa-**Si**-fa ram-**lee**-ya	توجـد عاصفة رمليـة
It's humid.	fee ru-**Too**-ba	الطقس رطب
It's raining.	bit-**maT**-Tar	الطقس ممطر
It's snowing.	bi-**yin**-zil talg	يسقط الثلج

COUNTRIES AND NATIONALITIES

Where are you from?	**in**-ta [**in**-tee] mi-**neyn**?	من اين انت ؟
I am from — .	**a**-na min — .	انا من —
I am — .	**a**-na — .	انا —

COUNTRY		NATIONALITY
Note: When there is not an accepted adjective for the nationality, the expression would be "from (min)" + the country.		
Africa	af-**reeq**-ya	af-**ree**-qee [af-**ree**-**qee**-ya]
	افريقيا	افريقي

COUNTRY		NATIONALITY
America	am-**ree**-ka	am-**ree**-kee/am-ree-**keh**-nee
		[am-**ree**-kee-ya/am-ree-ka-**nee**-ya]
	أمريكا	أمريكي
Asia	**as**-ya	as-**yeh**-wee [as-ya-**wee**-ya]
	آسيا	آسيوي
Australia	us-**tral**-ya	us-**traa**-lee [us-tra-**lee**-ya]
	استراليا	استرالي
Austria	in-**nim**-sa	nim-**seh**-wee [nim-sa-**wee**-ya]
	النمسا	نمساوي
Belgium	bal-**jee**-ka	bal-**jee**-kee [bal-jee-**kee**-ya]
	بلجيكا	بلجيكي
Brazil	ba-ra-**zeel**	ba-ra-**zee**-lee [ba-ra-zee-**lee**-ya]
	برازيل	برازيلي
Britain	bri-**Tan**-ya	bri-**Taa**-nee [bri-Ta-**nee**-ya]
	بريطانيا	بريطاني
Canada	**ka**-na-da	**ka**-na-dee [ka-na-**dee**-ya]
	كندا	كندي
China	iS-**Seen**	**See**-nee [See-**nee**-ya]
	الصين	صيني
Denmark	id-**di**-ni-mark	di-ni-**mar**-kee [di-ni-mar-**kee**-ya]
	الدنمرك	دنمركي
England	in-gil-**ti**-ra	in-gi-**lee**-zee [in-gi-lee-**zee**-ya]
	انجلترا	انجليزي
Europe	u-**rub**-ba	u-**rub**-bee [u-ru-**bee**-ya]
	أوروبا	أوروبي
Finland	fin-**lan**-da	fin-**lan**-dee [fin-lan-**dee**-ya]
	فنلندا	فنلندي

COUNTRY		NATIONALITY
France	*fa-ran-sa* فرنسا	*fa-ran-seh-wee [fa-ran-sa-wee-ya]* فرنسي
Germany	*al-man-ya* المانيا	*al-meh-nee [al-ma-nee-ya]* الماني
Greece	*il-yu-nehn* اليونان	*yu-neh-nee [yu-na-nee-ya]* يوناني
Holland	*ho-lan-da* هولندا	*ho-lan-dee [ho-lan-dee-ya]* هولندي
Hungary	*il-ma-gar* المجر	*ma-ga-ree [ma-ga-ree-ya]* مجري
India	*il-hind* الهند	*hin-dee [hin-dee-ya]* هندي
Iran	*i-raan* ايران	*i-raa-nee [i-raa-nee-ya]* ايراني
Ireland	*ayr-lan-da* ايرلندا	*ayr-lan-dee [ayr-lan-dee-ya]* ايرلندي
Israel	*is-ra-'eel* أسرائيل	*is-ra-'ee-lee [is-ra-'ee-lee-ya]* اسرائيلي
Italy	*i-Taal-ya* ايطاليا	*i-Taa-lee/i-Tal-yeh-nee* *[i-Taa-lee-ya/i-Tal-ya-nee-ya]* ايطالي
Japan	*il-ya-behn* اليابان	*ya-beh-nee [ya-ba-nee-ya]* ياباني
Luxembourg	*luk-sum-burg* لوكسمبرج	*mn ...* من ...
Malaysia	*ma-leyz-ya* ماليزيا	*ma-ley-zee [ma-ley-zee-ya]* ماليزي

COUNTRY		NATIONALITY
New Zealand	*nyoo zee-**lan**-da* نيوزيلندا	*nyoo zee-**lan**-dee [nyoo-zee-lan-**dee**-ya]* نيوزيلندي
Norway	*in-nur-**weyg**￼* النرويج	*nur-**wey**-gee [nur-wey-**gee**-ya]* نرويجي
the Philippines	*il-fi-li-**been*** الفيليبين	*fi-li-bee-**nee** [fi-li-bee-**nee**-ya]* فيليبيني
Portugal	*il-bur-tu-**ghehl*** البرتغال	*bur-tu-**ghehl**-lee [bur-tu-gha-**lee**-ya]* برتغالي
Russia	***roos**-ya* روسيا	***roo**-see [roo-**see**-ya]* روسي
Scotland	*is-kut-**lan**-da* اسكتلندا	*is-kut-**lan**-dee [is-kut-lan-**dee**-ya]* اسكتلندي
South America	*am-**ree**-ka l-ga-noo-**bee**-ya* من ... أمريكا الجنوبية	*min ...* من ...
Soviet Union	*il-'it-ti-**Hehd** is-soov-**yey**-tee* الاتحاد السوفييتي	*min ...* من ...
Spain	*as-**ban**-ya* اسبانيا	*as-**beh**-nee [as-ba-**nee**-ya]* اسباني
Sweden	*is-su-**weyd*** السويد	*su-**wey**-dee [su-wey-**dee**-ya]* سويدي
Switzerland	*su-**wis**-ra* سويسرا	*su-**wis**-ree [su-wis-**ree**-ya]* سويسري
Turkey	*tur-**kee**-ya* تركية	***tur**-kee [tur-**kee**-ya]* تركي

COUNTRY		NATIONALITY
United States	*il-wi-lay-yeht* *il-mut-ta-Hi-da* من ...الولايات المتحدة	*min ...*
Wales	*weylz* ويلز	**weyl**-zee [weyl-zee-ya] ويلزي
Yugoslavia	*yu-ghus-laf-ya* يوغسلافيا	yu-ghus-**leh**-fee [yu-ghus-la-fee-ya] يوغسلافي

The Arab World

COUNTRY		NATIONALITY
Algeria	*al-ga-zeh-'ir* الجزائر	ga-zeh-'i-ree [ga-zeh-'i-ree-ya] جزائري
Bahrain	*baH-reyn* البحرين	baH-rey-nee [baH-rey-nee-ya] بحريني
Djibouti	*ji-boo-tee* جيبوتي	*min ...* من ...
Egypt	*maSr* مصر	maS-ree [maS-ree-ya] مصري
Iraq	*il-ʿi-reh"* العراق	ʿi-reh-"ee [ʿi-ra-"oo ya] عراقي
Jordan	*il-'ur-dun* الأردن	'ur-du-nee ['ur-du-nee-ya] أردني
Kuwait	*ik-ku-weyt* الكويت	ku-wey-tee [ku-wey-tee-ya] كويتي

COUNTRY		NATIONALITY
Lebanon	*lib-**nehn***	*lib-**neh**-nee [lib-na-**nee**-ya]*
	لبنان	لبناني
Libya	***lib**-ya*	***lee**-bee [lee-**bee**-ya]*
	ليبيا	ليبي
Mauritania	*mu-ri-**tan**-ya*	*mu-ri-**teh**-nee [mu-ri-teh-**nee**-ya]*
	موريتانيا	موريتاني
Morocco	*il-**magh**-rib*	***magh**-ri-bee [magh-ri-**bee**-ya]*
	المغرب	مغربي
Oman	*ᶜu-**mehn***	*ᶜu-**meh**-nee [ᶜu-ma-**nee**-ya]*
	عمان	عماني
Palestine	*fa-laS-**Teen***	*fa-laS-**Tee**-nee [fa-laS-Tee-**nee**-ya]*
	فلسطين	فلسطيني
Qatar	***qa**-tar*	*qa-**Ta**-ree [qa-Ta-**ree**-ya]*
	قطر	قطري
Saudi Arabia	*il-ᶜa-ra-**bee**-ya is-su-ᶜu-**dee**-ya*	*su-ᶜ**oo**-dee [su-ᶜoo-**dee**-ya]*
	العربية السعودية	سعودي
Somalia	*iS-Su-**maal***	*Su-**maa**-lee [Su-maa-**lee**-ya]*
	الصومال	صومالي
Sudan	*is-su-**dehn***	*su-**deh**-nee [su-da-**nee**-ya]*
	السودان	سوداني
Syria	***soor**-ya*	***soo**-ree [soo-**ree**-ya]*
	سوريا	سوري
Tunisia	***too**-nis*	***too**-ni-see [too-ni-**see**-ya]*
	تونس	تونسي

COUNTRY		NATIONALITY
United Arab Emirates	*il-'i-maa-raat* الامارات	*min . . .* من . . .
Yemen	*il-ya-man* اليمن	*ya-ma-nee [ya-ma-nee-ya]* يمني

DIRECTIONS

north	*ish-sha-**mehl***	الشمال
south	*il-ga-**noob***	الجنوب
east	*ish-**shar"***	الشرق
west	*il-**gharb***	الغرب

COUNTING TIMES

once	***mar**-ra **waH**-da*	مرة واحدة
twice	*mar-ri-**teyn***	مرتان
three times	***ta**-lat mar-**raat***	ثلاث مرات
four times	***ar**-baᶜ mar-**raat***	اربع مرات

FOR THE BUSINESS TRAVELER

[See also the section on Banking and Money Matters.]

Personal contacts and personal relationships will be a crucial factor in the success or failure of any business venture in the Middle East. There, one rarely finds the strict division between work and leisure so common in the West. Thus patience is needed to nurture a social/business relationship. Avoid a high-pressure approach, which may be perceived as crude and undignified. For instance, you may arrive for a business appointment to find other people in the office — friends, relations, or business associates. Be prepared for the exchange of quite lengthy social preliminaries before you can broach the topic you want to discuss.

So many stereotypes and prejudices have become associated with the Middle East that people will find it refreshing to do business with a foreigner who has actually taken the trouble to learn about the area. Read as much as you can about the social and political system of the countries you are going to visit, talk with people who know them well, and be ready to learn while you are there.

You will certainly be offered hospitality by business colleagues and should be ready to reciprocate enthusiastically on your home ground.

How you dress is important. Err on the side of formality — that means a jacket and tie despite high temperatures and humidity (you will understand the purpose of the traditional loose cotton robes of Saudi Arabia and the Gulf states!). A safari suit is acceptable daytime wear for a young businessman. It is rather unusual for women to do business in Saudi Arabia and the Gulf, though they are employed in high positions in hospitals, schools, universities, and so on. Being respectably dressed for a foreign woman means sleeves to below the elbow, skirts to below the knee, and not too much décolleté. In Saudi Arabia (except in Jedda) all women are expected to wear the voluminous *abaya* when they go out in the street.

It is best to try to schedule a business trip during the winter, spring, or autumn, because in the summer months there is a mass exodus from the big cities and the people you were hoping to contact may be at the seaside or vacationing in Europe.

Avoid traveling to the Middle East on business during the month of Ramadan (see p. 197), because the pace of life is so much slower. Don't expect to accomplish much during the two big religious festivals of the muslim year (p. 198), which are national holidays and a time for family celebrations and reunions.

MINI DICTIONARY FOR BUSINESS

account	*Hi-sehb*	حساب
accounts, accounting	*Hi-seh-beht*	حسابات
◼ deposit account	◼ *Hi-sehb 'i-deh*ᶜ	حساب إيداع
◼ current account	◼ *Hi-sehb geh-ree*	حساب جاري
amount	*mab-lagh*	مبلغ
bank notes	*'aw-reh" na"d*	أوراق نقد
bill (noun)	*fa-too-ra*	فاتورة
bill of exchange	*kam-bee-yeh-la*	كمبيالة
bill of lading	*bu-lee-Sit shaHn*	بوليصة شحن
bill of sale	ᶜ*a"d rahn il-man-"oo-leht*, ᶜ*a"d il-bee*ᶜ	عقد رهن المنقولات ،عقد البيع

boycott	*mu-"aT-^{c}a*	مقاطعة
business operation	*^{c}a-ma-**lee**-ya ti-ga-**ree**-ya*	عملية تجارية
cash (noun)	*na"d*	نقد
cash on delivery	*id-**daf** $^{c\,c}$and it-tas-**leem***	
		الدفع عند التسليم
cash payment	*daf ^{c} na"-dee*	دفع نقدي
I (you) cash a check	*a**S**-rif (**tiS**-rif) sheek*	أصرف (تصرف) شيكا
certified check	*sheek ma"-**bool** id-**daf** ^{c}*	شيك مقبول الدفع
chamber of commerce	*il-**ghur**-fa it-ti-ga-**ree**-ya*	الغرفة التجارية
company (companies)	*shir-ka (sha-ri-**keht**)*	شركة (شركات)
compensation (for damage)	*ta^c-**weeD*** (^{c}an it-**ta**-laf)	تعويض (عن التلف)
competition	*mu-**naf**-sa*	منافسة
competitive price	*si^{c}r mu-**neh**-fis*	سعر منافس
contract	*^{c}a"d*	عقد
contractual obligations	*il-ti-za-**meht** it-ta-^{c}**eh**-qud*	إلتزامات التعاقد
controlling interest	*Hi**S**-Sa mu-say-**Ti**-ra*	حصة مسيطرة
co-owner	*meh-lik mush-**ta**-rak*	مالك مشترك

co-partner	sha-**reek** mush-**ta**-rik	شريك مشترك
credit	'**i**c-ti-**mehd**	إعتماد
delivery	it-tas-**leem**	التسليم
discount	khaSm	خصم ، تخفيض
dishonored check	sheek mar-**fooD**	شيك مرفوض
distribution	it-taw-**zee**c	التوزيع
down payment	**duf**-ca mab-da-'**ee**-ya	دفعة مبدئية
duty	ru-**soom** gum-ru-**kee**-ya	رسوم جمركية
enterprise (project)	mash-**roo**c	مشروع
enterprise (company)	**shir**-ka	شركة
expenses	maS-roo-**feht**	مصروفات
export	it-taS-**deer**	التصدير
free on board	it-tas-**leem** c**a**-la l-beh-**khi**-ra	التسليم على الباخرة
free trade zone	man-**Ti**-qit ti-**gaa**-ra **Hur**-ra	منطقة تجارة حرة
goods	il-ba-**Daa**-yic	البضائع
head office	il-**mak**-tab ir-ra-'**ee**-see	المكتب الرئيسي
import	il-'is-ti-**raad**	الاستيراد
infringement of patent rights	'**ikh-lehl** bi Ha"" il-'ikh-ti-**reh**c	إخلال بحق الاختراع
insurance	ta'-**meen**	تامين

insurance against all risks	*ta'-**meen** ^camm*	تأمين عام
international law	*il-qa-**noon** id-**daw**-lee*	القانون الدولي
lawful ownership	*mil-**kee**-ya qa-noo-**nee**-ya*	ملكية قانونية
lawsuit	*qa-**Dee**-ya*	قضية
lawyer	*mu-**Heh**-mee*	محامي
letter of credit	*ri-**seh**-lit i^c-ti-**mehd***	رسالة إعتماد
manager	*il-mu-**deer***	المدير
manufacturers	*iS-Si-**naa**-^ca*	الصنّاع
the Middle East market	*soo" ish-**sharq** il-'**aw**-SaT*	سوق الشرق الأوسط
market value	*il-**qee**-ma is-soo-**qee**-ya*	القيمة السوقية
owner of company	***Saa**-Hib ish-**shir**-ka*	مالك الشركة
partner	*sha-**reek***	شريك
past due	*mus-ta-**Hi**" " id-**daf** ^c*	مستحق الدفع
payment	*id-**daf** ^c*	الدفع
partial payment	***duf**-^ca guz-'**ee**-ya*	دفعة جزئية
we pay (you pay) customs	***nid**-fa^c (tid-**fa**-^coo) ig-ga-**meh**-rik*	ندفع (تدفعوا) الجمارك
percentage	***nis**-ba mi-'a-**wee**-ya*	نسبة مئوية
post office box	*san-**doo**" ba-**reed***	صندوق بريد
profit	*ribH*	ربح

profitable	**mur**-biH	مربح
property	'**am-lehk**	أملاك
purchasing agent	wa-**keel** mush-ta-ra-**yeht**	وكيل مشتريات
refund (noun)	'**i-ᶜeh**-dıt il-**mehl**	إعادة المال
sale	il-**bee**ᶜ	البيع
we (you) sell	ni-**bee**ᶜ (ti-**bee**-ᶜoo)	نبيع (تبيعوا)
we (you) send	**nib**-ᶜat (tib-**ᶜa**-too)	نرسل (ترسلوا)
shipment	**shiH**-na	شحنة
shipper	**sheh**-Hin	شاحن
spare parts	qi-Taᶜ gha-**yaar**	قطع غيار
supplier	mu-**war**-rid	مورّد
taxes	Da-**raa**-yib	ضرائب
sales tax	Da-**ree**-bit il-**bee**ᶜ	ضريبة البيع
luxury tax	Da **ree**-bit il-'is-tih-**lehk**	ضريبة الاستهلاك
tax-exempt	**ma**ᶜ-fee min iD-Da-**raa**-yib	معفي من الضرائب
trade fair	**ma**ᶜ-raD ti **geh**-ree	معرض تجاري
trade union	ni **qaa**-bu	نقابة عمال
we (you) transfer	ni **Haw**-wil (ti-Haw-**wi**-loo)	نحول (تحولوا)
transportation charges	'**u-goor** in-**na"**l	أجور النقل

| via | *^can Ta-**ree**"* | عن طريق |
| wholesale | *il-**bee**^c bil-**gum**-la* | البيع بالجملة |

The Petrochemical Industry

crude oil	*zeyt khehm*	بترول خام
the price of crude	*si^cr iz-**zeyt** il-**khehm***	سعر البترول الخام
per barrel	*il-bar-**meel***	البرميل
drilling	*il-**Hafr***	الحفر
exploratory drilling	*Hafr is-tik-**sheh**-fee*	حفر إستكشافي
local branch	*far^c ma-**Hal**-lee*	فرع محلي
natural gas	*ghehz Ta-**bee**-^cee*	غاز طبيعي
oil	*bit-**rohl***	بترول
oil company	*shir-kit bit-**rohl***	شركة بترول
oil fields	*Hu-**qool** il-bit-**rohl***	حقول البترول
oil rig	*gi-**hehz** il-**Hafr***	جهاز الحفر
offshore oil	*bit-**rohl** baH-ree*	بترول بحري
oil well	*beer bit-**rohl***	بئر بترول
OPEC	*oh-pek, mu-naZ-**Za**-mit il-bi-**lehd** il-mu-Sad-**di**-ra lil-bit-**rohl***	أوبك، منظمة البلدان المصدرة للبترول
pipeline	*khaTT 'a-na-**beeb***	خط انابيب
production	*'in-**tehg***	إنتاج

(petroleum) products	*mun-ta-***geht** *bit-ro-***lee**-*ya*	منتجات بترولية
refined oil	*bit-***rohl** *mu-***kar**-*rir*	بترول مكرر
refinery	**ma**^c-*mal tak-***reer**	معمل تكرير

ISLAM

The Koran, the holy book of Islam, which contains the divine revelations received by the prophet Mohammed, is the cornerstone of the Muslim faith. The fundamental religious observances of Islam consist of the profession of faith, prayer, fasting, almsgiving, and the pilgrimage to Mecca in Saudi Arabia, birthplace of the prophet. Like Judaism and Christianity, Islam is monotheistic, believing in an omnipotent creator to whom all must answer.

A Muslim prays after ritual ablutions five times a day — at dawn, noon, in the afternoon, at sunset, and in the evening—facing the direction of Mecca. The call to prayer, or *a-thehn*, will become a familiar sound, as it is chanted or broadcast via loudspeakers from minarets all over town. A Muslim may pray in any quiet and secluded place, kneeling and prostrating himself on a small rug kept especially for that purpose. It is however considered important to attend midday prayers at the mosque on Fridays, when a sermon is preached. Sometimes the mosque is so full that the worshippers overflow onto the pavement outside.

There is no priesthood in Islam, no mediator between the worshipper and God. Prayers may be led by any Muslim well-versed in the ritual, though a sizeable community will appoint an Imam or religious teacher to officiate. Although there is no equivalent of an established church, schools of theologians and jurists (*ʿu-la-ma*) evolved, differing in their precise interpretations of Muslim doctrine.

Dissension within the Islamic state has focussed mostly on the rights and duties of the successive Caliphs. These elected successors to the Prophet played an essentially political and administrative rather than religious role. The Caliphates were transformed into something more akin to traditional Middle Eastern dynasties, with the right to succession being violently disputed at many points in history. The last Caliphate of any real power was the Ottoman Empire based in Turkey, which finally collapsed in the early twentieth century, after a long period of decline.

The ancient Islamic state, stretching in Medieval times from Spain to China, has long since fragmented into independent states. These have been secularized to varying degrees. Saudi Arabia, an absolute monarchy, retains the sharia (*sha-ree-^{c}a*), or Islamic legal system, while others are republics and have adopted and adapted western legal systems. Sometimes the two operate in parallel, depending on the nature of the legal matter at issue.

The Prophet Mohammed

Mohammed was born in Mecca in West Arabia in about 571 A.D., into an essentially nomadic, tribal society in which a variety of local gods were worshipped. The Koran was revealed to him when he was about forty years old, by the angel Gabriel. As more and more conversions took place, Mohammed was obliged to leave Mecca, and was welcomed with his followers in Medina, where he became a ruler and military leader as well as a religious teacher. His influence gradually spread throughout the peninsula, until at his death he left an organized and well-armed state unified in its adherence to the new faith.

According to Islam, Mohammed is the last and greatest of the line of prophets in the Judeo-Christian tradition. Abraham, Moses, and Jesus are all venerated as bearers of God's word, but the Koran is seen as the last in this series of divine revelations, completing and superseding all previous scriptures. Christians and Jews, as "people of the pact," traditionally enjoyed certain rights and privileges within the Islamic state, including freedom of worship.

Islamic Civilization

The Arabs founded, but were by no means the exclusive contributors to, a rich civilization that lasted for over a thousand years. There were two great waves of conquest, one immediately following the death of Mohammed, which took the Muslim armies North into Syria, West into Egypt, and across North Africa, and into Persia in the East. Two centuries later, most of Spain came under Muslim rule, as did northern India and parts of China. The Arabs assimilated and built upon the scientific and technical knowledge of their subject nations, translating into Arabic works on mathematics, philosophy, astronomy, and medicine from the ancient Greek, Persian, and Indian civilizations. During what were the Dark Ages in Europe, great advances were also being made in the fields of chemistry, anatomy, geography, optics, and mechanical engineering. Universities, libraries, and hospitals flourished, often in close association with the great mosques of the period.

So in the Middle Ages it was to the East that Europe looked for scientific knowledge. (Our system of numerals for example, was borrowed from the Arabs, who had themselves borrowed and adapted the system from an Indian source.)

In the arts, Islamic civilization can be seen at its most impressive in its great architectural creations, from the Taj Mahal in India to the Alhambra palace in Spain. In both, formal gardens, pools, and fountains perfectly complement the graceful architecture. (Garden motifs as well as complex geometric patterns often recur in textiles, ceramics, and carpet designs.) The bold and elegant shapes of dome, minaret, and monumental gateway are generally left unadorned; decoration is concentrated on interior surfaces, in the form of tiling, mosaic, and elaborate plasterwork.

In the museums of the Arab world you will see examples of other great artistic achievements of Islamic civilization, in the form of pottery, glassware, pierced and inlaid metalwork, carpets, and textiles—art forms that continue to flourish today.

Since pre-Islamic times poetry had been the favored literary genre, and the themes and forms of Arabic poetry are clearly reflected in the work of the Medieval poets of southern Europe. Many believe that it was contact with this rich and varied culture that fostered new ideas in both the arts and sciences in Europe, culminating in the great flowering of the Renaissance.

The Muslim Calendar

The calendar is based on a key event in the history of the Islamic faith, the migration from Mecca to Medina by the Prophet and his followers in 622 A.D. This is therefore taken as the beginning of the Islamic era. In everyday conversation the years and months of the Western calendar are used, but for religious purposes and in published material of all kinds, Islamic dates are referred to. Both are used in newspapers.

The year is divided into 12 lunar months, each starting at the new moon, and consisting of about 29 days. This means that the Muslim year starts about 10 days earlier each year in relation to the Western calendar.

Here are the names of the months:

mu-**Har**-ram	محرّم
Sa-far	صفر
ra-**bee**ᶜ il-'**aw**-wal	ربيع الأول
ra-**bee**ᶜ it-**teh**-nee	ربيع الثاني
gu-**mehd** il-'**aw**-wal	جمادى الأولى
gu-**mehd** it-**teh**-nee	جمادى الآخرة
ra-gab	رجب
shaᶜ-**behn**	شعبان
ra-ma-**Daan**	رمضان
shaw-**wehl**	شوّال
zul-**qa**ᶜ-da	ذو القعدة
zul-**Hig**-ga	ذو الحجة

Ramadan is the month of fasting, when Muslims neither eat, drink, nor smoke from dawn till sunset. Special dishes are eaten at the evening meal known as *il-fi-**Taar***, which breaks the fast. In the early hours before dawn a second meal — *is-su-**hoor*** — is taken, to see people through the hours of fasting ahead.

Fasting is considered both a spiritual discipline and a reminder of those less fortunate than yourself who are hungry all year round. So it is a time to give generously to poor people in one's neighborhood. Devout Muslims gather to read aloud from the Koran, and go to the mosque more frequently during Ramadan.

The pace of life tends to slow down, with many people sleeping during the morning hours. In the evening, and often late into the night, there is a holiday atmosphere in the downtown areas of the cities, where shops and cafés stay open and the streets are thronged with people.

Hotels and all places catering to tourists function normally, but many neighborhood restaurants and cafés are closed during daylight hours. Non-Muslims are certainly not expected to fast, but it is polite not to eat, smoke, or drink in the street.

Muslim Festivals

Ramadan ends in the Feast of the Breaking of the Fast or the Small Feast — ^c*eed il-**fiTr*** or *il-^ceed iS-Sugh-**ghay-**yar*, which is associated with all kinds of local customs, such as providing one's children with new clothes. The culminating day of the pilgrimage to Mecca is on the tenth of *zul **Hig**-ga*. This is known as the Great Feast, or Feast of Sacrifice — *il-^c**eed** il-ki-**beer*** or ^c*eed il-'**aD**-Ha*, when every family that can afford it slaughters a sheep, in remembrance of the story of Abraham and Isaac, and meat is distributed to the poor.

The prophet's birthday — ***moo**-lid in-**na**-bee* — on the twelfth of *ra-**bee**^c il-'**aw**-wal* — is also celebrated; for days in advance mosques are illuminated and ceremonies and festivities abound.

During Ramadan, and on the occasion of any religious or secular festival — including birthdays — the equivalent to "Merry Christmas," "Happy Birthday," and so on is:

*kul-li sa-na win-ta **Tay**-yib [**win**-tee Tay-**yi**-ba]*

To which the reply is:

*win-ta **Tay**-yib [**win**-tee Tay-**yi**-ba]*

Or the more formal greeting is:

*kul-li ᶜehmm win-tum bi-**kheyr***

Saints Days

In Egypt and North Africa especially there is a long tradition — probably dating back to pre-Islamic times — of venerating the memory of men and women of great piety and learning. Their tombs have become shrines, and even mosques have been founded to commemorate them, which may become places of pilgrimage. One of the liveliest public celebrations is a saint's day or *moo-lid*; miniature fairgrounds for children are set up, as well as street stalls selling food, toys, and souvenirs. Shops and cafés stay open till late at night, and bands of musicians and singers provide religious and secular music.

Secular Festivals

The Western New Year — *raas is-sa-na* — is celebrated wherever Western influence has made itself felt, but it is not generally an official holiday. May 1, Labor Day (May Day), is also accorded varying degrees of importance in different countries.

In Egypt an ancient spring festival, that of *shamm in-ni-seem*, is celebrated on Coptic Easter Monday throughout the country. Everyone flocks to the fields, parks, and gardens in their newest clothes, and huge amounts of spring onions and salted fish are consumed.

Christian Festivals

Large Christian communities are to be found throughout the Middle East; in Lebanon they constitute about half the population. Roughly 15 percent of Egyptians belong to the Coptic church, one of the earliest established forms of Christianity, even today using the language of Ancient Egypt in its liturgy. The Coptic and Eastern Orthodox calendar does not coincide with the Western Christian calendar. The Eastern Christmas — *ˁeed il-mi-lehd* (literally, "Feast of the Birth") — and Easter — *ˁeed il-qi-yeh-ma* ("Feast of the Resurrection") — are celebrated about 12 days later than their Western equivalents.

THE ARAB WORLD TODAY

The Arab world has a degree of cultural unity, based on shared religious beliefs, a common literary language of great prestige, and many shared social institutions such as the extended family, with its elaborate system of rights and obligations. But within this framework there is great diversity — of race, of wealth, of political systems, of attitudes to the West, and to modern technology.

In the West the stereotype Arab as an oil-rich sheikh jet-setting round the capitals of Europe has tended to replace the more romantic image of the keen-eyed son of the desert, ascetic, proud and bound by a strict code of honor. Both exist, but only as tiny pieces in a much larger mosaic. They are both vastly outnumbered by the hardworking fellahcen (*fel-la-***Heen***), or peasant farmers, who still provide the economic base of the more populous Arab countries.

Urban centers increasingly attract workers to the factories from country towns and villages. Cairo, the townplanner's nightmare — or ultimate challenge — has exploded from being a sizeable city of 3 million to a vast agglomeration of 13 million in the space of twenty years. Armies of government clerks (*mu waZ-Zu-***feen***) — often university graduates — find it hard to make ends meet on their slender salary, and will often take a second job in the afternoon or evening.

There has been a massive emigration of the working population from the poorer to the richer countries within the Arab world and beyond, with all the social and economic turmoil that entails. Economists and sociologists are currently trying to calculate the likely longterm effects of the slump in oil prices and the continuing Gulf war on this migrant labor force and the region as a whole.

In this shifting scene two factors at least remain constant, which favor the foreign visitor: the innate sociability of the Arab people, and their abiding tradition of hospitality to strangers.

Women in Islam

Saudi Arabia, as the birthplace of the prophet Mohammed, sees itself as the guardian of traditional values, accepting changes to the established order with extreme caution. Attitudes that seem reactionary to Westerners, such as requiring women to go heavily veiled in public places and forbidding them to drive, should be viewed against some truly dramatic social reforms, like the provision of education for women at all levels, within the space of one generation.

Throughout the Middle East the trend has been toward greater emancipation for women and their increasing participation in every area of public life. In many ways they have enjoyed fuller legal rights than their Western sisters, from the early days of Islam, since they have always had individual property rights and legal protection against ill-treatment by their husband.

Polygamy is still practiced in most Arab countries, although it is unusual among the mass of the population — as wives must be treated equally in every respect few men can afford more than one! A woman must enter freely into the marriage contract, though frequently social and family pressures may mean that personal preference is not a major factor in the arrangement for either partner.

TRADITION AND CHANGE

In recent years, even in countries like Egypt which have been open to Western influences for more than a century, a profound re-evaluation of social and religious attitudes is taking place. The West is no longer synonymous with progress and enlightenment. The strength and stability offered by traditional values is increasingly appreciated, particularly among the younger generation. Fashions in dress — like the adoption of the nunlike headcovering (the *Hi-gehb*) and long skirts by young women, and the chin-strap beard of the young men — are outward signs of these changing attitudes.

THE ARABIC LANGUAGE

THE ARABIC SCRIPT

This section explains the general principles on which the writing system works, and will help you to recognize the common signs and notices that you will see on any trip to an Arab country.

Arabic is written from right to left, and it is a "cursive" script — that is, the letters of the word are usually joined up, whether in print or handwriting.

Many different styles exist, just as many different type-faces are used to print the Roman alphabet. Calligraphy is one of the great art forms of Islamic civilization, and some highly elaborate styles have been evolved, which you will see incorporated in metalwork, ceramics, architectural decoration, and so on. The style used in this book is simple, and one of the most common in everyday use.

The table below shows the 29 letters of the alphabet as they would occur in isolation. Their order (from right to left) is that used traditionally in Arabic dictionaries. You will notice that the letters which are very similar in shape are grouped together.

The transcription of the letters follows that used in this book, although two extra sounds occur that are not found in Egyptian Arabic: **th** as in "thing" and **<u>th</u>** as in "this." In Egyptian the first **th** is pronounced either **s** or **t**, and the second **<u>th</u>** as either **z** or **d**.

$\leftarrow$

kh	H	j or g	th	t	b	eh or aa	'
خ	ح	ج	ث	ت	ب	ا	ء

D	S	sh	s	z	r	<u>th</u>	d
ض	ص	ش	س	ز	ر	ذ	د

k	q	f	gh	c	Z	T
ك	ق	ف	غ	ع	ظ	ط

	y	w	h	n	m	l
	ي	و	ه	ن	م	ل

ي (**y**) and و (**w**) can also be used to represent the long vowels **ee** and **oo** respectively.

Besides these 29 letters there are three additional "vowel marks," two written above, and one below the consonant they follow:

فَ = fa   فِ = fi   فُ = fu

بَ = ba   بِ = bi   بُ = bu

These short vowels are not generally written in, because Arabic speakers can recognize the word quite well without them (just as you don't usually need to put in the vowel marks in English shorthand).

Another "optional" symbol — ّ — is one used over a letter to indicate that letter is doubled, or long:

جزّار = gaz-**zaar**   شبّاك = shib-**behk**

The glottal stop symbol ء (') rarely occurs by itself but is usually "carried" by ا ، و ، or ي : أ ؤ ئ

In the "joining up" process letters tend to change their shape. Typically, letters coming at the end of a word (or occurring in isolation, as above) end in a flourish or "tail." They lose this tail if they occur at the beginning or in the middle of a word.

First the letters that *don't* join up with the letters that follow them, and therefore do *not* change their shape:

ا   د   ذ   ر   ز   و

The following lose their tails:

ب   ت   ث   ج   ح   خ   ص   ض

ع   غ   ف   ق   ل   م   ن   ي

So if we were to join up   ت + ح + ت   (*taHt* — "under, below"), this would give   تحت   with only the final **t** ending in a flourish. Notice that dots are placed above or below the middle of the flourish if there is one. The same is true for the two forms of   ب   (**b**) and   ث   (**th**):

باب = *behb* ("door")   and   ثلث = *thilth* ("third")

Final   ي   sometimes loses its two dots: ى

Here are a few more examples of letters written first in their "full" form, and then as they would look joined up into words:

ب ح ر   ج م ي ل   ب ل د

بحر (*baHr*)   جميل (*ga-meel*)   بلد (**ba**-lad)

ش خ ص   ض ا ن ي   ف و ل

شخص (*shakhS*)   ضاني (**Daa**-nee)   فول (*fool*)

k has *three* variant forms, depending on whether they are initial, medial, or final in a word:

	FINAL	MEDIAL	INITIAL
k	ك	كـ	كـ

Three other letters have initial, medial, and final shapes, the final one varying slightly if it is unjoined:

	FINAL		MEDIAL	INITIAL
	Unjoined	Joined		
ᶜ	ع	‍ع	‍ع‍	ع‍
gh	غ	‍غ	‍غ‍	غ‍
h	ه	‍ه	‍ه‍	ه‍

This last letter may be written with two dots over it in final position: ة or ‍ة . Then it represents the feminine ending -**a**, as in طبيبة Ta-**bee**-ba — doctor (fem.) جميلة ga-**mee**-la — beautiful (fem.) Some examples of these last few letters in words:

(ᶜ**an**-dee)	(**gum**-ruk)	(say-**yaa**-ra)
عندي	جمرك	سيارة
(**ma**-ᶜa)	(Say-da-**lee**-ya)	(ma**T**-ᶜam)
مع	صيدلية	مطعم
(is-seh-ᶜa)	(ik-**kil**-ma)	(il-ᶜin-**wehn**)
الساعة	الكلمة	العنوان

The last three examples all begin with the definite article **il-** الـ (see Grammar Notes). Notice this is always written the same way, even if the **l** changes to match the following consonant in spoken Arabic.

You will occasionally come across three relatively new letters, which have been invented to cope with borrowed, foreign sounds. Arabic doesn't normally have a **v** sound, but this does occur in foreign borrowings such as "video." A variant of **f** with three dots is sometimes used: ڤ *vi-dyoo* ڤيديو . Egyptian uses **g** rather than **j** in words like *ga-meel* جميل (beautiful) or *ga-mal* جمل *(camel)*, but **j** may occur in foreign words such as "jeans." To make the difference clear, three dots can again be used:

چينز *jeenz* مكياچ *mak-yaaj* (makeup)

A **p** in foreign borrowings is usually Arabized to a **b**, as in *bu-loh-var* (pullover). But it can be represented by a modification of the **b** symbol ب again using three dots:

پ . For example:

سڤن اپ Seven-Up

So you may find a word such as "jeep" being written

جيب or چيب , or چيپ or جيپ !

Dialects of the Arab World

Considerable differences exist between the varieties of Arabic spoken throughout the Arab world; even within one country a good deal of local variation can be found. Although you will be able to make yourself understood very well with Egyptian Arabic, as the most widely known and prestigious form of the spoken language, if you are visiting other countries you may want to try and approximate the local dialect.

The differences lie in pronunciation and use of vocabulary rather than in grammatical structure. The following notes, indicating the most striking of these features, should help you "tune in" rapidly to another dialect. Dialects have been grouped together to simplify the picture, but it should be remembered that this simplification masks a lot of internal variation.

Egyptian Arabic

What identifies a speaker immediately as an Egyptian is his or her use of g as in ga-**meel** (beautiful), **gid**-dan (very) and so on; in virtually all other dialects (and in literary Arabic) this is a j, either as in "*jam*" or "*measure*": ja-**meel**, **jid**-dan, and so on.

The other feature (shared by some of the more Eastern dialects) is the use of the glottal stop " to replace what is elsewhere a q. The q has only survived in Egyptian in relatively few (usually rather learned) words. So other dialects will differentiate between **qa**-lam (pen) and '**a**-lam (pain), whereas in Egyptian they are pronounced the same, both with a glotal stop: "**a**-lam = '**a**-lam. Two slightly different symbols have been used for the Egyptian glottal stop, so that you will know where you should switch to q in another part of the Arab world. So "**ul**-lee (tell me) will be pronounced **qul**-lee elsewhere, but '**is**-**boo**ᶜ (week) will stay the same.

South of Cairo a rather different dialect is spoken, in which j is used for g and q for ". This Upper Egyptian, or '**sa**-ᶜ**ee**-**dee**', Arabic (sometimes made fun of by the educated city dweller) in fact has much in common with Sudanese.

Dialects of the Eastern Mediterranean
(Lebanon, Jordan, Syria, Palestine)

Egyptian g ⇒ j (as in measure, rather than jam)

Some unstressed vowels are dropped. For example, Egyptian ki-**teer**, = EM kteer (much, many).

As in Egyptian, q is usually replaced by ".

Here are some common expressions:

Not   *mish* or *ma*
Where?   *weyn?*
What?   *shoo?* or '*ehsh?*
Why?   *leysh?*
How much?   "*ad-***dehsh**?
How?   *keyf?*

How are you? **key**-fak [**key**-fik]?
Thing, something shey'
Thus, so heyk
Yes 'eyh
Nice, good ma-**leeH**
I want **bid**-dee or **bad**-dee
(You want . . ., etc.: the ending changes as after "**ud**-**dehm**- (in front of); see p. 218: **bid**-dak, **bid**-dik, **bid**-doo, etc.)

Sudanese

Very similar to Egyptian, except that j (as in "jam") is used instead of g, so gi-**deed** = Sudanese ja-**deed**, and Egyptian " is either q or g; for example, Egyptian "**ah**-wa = Sudanese **gah**-wa (coffee), "i-**zeh**-za =gi-**zeh**-za.

Iraqi

Additional sounds: th as in "thing," corresponding to Egyptian t (hence ka-**theer** = ki-**teer**) or s, and <u>th</u> as in "this" corresponding to Egyptian d or z.
Egyptian g = Iraqi j (as in "jam").
Egyptian " = q or g : Ta-**ree**" = Iraqi Ta-**reeq**, "**ah**-wa = Iraqi **gah**-wa.
k next to a , or i often becomes tsh: Egyptian kam = Iraqi tshehm.

Here are some common expressions:
What? shi-**noo?**
Who? min?
How? keyf? shlohn?
How much? kehm? tshehm?
Where? weyn?
Why? leysh?
When? **mi**-ta?
Fine, good zeyn
Bad baT-**Taal**
Thus, so **hee**-tshee
This, that **heh**-<u>th</u>a
I want a-**reed**
Not moo, mush

Dialects of Saudi Arabia and the Gulf

th and <u>*th*</u> are used (as in "think" and "this"): *tha-**leh**-tha* (three), **heh**-<u>tha</u> (this, that).

k often becomes *tsh* next to *a, e, i: kam = tshehm, keyf = tsheyf*. Egyptian *"* is usually *g*, occasionally *q*: **gah**-*wa*, **fun**-*dug*, ga-**leel**. Egyptian *g = j* (as in "jam").

Here are some common expressions:

What? *shoo?*
Where? *weyn?*
How? *keyf?, tsheyf?, shlohn?*
How are you? **shloh**-*nak [**shloh**-nik]?*
How much? *kehm?, tshehm?*
Much, very *ka-**theer***
I want *a-**reed**, **a**-bee, **ab**-gha*
Good, fine *zeyn*
Yesterday *'ams*
This, that **heh**-<u>tha</u> *[**heh**-thee]*
Thanks *mash-**koor***

North African dialects (*Moroccan, Algerian, Tunisian, Libyan*)

These are possibly the furthest from Egyptian, particularly Moroccan, where there is a strong Berber influence.
Egyptian *g = j*
Egyptian *" = q* or *g*: *"alb = qalb, "**ah**-wa = **gah**-wa.*

Many unstressed vowels are lost: Egyptian *ta-**leh**-ta =* NA **tleh**-ta, *"a-**deem** = qdeem.*

Here are some common expressions:

Yes *yeh*
Thank you *ba-ra-kal-**lau**-hu feek*
What? *'ehsh? shnoo?*
Why? *ᶜa-**lehsh**?*
When? *waq-**tehsh**? foh-**gehsh**?*
How much/many? *gad-**dehsh**? sh-**hehl**?*
How? *keyf? key-**fehsh**?*
Who? *shkoon?*
Good, well *la-**behs**, **beh**-hee*
Nice, pleasant *mleeH, miz-**yehn***

Bad   *doo*-nee, *kheh*-yib
Much, very   *yeh*-sir, biz-*zehf*
I want   ni-**Hibb**, *beh*-ghee [*bagh*-ya]
Food   *mak*-la
Tomorrow   *ghud*-wa, *ghed*-da
To form a "yes/no" question, add -*shee* to the verb or adjective: *beh-hee-shee?* — (Is it) O.K.?

GRAMMAR NOTES

The rules outlined here are those of spoken Egyptian Arabic, but most apply to other spoken forms of Arabic as well. The differences between the modern dialects are ones of pronunciation and vocabulary rather than of grammar.

Consonantal Roots

The most striking feature of Arabic, like other Semitic languages, is the way a series of (usually three) consonants is used as the basis for forming many closely related words. Take the series *d - r - s*; from this are formed the words *dars* — "lesson," *da*-ras — "he studied," *dar*-ras — "he taught," *mad-ra-sa* — "school," *mu-dar-ris* — "teacher," and many others, all related to the concept of study. Once you know the meaning of a root you can often guess at the meaning of a word containing it, because the addition of particular patterns of vowels, plus prefixes or suffixes, modifies the meaning of the root in predictable ways. For example *mak-ta-ba* follows the same pattern as *mad-ra-sa*; once you know that *k - t - b* involves writing and books (*ka-tab* — "he wrote," *keh*-tib — "clerk," *ki-tehb* — "book," etc.), it's not surprising to find that *mak-ta-ba* means "library" or "bookshop." This system of roots plus predictable patterns makes acquiring new vocabulary in Arabic relatively easy.

Word Order

The order of words in sentences is much the same as in English; the only major difference is that adjectives follow the noun they modify:

*bint ga-**mee**-la*   lit. a girl beautiful
                             i.e., a beautiful girl

If a word such as *very* modifies the adjective, it too follows:
*bint ga-**mee**-la **gid**-dan*   lit. a girl beautiful very
                             i.e., a very beautiful girl

NOUNS

Nouns are either masculine or feminine. Feminine nouns usually end in *-a*:

mu-dar-ris a teacher (masc.) *mu-dar-ris-sa* a teacher (fem.)

Notice the above nouns are *indefinite*. To make them *definite* ("the . . .") the prefix *il-* is put at the beginning of the word:

*il-mu-**dar**-ris* the teacher   *il-**bee**-ra* the beer

The *l* of this prefix sometimes changes to match the first consonant of the noun:

*is **suk**-kar* (the sugar)   — not *il-**suk**-kar*
*in-**nehs*** (the people)   — not *il-**nehs***

The consonants that trigger this change are:
    t d n s z sh r T D S Z
For *k*, *g*, and *j* the change is optional. So:

*il-**kart*** (the card)   or *ik-**kart***

Plurals

Sometimes an ending is added to make a noun plural (as in English):

*mu-dar-ri-**seen*** (teachers)   *do-la-**raat*** (dollars)

-een and *-aat* are among the most common plural endings. But even more frequently, the whole shape of the word changes, with only the consonantal root remaining intact. There are over a dozen different plural "patterns"; the most common are:

SINGULAR	PLURAL	SINGULAR	PLURAL
1 *wa-ra*" (paper)	'*aw-reh*"	*wa-lad* (boy)	'*aw-lehd*
2 '*is-boo*ᶜ (week)	'*a-sa-bee*ᶜ	*mif-tehH* (key)	*ma-fa-teeH*
3 *mak-tab* (office)	*ma-keh-tib*	*taz-ka-ra* (ticket)	*ta-zeh-kir*
4 *kart* (card)	*ku-root*	*Deyf* (guest)	*Du-yoof*
5 *sik-ka* (road)	*si-kak*	*nim-ra* (number)	*ni-mar*

Unfortunately, most of the time you can't predict the plural from the singular; it just has to be learned. This is the hardest part of Arabic grammar, but if you use the wrong plural pattern or ending, people will probably still understand!

Duals
If two objects or people are being referred to, a special form of the noun is used. For masculine nouns the ending *-eyn* is added:

yohm	*yoh-meyn*	'*alf*	'*al-feyn*
(day)	(2 days)	(1000)	(2000)

For feminine nouns ending in *-a*, the *a* is removed and *-teyn* added:

seh-ᶜa	*saᶜ-teyn*	*Ha-ga*	*Hag-teyn*
(hour)	(2 hours)	(thing)	(2 things)

Noun + Noun
When one noun immediately follows another, it usually indicates possession or the notion "of ":

*beyt mu-**Ham**-mad* Muhammed's house
***Saa**-Hib **ley**-la* Leila's friend

When the first noun is feminine, the *-a* ending changes to
-it:

***shur**-ba* (soup) but ***shur**-bit **ba**-Sal*
(onion soup)

*"i-**zeh**-za* (bottle) but *"i-**zeh**-zit **bee**-ra*
(a bottle of beer)

Numbers

The numbers are given on page 17. 1 is the only
number to have separate masculine and feminine forms,
***weh**-Hid* and ***waH**-da:* *yohm **weh**-Hid* one day, *sa-na*
***waH**-da* one year

Numbers 3 to 10 are followed by a plural noun:

*ta-lut 'a-sa-**bee**ᶜ* (3 weeks) *ar-baᶜ si-**neen*** (4 years)

Notice the final *-a* has been dropped before these plural
nouns.

With all higher numbers, a *singular* noun is used:

*ta-la-**teen** sa-na* (30 years) *it-**naa**-shar shahr* (12 months)

When ordering in a restaurant, however, or when currency is being referred to, the singular is *always* used:

*ta-**leh**-ta **bee**-ra* (3 beers) ***kham**-sa do-**laar*** (5 dollars)

When the hundreds are followed by a noun, ***mee**-ya*
becomes *meet*:

300 dollars	*tul-tu-meet do-**laar***
500 pounds	*khum-su-meet gi-**ney***

ADJECTIVES

Like nouns, adjectives have three different forms —
masculine, feminine, and plural:

kway-yis (good) masc. *kway-yi-sa* fem.
                        kway-yi-seen pl.

Tay-yib (kind) masc. *Tay-yi-ba* fem.
                        Tay-yi-been pl.

The feminine ending is always *-a*, but as with nouns the plural may take many forms:

la-Teef (pleasant) masc. *la-Tee-fa* fem. *lu-Taaf* pl.

mag-noon (crazy) masc. *mag-noo-na* fem.
                          ma-ga-neen pl.

Adjectives agree with the nouns they modify:

wa-lad la-Teef (a nice boy) *bint la-Tee-fa* (a nice girl)

Fortunately there is a strong tendency toward using the (regular!) feminine form with plural nouns as well. So you can say *either*

nehs lu-Taaf (nice people) **or** *nehs la-Tee-fa*

Adjectives also agree with the noun in being definite or indefinite, so the same definite prefix *il-* must be added to adjectives next to a definite noun:

wa-lad la-Teef   **but**   *il-wa-lad il-la-Teef*
(a nice boy)   (the nice boy —
                             lit., the boy the nice)

Comparatives and Superlatives

To say "bigger, biggest" "cheaper, cheapest" and so on, a special pattern is used:

ki-beer (big)   *'ak-bar* (bigger, biggest)
ri-kheeS (cheap)   *'ar-khaS* (cheaper, cheapest)
ga-meel (beautiful) *'ag-mal* (more, most beautiful)

When it means "the most . . ." it *precedes* the noun:

'ar-khaS siᶜr   *siᶜr 'ar-khaS*
(the cheapest price)   (a cheaper price)

Comparative/superlative adjectives are invariable:

'ak-bar wa-lad	(the biggest boy)
'ak-bar bint	(the biggest girl)
'ak-bar 'aw-lehd	(the biggest boys)

NONVERBAL SENTENCES

There is no equivalent in Arabic to "am, is, are"; the subject is just followed directly by the rest of the sentence:

*mu-**H**am-mad **maS**-ree*	Muhammed is Egyptian.
*a-na min **lan**-dan*	I'm from London.

To make these negative *mish* is placed after the subject:

*mu-**H**am-mad mish **maS**-ree*	Muhammed isn't Egyptian.
*a-na mish min **lan**-dan*	I'm not from London.

PRONOUNS

Personal Pronouns

These pronouns take the following form as subject of a sentence:

a-na	I	*i**H**-na*	we
in-ta	you (masc.)		
in-tee	you (fem.)	*in-**tum**-ma*	you (pl.)
*hu**w**-wa*	he		
hee ya	she	*hum-ma*	they

As in Spanish and Italian, these pronouns are used optionally with verbs — usually only when you want to emphasize the subject:

*(**a**-na) ᶜ**a**-wiz 'eh-kul*	I want to eat.
*(**hee**-ya) ᶜ**aw**-za teh-kul*	She wants to eat.

Following a noun or preposition they take the following forms:

-ee	*"ud-**deh**-mee*	in front of me
-ak	*"ud-**deh**-mak*	in front of you (masc.)
-ik	*"ud-**deh**-mik*	in front of you (fem.)
-oo	*"ud-**deh**-moo*	in front of him
-ha	*"ud-**dehm**-ha*	in front of her
-na	*"ud-**dehm**-na*	in front of us
-kum	*"ud-**dehm**-kum*	in front of you (pl.)
-hum	*"ud-**dehm**-hum*	in front of them

After a noun they have a possessive meaning:

bey-*tee* my house   *'***ukh**-*tak* your sister
                                                     (to a man)

After verbs, the same forms are used:

*yi-**shoof**-ha* he sees her   *ba-**Hib**-boo* I like him.

The only exception is the "me" form, which is *-nee* after verbs:

*yi-**shoof**-nee* he sees me.

Demonstrative Pronouns

To say "this one" or "that one," *da* or *dee* is used (depending on whether the noun referred to is masculine or feminine):

*da **kway**-yis*   *dee kway-**yi**-sa*
that (masc.) one is good   that (fem.) one is good

The plural "these" or "those" is *dohl*:

*dohl kway-yi-**seen***   those are good

da, *dee*, and *dohl* can be added to a definite noun to make it demonstrative:

*il-**wa**-lad* the boy   *il-**wa**-lad da* that boy
*il-**bint*** the girl   *il-**bint** dee* that girl

Possessive Particle

The word *bi-teh^c* means "belonging to." This particle can be used after a noun to indicate possession of the noun:

*il-**beyt** bi-**teh**^c mu-**Ham**-mad* the house belonging to Mohammed, Mohammed's house

It agrees with the noun it follows in number and gender. The feminine form is *bi-teh-^cit:*

*il-^ca-ra-**bee**-ya bi-**teh**-^cit* Mohammed's car
*mu-**Ham**-mad*

The plural form is *bi-**too**^c:*

*il-bu-**yoot** bi-**too**^c* Mohammed's houses
*mu-**Ham**-mad*

As with ordinary adjectives, the feminine singular may also be used after plural nouns:

*il-bu-**yoot** bi-**teh**-^cit* Mohammed's houses
*mu-**Ham**-mad*

When the possessor is a pronoun — "me, you, him, etc." — the suffixed forms given on p. 218 are added:

*il-**beyt** bi-**teh**-^cee* the house belonging to me, my house

Notice the feminine *bi-**teh**-^cit* gets shortened to *bi-**ta**^ct* if what follows begins with a vowel:

*il-^ca-ra-**bee**-ya bi-**ta**^c-tee* my car
*il-^ca-ra **bee**-ya bi-**ta**^ct* the engineer's car
*il-mu-**han**-dis*

VERBS

Present Tense

In the dictionary the verbs are given in the third person form of the present ("he goes," "he sees," and so on), beginning with y-. All forms of a regular present tense verb are as follows:

ash-rab I drink   **nish**-rab we drink

tish-rab you (masc.) drink
                                          tish-**ra**-boo you (pl.) drink
tish-**ra**-bee (fem.) drink

yish-rab he drinks
                                          yish-**ra**-boo they drink
tish-rab she drinks

These are the forms of the verb that follow words such as **mum**-kin (it is/is it possible), ^c**a**-wiz (I want), **leh**-zim (it is necessary), 'in shaa' al-laah (I hope):

^c**a**-wiz **ash**-rab shayy   I want to drink tea.

leh-zim **tish**-rab "**ah**-wa   You (masc.) must drink
                                              coffee.

mum-kin **yish**-rab **may**-ya?   Can he drink some water?

If the verb is being used by itself to indicate an habitual or ongoing action, it is usually prefixed by b(i)-:

bi-**yish**-rab   he drinks, is drinking

bash-rab   I drink, am drinking

Imperatives

Take the second person and omit the initial t-:

ish-rab!   drink! (masc.)

ish-**ra**-bee!   drink! (fem.)

ish-**ra**-boo!   drink! (pl.)

Future Tense

h(a)- is prefixed to the basic present:

ha-**yish**-rab   he will drink

hash-rab   I will drink

Negatives

In the present tense, *ma-* is added to the beginning, and *-sh* to the end of the verb:

*ma-bi-yish-**rabsh***   he doesn't drink/
                                     isn't drinking

With the future, *mish* is placed before the verb:

*mish **hash**-rab*   I shan't drink

Past Tense

This will not be widely used in situations expressing immediate needs and feelings. The same consonantal root is combined with a set of suffixes:

*shi-**ribt*** I drank	*shi-**rib**-na* we drank
*shi-**ribt*** you (masc.) drank	*shi-**rib**-too* you (pl.) drank
*shi-**rib**-tee* you (fem.) drank	
***shi**-rib* he drank	***shir**-boo* they drank
***shir**-bit* she drank	

"Want" and "Need"

"Verbs" such as *ᶜa-wiz [ᶜcaw-za]* (want) and *miH-tehg [miH-teh-ga]* (need) in fact behave more like adjectives, because they have only masculine, feminine, and plural forms. The plurals are *ᶜaw-**zeen*** and *miII-teh-**geen***. They are negated by *mish* before the verb:

*(**a**-na) mish ᶜa-wiz* I don't want

"Have"

There is no verb "to have" in Arabic; a preposition "with" (*ᶜand* or ***ma**-ᶜa*) is used with the object pronouns given above:

*ᶜ**an**-doo fi-**loos***   lit., with him money, that is,
                                   He has money.

*ᶜ**an**-dee wa"t*   lit., with me time,
                                   that is, I have time

These are negated like verbs, with -*ma* and -*sh* around the word:

ma-*c*an-**doosh** fi-**loos**	he has no money
ma-*c*an-**deesh** wa"t	I have no time

QUESTIONS

Questions requiring "yes" or "no" as an answer have the same form as statements, but the voice rises at the end of the sentences.

mu-**Ham**-mad min maSr ↓	Muhammed is from Egypt (falling intonation)
mu-**Ham**-mad min maSr? ↑	Is Muhammad from Egypt? (rising intonation)

Questions beginning in English with "what," "where," "why," "how," and so on often have the question word at the beginning in Arabic too:

feyn il-'u-tu-**bees**?	Where is the bus?
iz-**zayy** il-'aw-**lehd**?	How are the children?

But many speakers put the question word at the end of the sentence:

il-'u-tu-**bees** feyn?	Where is the bus?
'is-mak 'eyh?	What is your name?
in-ta za*c*-**lehn** leyh?	Why are you angry?

OTHER COMMON PATTERNS

Past participles:

mak-**toob** (written)	maf-**tooH** (open)
ma"-**fool** (closed)	mam-**noo***c* (forbidden)

Adjectives:

1 *la-**Teef*** (kind)   *la-**zeez*** (delicious)
  *kha-**feef*** (light)   *fa-"**eer*** (poor)

2 *bar-**dehn*** (cold)   *mal-**yehn*** (full)
  *zaᶜ-**lehn*** (angry)   *kas-**lehn*** (lazy)

Professions and occupations:

  *ba"-"**ehl*** (grocer)   *khay-**yaaT*** (tailor)
  *saw-**weh"*** (driver)   *Tay-**yaar*** (pilot)

ENGLISH-ARABIC DICTIONARY

The feminine form is given in square brackets. When a plural is given, it is preceded by (pl.). Verbs are given in the third person singular present form ("he goes," etc.), beginning with *yi-* . For other forms of the verbs see the Notes on Grammar on page 212 .

A

able *"eh-dir ["ad-ra]* قادر [قادرة]

about (approximately) *Ha-weh-lee* حوالي، تقريبا

above *foh"* فوق

accident *Had-sa* حادثة

account (financial) *Hi-sehb* (pl.) *Hi-seh-beht* حساب، حسابات

ache (noun) *wa-ga^c/'a-lam* وجع / ألم

(verb) *yiw-ga^c* يوجع

head — *Su-daa^c* صداع

adapter plug *mu-Haw-wil* محول، وصيلة

address *^cin-wehn* عنوان

advice *na-See-Ha* نصيحة

advise *yin-SaH* ينصح

Africa *af-reeq-ya* افريقيا

after *ba^cd* بعد

afternoon *ba^cd iD-Duhr* بعد الظهر

afterwards *ba^c-deyn* بعد ذلك

again *teh-nee* مرة اخرى، ثانية

agent *wa-keel* (pl.) *wu-ka-la* وكيل، وكلاء

— ago *min* — منذ —

air conditioning *tak-yeef ha-wa* مكيف، تكييف الهواء

(by) air mail *bil-ba-reed ig-gaw-wee* بالبريد الجوي

airplane *Tay-yaa-ra* طائرة

airport *ma-Taar* مطار

Alexandria *is-kin-di-ree-ya* اسكندرية

all *kull* كل

all right *Tay-yib* طيب

almonds *lohz* لوز

almost *ta"-ree-ban* تقريبا

also *ka-mehn/bar-Doo* ايضأ

always *ta-mal-lee/day-man* دائمأ

ambulance *il-'is-^cehf* سيارة الاسعاف

America *am-ree-ka* امريكا

American *am-ree-keh-nee* امريكي

and *wi* و

ankle *kaᶜb* كعب القدم

annual *sa-na-wee* سنوي

another *teh-nee* آخر، أخرى
[*tan-ya*]

answer (noun) *radd* رد، اجابة

(verb) *yi-rudd* يرد

antiseptic *mu-Tah-hir* مُطَهِّر

any *'ayy* أي

anyone *Hadd* أي شخص

apartment *sha"-"a* شقة، شقق
(pl.) *shu-"a*

appetite *sha-hee-ya* شهية

appetizers *maz-za* مزة

apples *tuf-fehH* تفاح

appointment *ma-ᶜehd* موعد،
ميعاد

apricots *mish-mish* مشمش

April *'ab-reel* ابريل

Arab *ᶜa-ra-bee* عربي، عرب
(pl.) *ᶜa-rab*

Arabic *ᶜa-ra-bee* عربي

area *man-Ti-"a* منطقة

arm *diraaᶜ* ذراع

army *geysh* جيش

around (approximately) تقريبا
Ha-weh-lee

arrival *wu-Sool* وصول

arrive *yiw-Sal* يصل

ashtray *Ta"-Too-"a* طفاية،
طقطوقة

ask *yis-'al* يسأل

ask for *yuT-lub* يطلب

aspirin *as-bee-reen* أسبيرين

Aswan *'aS-waan* أسوان

at (place) *fi* في / ب

aubergine *bi-din-gehn* باذنجان

August *a-ghuS-Tus* أغسطس

aunt (paternal) *ᶜam-ma* عمة

(maternal) *kheh-la* خالة

Australia *os-tral-ya* استراليا

auto repair shop *war-sha* ورشة

autumn *kha-reef* خريف

awake *Saa-Hee* صاحي

awful *fa-Zeeᶜ* فظيع

B

baby *Tifl* (pl.) *'aT-faal* طفل،
أطفال

back (noun) *Dahr* ظهر

back of, behind *wa-ra* وراء

backgammon *Towleh* طاولة

backwards *wa-ra* الى الوراء

bad *wi-Hish* سيء، رديء

not — *mish baT-Taal* مش بطال

bag *shan-Ta* حقيبة، حقائب
(pl.) *shu-naT*

baggage *shu-naT/* حقائب، أمتعة
ᶜafsh

baked *fil-furn* في الفرن

bakery *furn/makh-baz* فرن، مخبز

ball *koh-ra* كرة

ball-point pen *"al-lam gaff* قلم جاف

bananas *mohz* موز

bandages *ru-baaT* رباط

bank *bank* بنك، بنوك
(pl.) *bu-nook*

bar *baar* بار

barber *Hal-leh"* حلاق

bath *ban-yoo* بانيو

bathroom *Ham-mehm,* حمام،
twa-litt تواليت

bathe *yis-ta-Ham-ma* يستحم

battery *baT-Ta-ree-ya* بطارية

bazaar, market *soo"* سوق

beach *plehj/shaTT* شاطىء

beach umbrella *sham-see-ya* شمسية

beans *fa-Sul-ya,* فاصولية
fool فول

beard *da"n* لحية

beautiful *Hilw / ga-meel* جميل

beauty parlor *Sa-lohn tag-meel* صالون تجميل

because *ᶜa-shehn, li-'ann* لأن

bed *si-reer* سرير، سراير
(pl.) *sa-reh-yir*

beef *laH-ma ba-"a-ree* لحم بقر

beer *bee-ra* بيرة

before (prep) *"abl* قبل

beforehand *"ab-li ki-da* من قبل

believe *yi-sad-da"* يصدق

bell *ga-ras* جرس

belt *Hi-zehm* حزام

better, best *'aH-san/kheyr* أحسن، أفضل

bicycle *ᶜa-ga-la* عجلة، دراجة

big *ki-beer* كبير

bigger, biggest *'ak-bar* أكبر

bill (check) *Hi-sehb* حساب،
(pl.) *Hi-seh-beht* حسابات

bills (currency) *'aw-reh" na"d* أوراق نقد

birthday *ᶜeed mi-lehd* عيد ميلاد

biscuit *bas-ka-weet* بسكويت

black *'is-wid* أسود
[soh-da] [سوداء]

blanket *baT-Ta-nee-ya* بطانية

blood pressure *DakhT id-damm* ضغط الدم

blouse *bloo-za* بلوزة

blue *'az-ra" [zar-"a]* ازرق [زرقاء]

board *looH* لوح

boat *mar-kib* (pl.) *ma-reh-kib* سفينة، سفن/مركب، مراكب

bobby pins *bi-nas* دبابيس للشعر

boiled *mas-loo"* مسلوق

bone *ᶜaDm* عظم

book *ki-tehb* (pl.) *ku-tub* كتاب، كتب

bookstore *mak-ta-ba* مكتبة

boss *ray-yis* رئيس

bottle *"i-zeh-za* زجاجة، (pl.) *"a-zeh-yiz* زجاجات

box *san-doo"* صندوق

bra *soo-tyehn* حمالة الصدر

bracelet *ghi-wey-sha* سوار

brakes *fa-raa-mil* فرامل

branch *farᶜ* فرع، فروع (pl.) *fu-rooᶜ*

Brazil *ba-ra-zeel* برازيل

Brazilian *ba-ra-zee-lee* برازيلي [*ba-ra-zee-lee-ya*]

bread *ᶜeysh/ khubz* خبز

break (verb) *yik-sar* يكسر

broken *mak-soor* مكسور [*mak-soo-ra*]

broken (out of order) *ᶜaT laan* [*ᶜaT laa na*] بعطل

breakfast (noun) *fi-Taar* إفطار

(verb) *yif-Tar* يفطر

bridge *kub-ree* كوبري، كباري (pl.) *ka-beh-ree*

bring *yi-geeb* يحضر

Britain *bri-Tan-ya* بريطانيا

British *bri-Taa-nee* بريطاني [*bri-Taa-nee-ya*]

broke (bankrupt) *mi-fal-lis* مفلس

brother *'akhkh* أخ، إخوة (pl.) *'ikh-weht*

brown *bun-nee* بني

brush *fur-sha* فرشاة

buffet (dining) car *bu-feyh* بوفيه، عربة الأكل

building *ᶜi-maa-ra* عمارة، عمارات (pl.) *ᶜi-maa-raat*

burn *yiH-ra"* يحرق

burned *maH-roo"* محروق

bus *'u-tu-bees* أوتوبيس، (pl.) *'u-tu-bee-seht* أوتوبيسات

bus stop *ma-HaT-Tit 'u-tu-bees* محطة أوتوبيس

business *ti-gaa-ra, 'aᶜ-mehl* تجارة، اعمال

businessman *teh-gir, raa-gil 'aᶜ-mehl* رجل أعمال، تاجر

busy *mash-ghool* مشغول

but *bass, leh-kin* لكن

butcher *gaz-zaar* جزار

butter *zib-da* زبدة

button *zu-raar* زر، ازرار (pl.) *za-raa-yir*

buy (verb) *yish-ti-ree* يشتري

by the hour *fis-seh-ᶜa* في الساعة

by the way ... *ᶜa-la fik-ra* على فكرة

C

cabaret *ka-ba-rey* كاباريه، عرض

cabbage *ku-rumb* كرنب

café *"ah-wa* مقهى

caftan *"uf-Taan* (pl.) *"a-fa-Teen* قفطان، قفاطين

Cairo *il-qaa-hi-ra, maSr* القاهرة، مصر

call (telephone) *mu-kal-ma* مكالمة

call (verb) *yi-kal-lim* يكلم

camel *ga-mal* جمل

camera *ka-me-ra* كاميرا، آلة التصوير

campsite *mu-khay-yam si-yeh-Hee* مخيم سياحي

can (noun) *'il-ba* (pl.) *'i-lab* علبة، علب

Canada *ka-na-da* كندا

Canadian *ka-na-dee* كندي [كندية] [*ka-na-dee-ya*]

capital (finance) *ra's mehl* رأس مال

capital (city) *'aa-Si-ma* عاصمة

car *'a-ra-bee-ya/ say-yaa-ra* سيارة

carat *"i-raaT* قيراط

card *kart* (pl.) *ku-root*/ *bi-Taa-qa* (pl.) *bi-Taa-qaat* كارت، كروت / بطاقة، بطاقات

(be) careful! *Heh-sib!* [*Has-bee!*] إحذر

carpet *sig-geh-da* (pl.) *sa-ga-geed* سجادة، سجاجيد

carriage (horsedrawn) *Han-Toor* حنطور

carry *yi-sheel, yiH-mil* يحمل

cash (noun) *na"d* نقد

cashier *Sar-raaf* صراف

cassette *ka-sitt* (pl.) *kasit-teht* كسيت، كسيتات

cassette player *gi-hehz ka-sitt* جهاز كسيت

center *wisT* وسط

center (institution) *mar-kaz* مركز

ceramics *fukh-khaar* فخار

certain (sure) *mit-'ak-kid* [*mit-'ak-ki-da*] متأكد [متأكدة]

certainly *Haa-Dir* حاضر، تحت أمرك

chain *sil-si-la* سلسلة

change (money) *yi-Haw-wil* يحول

change (verb intr.) *yit-ghay-yar* يتغير

(verb trans.) *yi-ghay-yar* يغير

change (remainder) *beh-"ee* باقي

small — *fak-ka* فكة

channel *qa-naah* قناة

chat (verb) *yi-dar-dish* يدردش

chauffeur *saw-weh* سائق، سواق

cheap *ri-kheeS* [*ri-khee-Sa*] رخيص [رخيصة]

cheaper, *'ar-khaS* أرخص
cheapest

cheat (verb) *yi-***ghishsh**   يغش

check, bill *Hi-***sehb**   حساب

check (personal) *sheek*
(pl.) *shee-***keht**   شيك، شيكات

traveler's checks *shee-***keht**
*si-ya-***Hee**-ya   شيكات سياحية

check (examine) *yi-***shoof**   يفحص

check in (baggage) *yi-***sag**-gil   يسجل

cheese *gib-***na**   جبنة

chemist's (druggist's)
'ag ƨa khoh na, Say da loo ya
أجزخانة، صيدلية

chest (box) *san-***doo"**   صندوق

chest (body) *Sidr*   صدر

chicken *fi-***rehkh**/da-**jehj**   فراخ /
دجاج

chicken soup *shur-bit fi-***rehkh**
/da-**jehj**   شربة فراخ / دجاج

child *Tifl* (pl.) *'aT-***faal**, *wa-***lad**
(pl.) *'aw-***lehd**   طفل، اطفال /
ولد، اولاد

China *iS-***Seen**   الصين

Chinese *See-nee* [*See-***nee**-ya]
صيني

chocolate *sho-ko-***laa**-ta   شكولاتة

choose *yikh-***taar**   يختار

cigarette *si-***gaa**-ra (pl.) *sa-***geh**-yir
سيجارة، سجائر

city *ba-***lad**/ *ma-***dee**-na   مدينة

class, classroom *faSl*   فصل

clean (adj.) *ni-***Deef**
[*ni-***Dee**-fa]   نظيف

clean (verb) *yi-***naD**-Daf   ينظف

cleansing cream *kreym li 'i-***zeh**-lit
*il-mak-***yaj**   كريم لازالة المكياج

clock *seh-*^c*a*   ساعة
alarm clock *mi-***nab**-bih   منبه

close (verb) *yi*"-*fil*   يغلق، يقفل
closed *ma*"-*fool*   مغلق، مقفول

clothes *hu-***doom**   ملابس

club *neh-***dee** (pl.) *na-***weh**-dee
نادي، نوادي

coffee *"ah-***wa**   قهوة
ground — *bunn*   بن

coffee shop *"ah-***wa**   مقهى

cold (things, weather) *beh-***rid**   بارد
(people) *bar-***dehn**
[*bar-***deh**-na]   بردان
(in the head) *zu-***kehm**/*bard*
زكام / برد

colleague *zi-***meel**   زميل، زملاء
(pl.) *zu-ma-la*

cologne *ko-lon-ya*   كلونيا

color *lohn* (pl.) *'al-***wehn**
لون، الوان

color chart *da-***leel** *'al-***wehn**
دليل ألوان

comb *mishT*   مشط

come *yee-***gee**   يجي

come! (imp.) *ta-*^c*eh-la!*   هيا بنا!
[*ta-*^c*eh-lee!*]

coming *gayy* [*gay*-ya] قادم / جاي

company *shir-ka* شركة، شركات
(pl.) *sha-ri-keht*

complete (entire) *keh-mil* كامل
[*kam*-la]

concert *Haf-la mu-si-qee-ya*
حفلة موسيقية

confectioner's *Ha-la-weh-nee* حلواني

confectionery *Ha-la-wee-yeht*
حلويات

conference *mu'-ta-mar* مؤتمر،
(pl.) *mu'-ta-ma-raat* مؤتمرات

congratulations! *mab-rook!*
مبروك !

constipation *'im-sehk* إمساك

consulate *qun-Su-lee-ya* قنصلية

contact (verb) *yiT-Ti-Sil (bi —)*
يتصل (بـ —)

contact lenses *ᶜa-da-seht* عدسات
soft — *— Ta-ree-ya* — لينة
hard — *— nash-fa* — صلبة

contract *ᶜa"d* عقد

cook (verb) *yuT-bukh* يطبخ

cookies *bas-ka-weet* بسكويت

copy (noun) *nus-kha* نسخة

coral *mur-gehn* مرجان

corner (of street) *naS-ya* ناصية

correct *maZ-booT* مضبوط

cosmetics *mak-yaj* مكياج

cost *ta-man / siᶜr* ثمن / سعر

cotton *"uTn* قطن

cough (verb) *yi-kuHH*, يسعل،
يكح

(noun) *kuH-Ha* سعال، كحة

country (nation) *ba-lad* بلد

countryside *reef* ريف

(of) course *Tab-ᶜan* طبعاً

crab *'a-boo ga-lam-boo* أبو جلمبو

crazy *mag-noon* مجنون
[*mag-noo-na*]

cream *"ish-Ta* قشطة

(cosmetic) cream *kreym* كريم

credit card *kri-dit kard /* كريدت
bi-Taa-qit ᶜ-ti-mehd كارد /
بطاقة اعتماد

crowded *zaH-ma* زحمة / مزدحم

crystal (watch) *"i-zehz* زجاج

cucumber *khi-yaar* قثاء، خيار

cup *fin-gehn* (pl.) *fa-na-geen*
فنجان، فناجين

currency *ᶜum-la* عملة
hard — *ᶜum-la Saᶜ-ba*
عملة صعبة

customer *zi-boon* (pl.) *za-beh-yin*
زبون، زبائن

customs *ig-gum-ruk* الجمرك

D

dance (verb) *yur-"uS* يرقص

dancing *ra"S* رقص

danger *kha-Tar* خطر

dangerous *kha-Teer* خطير

date *ta-reekh* تاريخ

date (appointment) *ma-ᶜehd* موعد، ميعاد

dates (fruit) *ba-laH* بلح

daughter *bint (pl.) ba-neht* بنت، بنات

dawn *fagr* فجر

day *yohm (pl.) 'ay-yehm* يوم، أيام

two days *yoh-meyn* يومان

day after tomorrow *baᶜ-di buk-ra* بعد غد

December *di-sim-bir* ديسمبر

delicious *la-zeez* لذيذ

deliver *yi-sal-lim* يسلم

dentist *Ta-beeb 'as-nehn* طبيب أسنان

depart, leave *yim-shee/ yi-seh-fir* يغادر، يسافر

department *qism (pl.) aq-sehm* قسم، أقسام

deposit (noun) *ta'-meen, ᶜar-boon* عربون، تأمين

desert *SaH-ra* صحراء

desserts *Ha-la-wee-yeht* حلويات

detour *taH-wee-la* تحويلة

develop (film) *yi-Ham-maD* يحمض

development *ta-Taw-wur* تطور

dialect *lah-ga (pl.) lah-geht* لهجة، لهجات

diamond *'al-maaz* الماس

diarrhea *'is-hehl* إسهال

dictionary *qa-moos* قاموس

die *yi-moot* يموت

diesel (gas) *dee-zil* ديزل

different *mukh-ta-lif [mukh-ta-li-fa]* مختلف

difficult *Saᶜb* صعب

difficulty *Su-ᶜoo-ba* صعوبة

dine *yit-ᶜash-sha* يتعشى

dining room (in hotel) *maT-ᶜam* مطعم

dinner *ᶜa-sha* عشاء

direct (adj.) *mu-beh-shir* مباشر

director *mu-deer* مدير

directory *da-leel* دليل

dirty *wi-sikh [wis-kha]* قذر، وسخ

discount *takh-feeD* تخفيض

disease (illness) *ma-raD (pl.) 'am-raaD* مرض، أمراض

distribution *taw-zeeᶜ* توزيع

do *yiᵉ-mil* يعمل

doctor *Ta-beeb, duk-toor* طبيب، دكتور

documents *'aw-reh"* أوراق

dog *kalb (pl.) ki-lehb* كلب، كلاب

dollar do-**laar** دولار، دولارات
(pl.) do-la-**raat**

door behb باب

doorman (doorkeeper) baw-**wehb** بواب
(pl.) baw-weh-**been**

down (stairs) taHt تحت

downtown fi wiST il-**ba**-lad في وسط المدينة

dress (noun) fus-**tehn** فستان

dressed leh-bis [lab-sa] لابس

get dressed yil-bis يلبس

drink (verb) yish-rab يشرب

drinks mash-roo-**beht** مشروبات

drive (verb) yi-soo" يسوق

drugstore 'ag-za-**kheh**-na, أجزخانة،
Say-da-**lee**-ya صيدلية

drunk sak-**raan** سكران
[sak-**raa**-na]

dry neh-shif [nash-fa] جاف،
ناشف

dry cleaning it-tan-**Deef** التنظيف
in-**neh**-shif الجاف

Dutch ho-**lan**-dee هولندي
[ho-lan-**dee**-ya]

E

each kull كل

ear widn أذن

early **bad**-ree مبكر، باكر

earrings Ha-la" حلق

East (Orient) shar " شرق

Middle East الشرق الأوسط
ish-**sharq** il-'**aw**-SaT

Eastern shar-"ee [shar-"ee-ya] شرقي

easy sahl سهل

eat yeh-kul ياكل

eggs beyD بيض

eggplant bi-din-**gehn** باذنجان

Egypt maSr مصر

Egyptian **maS**-ree مصري
[maS-**ree**-ya] (pl.) maS-ree-**yeen**

eight ta-**man**-ya ثمانية

electricity kah-ra-ba كهرباء

elevator 'a-san-**Seer** مصعد

embarrassed mak-**soof** مكسوف
[mak-**soo**-fa]

embassy sa-**faa**-ra سفارة

emergency Ta-**waa**-ri' طوارىء

empty **faa**-Dee, feh-righ فارغ

engine mo-**toor**, ʿid-da موتور، محرك

engineer mu-**han**-dis مهندس

engineering han-da-sa هندسة

England in-gil-**ti**-ra انجلترا

English in-gi-**lee**-zee انجليزي
[in-gi-lee-**zee**-ya]

enjoy yit-**mat**-taʿ (bi —) يتمتع (ب —)

enough *ki-feh-ya* كفاية

entertainment *ma-leh-hee* ملاهي

entrance *du-khool* دخول

   no entry
   mam-noo^c id-du-khool ممنوع الدخول

envelope *Zarf (pl.) Zu-roof* ظرف، ظروف

Europe *u-rub-ba* أوروبا

European *u-rub-bee* أوروبي

evening *mi-seh', magh-rib* مساء، مغرب

every *kull* كل

everything *kul-li Ha-ga* كل شيء

exact *maZ-booT* مضبوط

exactly *biZ-ZabT* تماما، بالضبط

exam *im-ti-Hehn* امتحان
   (pl.) im-ti-Heh-neht

(for) example *ma-sa-lan* مثلا

exchange (money) *yi-Haw-wil* يحول

exchange rate *si^cr it-taH-weel* سعر التحويل

Excuse me. *is-maH-lee* اسمح لي

exhibition *ma^c-raD* معرض

exit *khu-roog* خروج

   no exit mam-noo^c il-khu-roog ممنوع الخروج

expensive *gheh-lee* غالي
   [ghal-ya]

experience *khib-ra* خبرة

explain *yish-raH, yi-fah-him* يشرح

eye *^ceyn (pl.) ^ci-yoon* عين، عيون

eyeglasses *naD-Daa-ra* نظارة

F

face *wishsh* وجه

facial massage *tad-leek* تدليك

factory *maS-na^c* مصنع، مصانع
   (pl.) ma-Saa-ni^c

fall (verb) *yu-"a^c* يقع

family *^cey-la/'us-ra* أسرة، عائلة

famous *mash-hoor* مشهور
   [mash-hoo-ra]

fan *mar-wa-Ha* مروحة

far *bi-^ceed* بعيد

fare *'ug-ra* أجرة

fast (adj.) *sa-ree^c* سريع

fast (adv.) *bi sur-^ca* بسرعة

fast (verb) *yi-Soom* يصوم

father *'abb* أب

   *my father *'a-boo-ya* أبي

feast *^ceed* عيد

February *fib-reh-yir* فبراير

ferry *mi-^cad-dee-ya* معدية

festival *^ceed* عيد

fever *su-khu-nee-ya* حمى

fill **yim-la** يملا

filling (tooth) **Hashw** حشو

film **film** (pl.) **'af-lehm** فلم، افلام

find **yi-leh-"ee** يلقى

fine (great) **mum-tehz** ممتاز

finger **Su-baac** (pl.) **Sa-waa-bic** أصبع، اصابع

finish **yi-khal-laS** يكمل

finish (intrans.) **yikh-laS** يخلص

finished! (it's over!) **kha-laas!** إنتـهى

first **'aw-wil** [**'oo-la**] اول [اولى]

first class **da-ra-ga 'oo-la** درجة اولى

first time **'aw-wil mar-ra** المرة الاولى

fish **sa-mak** سمك

five **kham-sa** خمسة

fix **yi-Sal-laH** يصلح

flashlight **kash-shehf** مصباح كهربائي

flat (apartment) **sha"-"a** (pl.) **shu-"a"** شقة، شقق

flies **dib-behn** ذباب

floor **dohr** (pl.) **'ad-waar** دور، طابق

floor show **carD, ka-ba-rey** عرض، كاباريه

florist **ma-Hall zu-hoor** محل زهور

flowers **zu-hoor, ward** زهور، ورد

folk dancing **ra"S shac-bee** رقص شعبي

food **'akl** طعام، اكل

foot **rigl, "a-dam** قدم

football **koh-ra** كرة القدم

for **li, ca-shehn** ل

for example **ma-sa-lan** مثلا

forbidden **mam-nooc** ممنوع

foreign(er) **'ag-na-bee** [**'ag-na-bee-ya**] اجنبي

forgive **yi-seh-miH** يسامح

fork **shoh-ka** شوكة

forward **"ud-dehm** الى الامام/قدام

four **ar-ba-ca** اربعة

France **fa-ran-sa** فرنسا

free (unoccupied) **faa-Dee** (for nothing) **bi ba-lehsh**, **mag-geh-nan** خالي، مجانا

freedom **Hur-ree-ya** حرية

French **fa-ran-seh-wee** [**fa-ran-sa-wee-ya**] فرنسي

fresh **Taa-za** طازج

Friday (yohm) **ig-gum-ca** يوم الجمعة

fried **ma"-lee** مقلي

friend **Saa-Hib, Sa-deeq** (pl.) **'aS-Haab** صاحب، صديق

from **min** من

in front of **"ud-dehm** امام، قدام

fruit **fak-ha** فاكهة

full *mal-yehn* [*mal-yeh-na*] ملء

G

galabiyya *gal-la-hee-ya* جلابية

garden *gi-ney-na* حديقة، جنينة
(pl.) *ga-neh-yin*

garlic *tohm* ثوم

gasoline *ban-zeen* بنزين

gas station *ma-HaT-Tit* محطة بنزين
ban-zeen

gears *na"-leht, tu-roos* تروس

generous *ka-reem* كريم، كرماء
[*ka-ree-ma*] (pl.) *ku-ra-ma*

German *al-meh-nee* الماني
[*al-ma-nee-ya*]

Germany *al-man-ya* المانيا

get *yi-geeb* يحضر

get in, on (vehicle) *yir-kab* يركب

gift *ha-dee-ya* هدية، هدايا
(pl.) *ha-deh-ya*

glass "*i-zehz* زجاج

glass (drinking) *kub-beh-ya* كأس

go *yi-rooH* يذهب

Let's go! *yul-la!* هيّا بنا

go away *yim-shee* يرحل، يغادر

go home *yi-raw-waH* يرجع للبيت

go in *yud-khul* يدخل

God '*al-laah* الله

gold *da-hab* ذهب

good (things) *kway-yis* جيد، كويس
[*kway-yi-sa*]

good (people) *Tay-yib* طيب
[*Tay-yi-ba*]

Good afternoon. *mi-seh' il-kheyr* مساء الخير

Goodbye. *ma-ᶜa s-sa-leh-ma* مع السلامة

Good evening. *mi-seh' il-kheyr* مساء الخير

Good morning. *Sa-baH il-kheyr* صباح الخير

Good night. *riS-baH ᶜa-la kheyr* تصبح على خير

grandfather *gidd* جد

grandmother *gid-da* جدة

grapes *ᶜi-nab* عنب

gray *ra-maa-Dee* رمادي

Greece *il-yu-nehn* اليونان

greedy *Tam-maaᶜ* طمّاع
[*Tam-maa-ᶜa*]

Greek *yu-neh-nee* يوناني
[*yu-neh-nee-ya*]

green '*akh-Dar* [*khaD-ra*] أخضر

grocery store *ba"-"ehl* محل بقالة، بقال

grilled *mash-wee* مشوي

guest *Deyf* ضيف، ضيوف
(pl.) *Du-yoof*

guide, guidebook *da-leel* دليل

gulf *kha-leeg* خليج

H

hair *sha^r* شعر

hairdresser *Hal-leh"*, حلاق
kwa-**feer**

half *nuSS* نصف

hand *'eed (pl.) 'a-yeh-dee* يد، ايدي

happen *yiH-Sal* يحصل

happy *mab-SooT* مبسوط
[*mab-Soo-Ta*,
far-**Haan** [far-**Haa**-na] فرحان

harbor *mee-na* ميناء

hat *bur-ney-Ta* قبعة، برنيطة

have *^and* — عند — ، مع —
or **ma**-^a — + pronoun
I have *^an-dee*, معي عندي، معي
ma-^**eh**-ya

hay fever *zu-kehm* زكام ربيعي
ra-bee-^ee

he *huw-wa* هو

head *raas* رأس

headache *Su-daa^* صداع

headlight *kash-shehf* النور الأمامي

hear *yis-ma^* يسمع

heart *"alb* قلب

heart attack *'az-ma qal-bee-ya* أزمة /نوبة قلبية

heavy *ti-"eel* ثقيل

heel *ka^b* كعب

Hello. (on the phone) *a-loh* آلو

help (verb) *yi-seh-^id* يساعد

Help! *il-Ha-"oo-nee!* النجدة !

here *hi-na* هنا

hide (verb) *yi-khab-bee* يخبىء

high *^eh-lee* عالي

highway *Ta-ree"* طريق رئيسي
ra-'ee-see

hire *yi-'ag-gar* يؤجر، يستاجر

historical *ta-ree-khee* تاريخي

history *ta-reekh* تاريخ

hit *yiD-rab* يضرب

holiday *'a-geh-za* عطلة / اجازة

Holland *ho-lan-da* هولندا

home *beyt* بيت، منزل
at home *fil-beyt* في البيت

honey *^a-sal* عسل

(I/we) hope so *'in shaa'-al-laah* إن شاء الله

hospital *mus-tash-fa* مستشفى

hot (weather) *Harr* حار
(food, etc.) *sukhn* ساخن

hot (spicy) *Heh-mee* متبل، حامي

hotel *'u-teel, fun-du"* اوتيل، فندق

hour *seh-^a* ساعة، ساعات
(pl.) sa-^eht
per hour *fis-seh-^a* في الساعة

house *beyt* بيت، منزل
(pl.) bu-yoot

housewife *sit-ti beyt* ربة بيت

how? *iz-zayy/keyf?* ازي، كيف ؟

How do you do? iz-**zay**-yak? ازيك؟
[iz-**zay**-yik?]

How are you? keyf il-**Hehl**?
كيف الحال؟

How much/many? kam? bi kam? كم، بكم؟

hubble bubble shee-sha شيشة
(water) pipe

humidity ru-**Too**-ba رطوبة

hundred mee-ya مئة، مئات
(pl.) mee-yeht

hungry ga-ʿehn جائع، جوعان
[gu-ʿeh-nu]

(in a) hurry mis-taʿ-gil مستعجل
[mis-taʿ-gi-la]

hurt yiw-gaʿ يؤلم، يوجع

husband gooz/zohj زوج

I

I a-na انا

ice talg ثلج

ice cream ays kreem أيس كريم

idea fik-ra (pl.) 'af-kaar فكرة،
أفكار

if law لو

ill ʿay-yehn [ʿay-yeh-na], مريض
ma-reeD [ma-ree-Da]

import is-ti-raad إستيراد

important mu-himm مهم

in fi في، ب

independence is-tiq-lehl استقلال

India il-hind الهند

Indian hin-dee [hin-dee-ya] هندي

indigestion Hu-moo-Da حموضة
سوء الهضم

inexpensive ri-kheeS رخيص

infection 'il-ti-hehb إلتهاب

influenza in-floo-in-za انفلونزا

information is-tiʿ-la-meht
معلومات، استعلامات

insect Ha-sha-ra حشرة، حشرات
(pl.) Ha-sha-raat

inside gow-wa في الداخل

insomnia ʿa-dam in-nohm أرق

insurance ta'-meen تامين

intelligent za-kee [za-kee-ya] ذكي

interested (in —)
muh-tamm (bi —) مهتم (ب)

interesting mu-himm مهم

interview, encounter (noun)
mu-"ab-la مقابلة

introduce X to Y yi-"ad-dim X li Y
يقدم X ل Y

invitation ʿu-zoo-ma عزومة

invite yiʿ-zim يعزم

Ireland ayr-lan-da ايرلندا

Irish (man) ayr-lan-dee ايرلندي
[ayr-lan-dee-ya]

iron mak-wa مكواة

ironer *mak-wa-gee* محل كي، مكوجي

ironing *kayy* كي

Islam *'is-lehm* إسلام

Islamic *'is-leh-mee* إسلامي

island *gi-zee-ra* جزيرة، جزر
(pl.) *gu-zur*

Israel *is-ra-'eel* إسرائيل

Israeli *is-ra-'ee-lee* إسرائيلي
[*is-ra-'ee-lee-ya*]

Italian *i-Taa-lee* إيطالي
[*i-Taa-lee-ya*]

Italy *i-Taal-ya* إيطاليا

ivory *sinn il-feel* سن الفيل

J

jack (car) *ku-reek, jehk* جك، مرفاع سيارة

jacket *ja-kit-ta* جاكيتة

jam *mu-rab-ba* مربى

January *ya-neh-yir* يناير

Japan *il-ya-behn* اليابان

Japanese *ya-beh-nee* ياباني
[*ya-beh-nee-ya*]

jewelry *ga-weh-hir,* مجوهرات
mu-gaw-ha-raat

jewelry store *ga-wa-hir-gee* جواهرجي

Jewish *yu-hoo-dee* يهودي
[*yu-hoo-dee-ya*]

job, post *wa-Zee-fa* وظيفة

juice *ᶜa-Seer* عصير

July *yul-yoo* يوليو

June *yun-yoo* يونيو

K

key *mif-tehH* مفتاح، مفاتيح
(pl.) *ma-fa-teeH*

kilo *kee-loo* كيلو

kind (noun) *Sanf* (pl.) صنف، نوع
(pl.) *'aS-naaf, noh*ᶜ *'an-weh*ᶜ

kind (adj.) *la-Teef* لطيف
[*la-Tee-fa*] (pl.) *lu-Taaf*

king *ma-lik* (pl.) *mu-look* ملك

kiosk *kushk* كشك، كشكات
(pl.) *kush-keht*

kiss *yi-boos* يبوس

knife *sik-kee-na* سكينة، سكاكين
(pl.) *sa-ka-keen*

know *yi*ᶜ*-raf* يعرف

L

laboratory *ma*ᶜ*-mal* معمل

lady *sitt* (pl.) *sit-teht* سيدة، سيدات

lake *bu-Hey-ra* بحيرة

lamb *Daa-nee* لحم خروف، ضاني

lamp *lam-ba* لمبة

land, earth *'arD*	ارض
language *lu-gha*	لغة
large *ki-beer [ki-bee-ra]*	كبير
larger, largest *'ak-bar*	اكبر
late *wakh-ree*, *mut-'akh-khir*	متأخر
later *ba^c-deyn*	بعد ذلك
laugh *yiD-Hak*	يضحك
laundry *gha-seel* (washing place) *magh-sa-la*	غسيل مغسلة
lavatory *twa-litt*, *doh-rit il-may-ya*	توالیت، دورة المياه
law *qa-noon*	قانون
lawyer *mu-Heh-mee*	محامي
laxative *mu-lay-yin*	ملين
lazy *kas-lehn*	كسول
leather *gild*	جلد
left *shi-mehl, yi-saar*	يسار
leg *rigl*	رجل
lemon *la-moon*	ليمون
lend *yi-sal-lif*	يسلف
lens *^c a da sa* (pl.) *^ca-da-seht*	عدسة، عدسات
lentils *^ca ds*	عدس
lesson *dars* (pl.) *du-roos*	درس، دروس
letter *ga-wehb* (pl.) *ga-weh-beht*	خطاب
library *mak-ta-ba*	مكتبة

license, permit *rukh-Sa*	رخصة
light *noor*	نور
light (in color) *feh-tiH [fat-Ha]*	فاتح
light (in weight) *kha-feef [kha-fee-fa]*	خفيف
lighter (noun) *wal-leh-^ca*	ولاعة
like (verb) *yi-Hibb*	يحب
like (prep.) *zayy/keyf*	زاي / مثل
limit (verb) *yi-Had-did*	يحدد
line *khaTT* (pl.) *khu-TooT*	خط، خطوط
liquor *kham-ra*	خمرة
list *"ay-ma*	قائمة
little *Su-ghay-yar*	صغير
(a) little *shway-ya*	قليل
live (verb) *yus-kun*, *yi-^ceesh*	يسكن، يعيش
loaf *ri-gheef* (pl.) *'ar-ghi-fa*	رغيف، أرغفة
local *ma-Hal-lee*	محلي
long *Ta-weel*	طويل
look, appearance *shakl* he (she) looks— *shak-loo [shak-la-ha]*	مظهر، شكل مظهره —، شكلها
look (at) *yit-far-rag (^ca-la)*	ينظر (الى)
look (for) *yi-daw-war (^ca-la)*	يبحث (عن)
loose (clothes) *weh-si^c*	واسع

lose *yi-Dee*^c   يفقد

(get) lost *yi-teeh*   يتيه، يضلل الطريق

a lot *ki-teer*   كثير

low *waa-Tee*   منخفض، واطىء

luck *bakht, HaZZ*   حظ

luggage *shu-naT/*^c*afsh*   أمتعة

lunch (noun) *gha-da*   غداء

    (verb) *yit-ghad-da*   يتغدى

M

magazine *ma-gal-la*   مجلة، مجلات
    (pl.) *ma-gal-leht*

magnificent ^c*a-Zeem*   عظيم

maid *khad-deh-ma*   خادمة

mail *ba-reed*   بريد

make *yi*^c*-mil*   يعمل

man *raa-gil*   رجل، رجال
    (pl.) *rig-geh-la*

manager *mu-deer*   مدير

mangoes *man-ga*   منجو

manicure *ma-ni-keer*   مانيكير

many *ki-teer*   كثير

map *kha-ree-Ta*   خريطة

March *meh-ris*   مارس

market *soo"*   سوق

married! *mit-gaw-wiz*   متزوج
    [*mit-gaw-wi-za*]

marry *yit-gaw-wiz*   يتزوج

massage *tad-leek*   تدليك

(football) match *matsh (koh-ra)*   مباراة (كرة)

matches *kab-reet*   كبريت

(it doesn't) matter   غير مهم
    may-him-mish

May *may-yoo*   مايو

maybe *yim-kin*   يمكن، ربما

meal *'akl*   طعام، أكل

measure *yi-"ees*   يقيس

meat *laHm*   لحم

medicine *da-wa*   دواء
    (pl.) *'ad-wee-ya*

meet *yi-"eh-bil*   يقابل

meeting *ig-ti-meh*^c   اجتماع

melon *sham-mehm*   شمام

mend *yi-Sal-laH*   يصلح

menu *min-yoo/"ay-ma*   منيو، قائمة

message *ri-seh-la*   رسالة

meter (taxi) ^c*ad-dehd*   عداد

meter (measurement) *mitr*   متر

military ^c*as-ka-ree*   عسكري

milk *la-ban/Ha-leeb*   لبن، حليب

million *mil-yohn*   مليون، ملايين
    (pl.) *ma-la-yeen*

(never) mind! *ma-*^c*a-lish!*   معلهش! لا بأس!

mind ^c*a"l*   عقل

mine *bi-teh-ʿee*   لي

minister *wa-zeer*   وزير

ministry *wi-zaa-ra*   وزارة

minute (time) *da-"ee-"a*,   دقيقة،
(pl.) *da-"eh-yi"*   دقائق

mirror *mi-reh-ya*   مرايا

Miss — *il-eh-ni-sa* —   — الآنسة

modern *ʿaS-ree/Ha-dees*   عصري، حديث

Monday *(yohm) lit-neyn*   يوم الاثنين

money *fi-loos*   فلوس

money exchange *mak-tab Sarf*   مكتب الصرف

month *shahr*, أشهر   شهر،
(pl.) *shu hoor*

monument *'a-sar*, آثار   أثر،
(pl.) *'a-saar*

morning *SubH/Sa-baaH*   صبح، صباح

in the morning *iS-SubH*   صباحاً

mosque *geh-miʿ*, جوامع   جامع،
(pl.) *ga-weh-miʿ*

mosquitoes *na-moos*   ناموس

mother *'umm*   أم

mountain *ga-bal*، جبال   جبل،
(pl.) *gi-behl*

Mr.— *is-say-yid* —   — السيد

Mrs.— *is-say-yi-da, ma-dehm* —   — السيدة، مدام

museum *mat-Haf*   متحف

music *mu-see-qa*   موسيقى

Muslim *mus-lim*   مسلم
[mus-li-ma] (pl.) *mus-li-meen*

(I, you, etc.) must — *leh-zim* —   — يجب أن —

mustache *sha-nab*   شنب، شارب

N

name *'ism*, أسماء   اسم،
(pl.) *'a seh mee*

napkin *foo-Ta*, منشفة   فوطة،
(pl.) *fo-waT*

sanitary napkin *foo-Ta*   فوطة صحية
siH-Hee-ya

narrow *day-ya"*   ضيق

national, nationalist *qaw-mee*   قومي

nationality *gin-see-ya*   جنسية

naughty *sha-"ee*   شقي، شرير

near (to) *"u-ray-yib (min)*   قريب (من)

nearby *"u-ray-yib*   قريباً

nearly *ta"-ree-ban*   تقريباً

(it is) necessary *leh zim*   يلزم

(I) need *ʿa-wiz* أحتاج   أريد،
[ʿaw-za]

never *'a-ba-dan*   أبداً

new *gi-deed*   جديد

newspaper *ga-ree-da*, جريدة، جرائد
(pl.) *ga-raa-yid*

next *gayy*   قادم

night *ley-la*   ليلة

Nile *in-neel*   النيل

nine *tis-ᶜa*   تسعة

no *la'*   لا

noise *daw-sha*   دوشة، ضخب

noon *Duhr*   ظهر

north *sha-mehl*   شمال

not *mish*   ليس، ما، لا

notebook *noh-ta*   دفتر جيب

nothing *wa-la Ha-ga*   لا شيء

November *nu-vim-bir*   نوفمبر

now *dil-wa"-tee*   الآن

number *nim-ra/ra-qam*   رقم

number (quantity) *ᶜa-dad*   عدد

nurse *mu-mar-ri-Da*   ممرضة

O

(I've/we've no) objection.   ليس
ma feesh meh-niᶜ   عندي مانع

obvious *waa-DiH*   واضح

October *ok-too-bar*   اكتوبر

of course *Tab-ᶜan*   طبعاً

office *mak-tab*   مكتب

office worker *mu-waZ-Zaf*   موظف
[*mu-waZ-Za-fa*]

oil *zeyt*   زيت
olive oil *zeyt zey-toon*   زيت زيتون

oil (petroleum) *bit-rohl*, *nafT*   بترول، نفط

old (people) *ki-beer*   كبير، كبار
[*ki-bee-ra*] (pl.) *ku-baar*

old (things) *"a-deem*   قديم
[*"a-dee-ma*]

I'm — years old.   عمري — سنة
ᶜan-dee — sa-na

How old are you? *ᶜan-dak*   عمرك كم سنة؟
[*ᶜan-dik*] *kam sa-na?*

on *ᶜa-la*   على

on foot *ᶜa-la rig-ley-na*   ماشياً، على الاقدام

on time *fil-ma-ᶜehd*   في الميعاد

once *mar-ra waH-da*   مرة واحدة

one *weh-Hid*   واحد، واحدة
[*waH-da*]

onions *ba-Sal*   بصل

only (just) *bass*   فقط

only (sole) *wa-Heed*   وحيد

open *yif-taH*   يفتح

open (adj.) *feh-tiH*, *maf-tooH*   مفتوح

optician *naD-Da-raa-tee*   محل نظارات

or *'aw*; *wal-la* (in questions)   او؛ أم

orange *bur-tu-"aan*   برتقال

order (verb) *yuT-lub*   يطلب

other **teh-nee [tan-ya]**, آخر
'**eh-khir ['ukh-ra]**

out of order **ʿaT-laan** معطل

outing, break **fus-Ha** فسحة

outside **bar-ra** في الخارج

oven **furn** فرن

over **foh"** فوق

It's over; that's it! **kha-laaS!** خلاص !

overcoat **bal-Too** بالطو، معطف

(on my) own **li waH-dee** وحدي

(on your) own **li waH-dak** وحدك
[li waH-dik]

P

package **Tard** طرد، طرود
(pl.) **Tu-rood**

packet **ʿil ba** (pl.) **ʿi-lab**, علبة،
beh-koo (pl.) **beh-ku-weht** علب

pain **wa-gaʿ/'a-lum** وجع، ألم

palace **"aSr** قصر

panties **kee-lott** سروال داخلي
نسائي

pants, trousers **ban-Ta-lohn** بنطلون

paper **wa-ra"** ورق، اوراق
(pl.) **'aw-reh"**

parcel **Tard** طرد، طرود
(pl.) **Tu-rood**

Pardon me, but — **is-maH-lee** —, إسمح لي
law sa-maHt —

park **gi-ney-na** حديقة
(pl.) **ga-neh-yin**

park (verb) **yu-"af** يقف

parking **'in-ti-Zaar** إنتظار

party **Haf-la** حفل

passport **bas-boor/** جواز السفر
ga-wehz is-sa-far

past (noun) **maa-Dee** ماضي

pastries **Ha-la-wee-yeht** حلويات

pastry shop **Ha-la-weh-nee** حلواني

peach **khokhkh** خوخ

peanuts **fool su-deh-nee** فول
سوداني

peasant **fal-lehH** فلاح
(pl.) **fal-la-Heen**

pen, pencil **"a-lam** قلم

people **nehs** ناس

pepper **fil-fil** فلفل

percentage **nis-ba mi-'a-wee-ya** نسبة مئوية

perhaps **yim-kin** يمكن، ربما

person **na-far** نفر، انفار
(pl.) **'an-faar**,
shakhS, (pl.) 'ash-khaaS شخص، أشخاص

personal **shakh-See** شخصي

personally **shakh-See-yan** شخصياً

petrol **ban-zeen** بنزين

Pharaonic **far-ʿoo-nee** فرعوني

pharmacy *'ag-za-kheh-na*, أجزخانة، صيدلية
Say-da-lee-ya

photograph, picture *Soo-ra* صورة ، صور
(pl.) *So-war*

photograph (verb) *yi-Saw-war* يصور

pickles *Tur-shee/* طرشي ، مخلل
mi-khal-lil

pillow *mi-khad-da* مخدة

pills *Hu-boob* حبوب

sleeping pills حبوب منومة
Hu-boob mi-naw-wi-ma

(what a) pity! *ya kh-Saa-ra!*
يا خسارة

place *ma-kehn* مكان ، أماكن
(pl.) *'a-meh-kin*

plants *na-ba-teht* نباتات

plate *Ta-ba"* طبق ، أطباق
(pl.) *'aT-baa"*

platform *ra-Seef* رصيف

play (verb) *yil-ᶜab* يلعب

play (theater) *mas-ra-Hee-ya*
مسرحية

pleasant (things) *Za-reef* ظريف

(people) *la-Teef* لطيف
[*la-Tee-fa*] (pl.) *lu-Taaf*

please — *min faD-lak* — من فضلك —
[*min faD-lik*]

pleased, happy *mab-SooT*, سعيد، فرحان،
far-Haan مبسوط

Pleased to meet you، فرصة سعيدة
it-shar-raf-na, تشرفنا
fur-Sa sa-ᶜee-da

police *bu-leeS/shur-Ta*
بوليس ، شرطة

policeman *ᶜas-ka-ree* شرطي
(pl.) *ᶜa-seh-kir*

poor *fa-"eer* فقير ، فقراء
(pl.) *fu-"a-ra*

popcorn *fi-shaar* فشار

popular (of the people) *shaᶜ-bee*
شعبي

porter *shay-yehl* شيال ، حمال

possible *mum-kin* ممكن

post *ba-reed* بريد

postcard *kart bus-tehl*
كارت بوستال، بطاقة بريدية

post office *mak-tab il-ba-reed*
مكتب البريد

potatoes *ba-Taa-Tis* بطاطس

pottery *fukh-khaar* فخار

pound (currency) *gi-ney* جنيه

pound (weight) *raTl* رطل

pray *yi-Sal-lee* يصلي

prefer *yi-faD-Dal* يفضل

pregnant *Heh-mil* حامل

prescription *ru-shit-ta* روشتة

present (gift) *ha-dee-ya* هدية
(pl.) *ha-deh-ya*

present (adj.) *maw-good* موجود

president *ra-'ees* رئيس

pretty *Hilw* حلو

price *ta-man, si^cr* ثمن ، سعر

print (photo) *nus-kha* نسخة

private *khaaS* خاص

problem *mush-ki-la* ، مشكلة
(pl.) *ma-sheh-kil* مشاكل

promise (verb) *yiw-^cid* يعد

public *^camm* عام

pupil *til-meez* تلميذ ، تلامذة
(pl.) *ta-lam-za*

purse, wallet *maH-fa-Za* محفظة

purse, bag *shan Ta* شنطة ، حقيبة
(pl.) *shu-naT*

pyramids *il-hu-ram* أهرام

Q

quantity *^ca-dad, qee-ma* عدد ، قيمة

quarrel (verb) *yi-kheh-ni"* يخانق

question (query) *su-'ehl,* سؤال ،
(pl.) *'as-'i-la* أسئلة

quick *sa ree^c* سريع

quickly *bi-sur-^cu* بسرعة

quiet *heh-dee* هادىء

R

radio *rad-yoo* راديو

railroad *is-sik-ka il-Ha-deed* السكة الحديدية

railroad station *ma-HaT-Tit* محطة القطار
il-"aTr

by rail *bil-"aTr* بالقطار

rain (noun) *ma-Tar* مطر

rare (unusual) *neh-dir* نادر

rate of exchange *si^cr it-taH-weel* سعر التحويل

rather (somewhat) *shway-ya* الى حد ما، قليلاً

raw *nayy* خام ، نيء

razor blades *'am-wehs Hi-leh-"a* أمواس حلاقة

read *yi"-ra* يقرأ

ready *geh-hiz [gah-za]* جاهز

really? *Sa-HeeH?* صحيح ؟

to the rear *wa-ra* الى الوراء

reason *sa-bab* سبب ، أسباب
(pl.) *'as-behb*

receipt *waSl* إيصال

record (music) *is-Ti-waa-na* اسطوانة

record (verb) *yi-sag-gil* يسجل

recover (health) *yi-khiff, yish-fa* يشفى

red *'uH-mar [Ham-ra]* أحمر

reduction *takh-feeD* تخفيض

relation *"a-reeb* قريب ، أقرباء
(pl.) *"a-raa-yih*

remember *yif-ti-kir* يفتكر ، يتذكر

remind yi-**fak**-kar   يفكر

rent (verb) yi-'**ag**-gar   يؤجر ، يستأجر

repair (verb) yi-**Sal**-laH   يصلح

  (noun) taS-**leeH**   تصليح

repeat yi-**kar**-rar   يكرر

reservation Hagz   حجز

reserve **yiH**-giz   يحجز

responsible mas-'**ool**   مسؤول

rest (verb) yis-ta-**ray**-yaH   يستريح

restaurant maT-**c**am   مطعم ، مطاعم
  (pl.) ma-**Taa**-c im

restroom twa-litt   تواليت ، دورة المياه

return (verb) **yir**-ga c   يعود ، يرجع

rice ruzz   أرز

rich **gha**-nee [gha-**nee**-ya]   غني
  (pl.) 'agh-**nee**-ya

right (correct) maZ-**booT**   صحيح ، مضبوط

right (direction) yi-**meen**   يمين

ring (jewelry) **kheh**-tim   خاتم

river nahr   نهر

road Ta-**ree**" (pl.) **Tu**-ru"   طريق ، طرق
  sik-ka (pl.) **si**-kak   سكة ، سكك

roast **mash**-wee   مشوي

robe, dressing gown rohb   ثوب ، روب

roof SatH   سقف ، سطح

room '**oh**-Da (pl.) '**o**-waD /   غرفة ، غرف
  ghur-fa (pl.) **ghu**-raf

rug sig-**geh**-da (pl.) sa-ga-**geed**,   سجادة ، سجاجيد ، كليم ، أكلمة
  ki-**leem** (pl.) 'ak-**li**-ma

Russia **roos**-ya   روسيا

Russian **roo**-see   روسي

S

sad Ha-**zeen**   حزين

safe **khaz**-na   خزنة

sailboat yakht, fa-**loo**-ka   يخت ، قارب

salad sa-la-Ta   سلطة

sale bee c   بيع

salt malH   ملح

(the) same — nafs il — — —   نفس الـ ـ ـ ـ

sand raml   رمل

sandstorm zaw-ba-c a عاصفة رملية

sandals **san**-dal (pl.) sa-na-**deel**   صندل

sandwich **sand**-witsh,   سندويتش ، سندويتشات
  (pl.) sand-wit-**sheht**

sanitary napkins fo-waT   فوط صحية
  SiH-**Hee**-ya

sardines sar-**deen**   سردين

Saturday (yohm) is-**sabt**   يوم السبت

sausages su-**gu**" "   سجق

say yi-"**ool**   يقول

scarf *'i-sharb*, *ku-fee-ya*   منديل الراس

schedule *gad-wal il-ma-wa-^ceed*   جدول المواعيد

school *mad-ra-sa* (pl.) *ma-deh-ris*   مدرسة ، مدارس

science *^cilm* (pl.) *^cu-loom*   علم ، علوم

scientific *^cil-mee*   علمي

scissors *ma-"aSS*   مقص

scotch (whiskey) *wis-kee*   ويسكي

screwdriver *mu-fakk ma-sa-meer*   مفك مسامير

sea *baHr*   بحر

seashore *shaTT* (البحر)   شاطىء

search for *yi-daw-war ^ca-lu*   يبحث عن

season *faSl*   فصل

second *teh-nee [tan-ya]*   ثاني

secretary *si-kir-teer* ، *[si-kir-tee-ra]*   سكرتير ، [سكرتيرة]

see *yi-shoof*   يرى

sell *yi-bee^c*   يبيع

send *yib-^cat*   يرسل ، يبعث

September *sib-tim-bir*   سبتمبر

serious *gadd*   جاد

seriously *bi-gadd*   بجد

service *khid-ma*   خدمة

seven *sab-^ca*   سبعة

shampoo *sham-poo*   شامبو

shark *"irsh* (pl.) *"u-roosh*   سمك القرش

shave *yiH-la"*   يحلق

she *hee-ya*   هـي

sheep (and goats) *gha-nam*   غنم

shells *Sa-daf*   صدف

ship *mar-kib/sa-fee-na*   مركب ، سفينة

shirt *"a-meeS* (pl.) *"um-Saan*   قميص ، قمصان

shoemaker *gaz-ma-gee*   جزمجي

shoes *gaz-ma*   حذاء ، جزمة

shop *duk-kehn* (pl.) *da-ka-keen*, *ma-Hall* (pl.) *ma-Hal-leht*   دكان ، دكاكين ، محل ، محلات

short *"u-Say-yar*   قصير

shoulder *kitf*   كتف

show (stage, floor) *^carD*   عرض

shower *dush*   دش

shy *mak-soof [mak-soo-fa]*   مكسوف

sick *^cay-yehn [^cay-yeh-na]*, *ma-reeD [ma-ree-Da]*   مريض

sight *man-Zar* (pl.) *ma-naa-Zir*   منظر ، مناظر

sign (verb) *yim-Dec*   يمضي

silent (of people) *seh-kit [sak-ta]*   ساكت

silk *Ha-reer*   حرير

silver *faD-Da*   فضة

sing yi-**ghan**-nee	يغني	soldier ᶜas-ka-ree (pl.) ᶜa-**seh**-kir	عسكري
singer mu-**ghan**-nee [mu-ghan-**nee**-ya]	مغني [مغنية]	some — baᶜD —	بعض —
sister 'ukht	أخت	somebody Hadd, **weh**-Hid	واحد
sit yu"-ᶜud	يقعد	something Ha-ga	شيء
six **sit**-ta	ستة	sometimes sa-ᶜeht, 'aH-**yeh**-nan	أحياناً
size ma-"ehs	مقاس	son 'ibn	ابن
skin gild/**bash**-ra	جلد ، بشرة	soon "u-**ray**-yib	قريباً
skirt gu-**nil**-la	جيبة ، جونلة	Sorry! 'eh-sif! ['as-fa!]	آسف !
sky **sa**-ma	سماء	sort, kind nohᶜ (pl.) 'an-**weh**ᶜ	نوع ، أنواع
sleep (verb) yi-**nehm** (noun) nohm	ينام توم	soup **shur**-ba	شربة
sleeping pills Hu-**boob** mi-naw-**wi**-ma	حبوب منومة	south ga-**noob**	جنوب
slippers **shib**-shib	شبشب	Spain as-**ban**-ya	إسبانيا
slow ba-**Tee'**	بطيء	Spanish as-**beh**-nee [as-ba-**nee**-ya]	إسباني
slowly bir-**raa**-Ha	ببطء		
Slow down! ᶜa-la **mah**-lak!		spark plugs boo-jey-**heht**	بوجيهات شمعة الشرارة
قلل السرعة ، على مهلك !		speak yit-**kal**-lim	يتكلم
small Su-**ghay**-yar [Su-ghay-**ya**-ra]	صغير	special makh-**SooS**	مخصوص
smoke (verb) yi-**dakh**-khan	يدخن	spend **yiS**-rif	يصرف
snow talg	ثلج	sponge si-**fing**	إسفنج
so, thus **ki**-da	هكذا	spoon maᶜ-**la**-"a	ملعقة
soap Sa-**boon**	صابون	sports ri-**yaa**-Da	رياضة
soccer **koh**-ra	كرة القدم	spring (season) ra-**beeᶜ**	ربيع
soccer match matsh **koh**-ra		square (place) mi-**dehn**	ميدان
مباراة في كرة القدم		stamps Ta-**waa**-biᶜ	طوابع
socialist ish-ti-**raa**-kee	اشتراكي	stand (up) yi-"**oom**	يقوم
socks sha-**raab**	شرابات ، جوارب		

start *yib-**ti**-dee*   يبدا

state (noun) ***daw**-la (pl.) **du**-wal*
دولة ، دول

station *ma-**HaT**-Ta*   محطة

stay (in, at) *yin-**zil** (fi)*، ينزل ، يبقى
yu"-^cud

steal *yis-**ra**"*   يسرق

stockings *shu-**raab***   ، شرابات
جوارب

stomach *mi^c-da, baTn*   معدة ، بطن

stone *Ha-gar*   حجر

stop *yu-**"af***   يقف

store *duk-**kehn** (pl.) da-ka-**keen**,*
،كان ، دكاكين،
*ma-**Hall** (pl.) ma-Hal-**leht***
محل ، محلات

story *fil-**keh**-ya*   قصة ، حكاية

straight (on) *dugh-ree* ،   إلى الأمام
دغري

strange *gha-reeb*   غريب

strawberries *fa-**raw**-la*   فراولة

street *sheh-ri^c*   شارع ، شوارع
*(pl.) sha-**weh**-ri^c*

strong *qa-wee [qa-**wee**-ya]*   قوي

student ***Taa**-lib [**Taa**-li-ba]*
*(pl.) **Ta**-la-ba*   طالب ، طلبة

study *yid-ris*   يدرس

stupid *gha-bee [gha-**bee**-ya]*   غبي

style *'us-**loob***   أسلوب

suddenly *biS-**Sud**-fa*   بالصدفة

sugar *suk-kar*   سكر

suit ***bad**-la, **kis**-wa*   كسوة ، بدلة

suitable *mu-**neh**-sib*   مناسب

summer *Seyf*   صيف

sun *shams*   شمس

Sunday (yohm) il-**Hadd**   يوم الأحد

sunglasses *naD-**Daa**-rit ish-**shams***
نظارة الشمس

suntan lotion *kreym li Hi-**meh**-yit*
*il-**bash**-ra*   كريم لحماية البشرة

sweater *bu-**loh**-var*   بلوفر

sweet *Hilw*   حلو

swim *yis-ta-**Ham**-ma, yi-^coom*
يستحم ، يسبح

swimming pool *Ham-**mehm***
*si-**beh**-Ha*   حمام سباحة

T

table *Ta-ra-**bey**-za*   طاولة ، طربيزة

tailor ***tar**-zee, khay-**yaaT***
ترزي ،
خياط

take *yeh-khud*   ياخذ

take off (plane) *yiT lu^c*   يقوم ، يقلع

take off (clothes) *yi"-la^c, yikh-la^c*
يخلع

take a picture *yi-**Saw**-war*   يصور

tapes *sha-**raa**-yiT*   شرائط

tax *Da-**ree**-ba*   ضريبة ، ضرائب
*(pl.) Da-**raa**-yib*

taxi *tak-see*   تاكسي

taxi stand *maw-"af tak-see*
موقف تاكسي

tea *shayy*
شاي

teach *yi-dar-ris*
يدرس

teacher *mu-dar-ris* [*mu-dar-ri-sa*]
مدرس ، معلم

T-shirt *fa-nil-la*
فانلة ، قميص نصف كم

telegram *til-li-ghrehf*
برقية ، تلغراف

telephone *ti-li-fohn*
تليفون

telephone call *mu-kal-ma*
مكالمة

telephone number *nim-rit*/ *ra-qam ti-li-fohn*
رقم تليفون

television *ti-li-viz-yohn*
تليفزيون

tell *yi-"ool*
يقول

tell me . . . *"ul-lee* . . . . . .
قل لي . . . .

temperature *Ha-raa-ra*
حرارة

the — *il* —
الـ —

there *hi-nehk*
هناك

there is/are — *fee* — is/are there? *fee?*
يوجد /توجد هل يوجد / توجد ؟

there isn't/aren't *ma feesh*
لا يوجد

think *yi-Zunn*
يظن

thousand *'alf* (pl.) *'a-lehf*
ألف ، آلاف

Thursday *yohm il-kha-mees*
يوم الخميس

thus *ki-da*
هكذا

tidy (adj.) *mu-rat-tab*
مرتب

tight *day-ya"*
ضيق

time *wa"t, za-man*
وقت ، زمن

What time is it? *is-seh-ᶜa kam?*
كم الساعة ؟

tip (gratuity) *ba"-sheesh*
بقشيش

together *sa-wa*
سوياً

tomb *ma"-ba-ra,* (pl.) *ma-"eh-bir*
مقبرة ، مقابر

tomorrow *buk-ra*
غداً

(on) top *foh"*
فوق

tooth *sinn* (pl.) *'as-nehn*
سن ، أسنان

tourist *saw-wehH* [*saw-weh-Ha*] (pl.) *suw-wehH*
سائح ، سواح

towel *foo-Ta* (pl.) *fo-waT*
منشفة ، مناشف ، فوطة ، فوط

traditions *ta-qa-leed*
تقاليد

traffic *mu-roor*
مرور

translate *yi-tar-gim*
يترجم

travel (verb) *yi-seh-fir*
يسافر

tree *sha-ga-ra* (pl.) *sha-gar*
شجرة ، شجر

true *Sa-HeeH*
صحيح

Tuesday (*yohm*) *it-ta-leht*
يوم الثلاثاء

typewriter *'eh-la kat-ba*
آلة كاتبة

U

ugly *wi-Hish* [*wiH-sha*]
قبيح

uncle (paternal) *ᶜamm*   عم

    (maternal) *khehl*   خال

under *taHt*   تحت

undershirt *fa-nil-la*   ، فانلة
    قميص تحتاني

understand *yif-ham*   يفهم

unfortunately **ma**-ᶜal-'a-saf   مع الأسف

United States *il-wi-la-yeht*
il-mut-ta-Hi-da   الولايات المتحدة

university *gam-ᶜa*   جامعة

unlikely *mish min il-muH-ta-mal*   بعيد الاحتمال

up *foh"*   الى فوق

use (verb) *yis-**ta**ᶜ-mil*   يستعمل

useful *mu-**feed***   مفيد

usually *ᶜa-**da**-tan*   عادةً

V

vacation *'a-**geh**-za*   عطلة ، إجازة

valley *weh-dee*   وادي

vegetables *khu-**Daar***   خضر

very *"a-wee, gid-dan*   جداً

video *vid-yo*   فيديو

view *man-Zar*   منظر ، مناظر
    (pl.) *ma-**naa**-Zir*

village *qar-ya*   قرية ، قرى
    (pl.) *qu-ra*

visit (verb) *yi-**Zoor***   يزور

voice, vote *Soht*   صوت ، أصوات
    (pl.) *'aS-waat*

voltage *volt*   فولت

W

wages *ma-**hee**-ya*   ماهية

wait *yis-**tan**-na/yin-**ti**-Zir*   ينتظر

walk *yim-shee, yit-**mash**-sha*   يمشي ، يتمشى

wallet *maH-fa-Za*   محفظة

want *ᶜa-wiz [ᶜaw-za]*   يريد

war *Harb*   حرب

warm *deh-fee*   دافئ

wash (verb) *yigh-sil*   يغسل

    (noun) *gha-seel*   غسيل

watch (verb) *yit-far-rag (ᶜa-la)*   ينظر الى

watch (noun) *seh-ᶜa*   ساعة

water *may-ya*   ماء ، مياه

    hot water *may-ya sukh-na*   مياه ساخنة

watermelon *baT-Teekh*   بطيخ

waves (water, air) *'am-wehg*   أمواج

we *iH-na*   نحن

weak *Da-ᶜeef*   ضعيف

wear *yil-bis*   يلبس

weather *gaww, Ta"S*   جو ، طقس

Wednesday (yohm) *lar-baᶜ*   يوم الأربعاء

eek *'is-boo^c* (pl.) *'a-sa-bee^c* أسبوع ، أسابيع

welcome! *mar-Ha-ba!* مرحباً !
You're welcome, don't mention it. *^{c}af-wan* عفواً

well *kway-yis* كويس ، بخير

well done (meat) *mis-ti-wee* تام النضج

West (Occident) *gharb* غرب

Western *ghar-bee* غربي [*ghar-bee-ya*]

wet *mab-lool* مبلول

What? *'eyh?* ما ؟

What!! (surprise) *ya sa-lehm!!* يا سلام !

What time? *is-seh-^{c}a kam?* كم الساعة ؟

wheel *^{c}a-ga-la* عجلة

When? *'im-ta?* متى ؟

when *lam-ma* لما

Where? *feyn?* أين ؟

Where from? *mi-neyn?* من أين ؟

Which? *'an-hee?* اي ؟

which (relative) *il-lee* الذي

whiskey *wis-kee* ويسكي

white *'ab-yaD* أبيض

Who? *meen?* من ؟

Why? *leyh?* لماذا ؟

wide *weh-si^c* [*was-^{c}a*] واسع

wife *ma-ra*, *sitt/zoh-ga* زوجة

window *shib-behk*, شباك ، شبابيك (pl.) *sha-ba-beek*

wine *ni-beet* نبيذ

winter *shi-ta* شتاء

with *ma-^{c}a, bi* مع ، ب

without *min-gheyr, bi-doon* بدون

woman *ma-ra* (pl.) *ni-seh'*, إمرأة ، *sitt* (pl.) *sit-teht* سيدة

wonderful *mum-tehz*, *^{c}a-Zeem* ممتاز ، عظيم

wood *kha-shab* خشب

wool *Soof* صوف

word *kil-ma* كلمة

work (verb) *yish-ta-ghal* يعمل ، يشتغل

work (noun) *shughl* عمل ، شغل

worried *"al-"ehn* قلق ، قلقان

wrap *yi-liff* يلف

write *yik-tib* يكتب

writer *keh-tib, mu-'al-lif* كاتب ، مؤلف

writing pad *blok noht* دفتر ، كراسة للكتابة

wrong *gha-laT* خطأ ، غلط

XYZ

X-rays *'a-shi^c-^{c}a* أشعة

year **sa**-na سنة ، سنوات
(pl.) si-**neen**

this year is-sa-**neh** dee هذه السنة

last year is-**sa**-na il-lee-**feh**-tit
السنة التي فاتت

yellow '**aS**-far [**Saf**-ra] أصفر

yes '**ay**-wa, na-ᶜam نعم

yesterday im-**beh**-riH/'ams أمس

you (sing.) **in**-ta [**in**-tee] أنت

you (pl.) ın-**tum**-ma أنتم

You're welcome, don't mention it.
ᶜ**af**-wan عفواً

young Su-**ghay**-yar صغير
[Su-**ghay**-ya-ra]

younger, youngest '**aS**-ghar أصغر

young man shabb شاب ، شباب
(pl.) sha-**behb**

yours bi-**teh**-ᶜak لك

zipper **sus**-ta سوستة

zone man-**Ti**-qa منطقة

zoo gi-**ney**-nit il-Ha-ya-wa-**neht**
حديقة الحيوان

ARABIC-ENGLISH DICTIONARY

The verbs are given in the third person singular present form ("he goes," etc.), beginning with *yi-* . For other forms of the verb see the Notes on Grammar on page 212.

As in the text, feminine forms are given in square brackets.

The following alphabetical order is used:

" or ', a, b, d, D, e, f, g, h, H, i, j, k, kh, l, m, n, p, q, r, s, S, sh, t, T, u, v, w, y, z, Z, ^c

" or '

'a-ba-dan never

'abb father

"abl before (prep.)

*"ab-li **ki**-da* before (now)

*'a-boo ga-**lam**-boo* crab

*'a-**boo**-ya* my father

*'ab-yaD [**bey**-Da]* white

*"a-**deem** ["a-**dee**-ma]* old

*'a-**gaa**-za* holiday, vacation

*ag-**na**-bee ['ag-na-**bee**-ya]* foreign

*'ag-za-**kheh**-na* pharmacy (chemist's)

'ah-lan! Hi!

*'ah-**raam*** pyramids

"ah-wa coffee, café

*'a**H**-mar [**Ham**-ra]* red

*'a**H**-san* better

'ak-bar bigger

'akl food

'akh-Dar [khaD-ra] green

*'al-**maaz*** diamonds

'a-lam pain

'al-"ehn worried

"a-lam pen, pencil

"a-lam gaff ball-point pen

"alb heart

*'alf (pl.) 'a-**lehf*** thousand

*"a-**meeS** (pl.) "um-**Saan*** shirt

*'am-**wehg*** waves

*'am-**wehs** Hi-**leh**-"a* razor blades

'an-hee? which?

'arD land, earth

'ar-khaS cheaper

'a-san-Seer elevator, lift

'a-sar (pl.) 'a-saar monument, ruin

'a-shi^c-^{c}a X-rays

'aS-far [Saf-ra] yellow

'aS-ghar smaller, younger

"aSr palace

"aS-waan Aswan

"aTr train

'aw or

'aw-reh" papers, documents, bills

'aw-reh" na"d paper money

'aw-wil ['oo-la] first

"ay-ma list, menu

'ay-wa yes

'ayy any

'az-ma qal-bee-ya heart attack

'az-ra" [zar-"a] blue

'eed (pl.) 'a-yeh-dee hand

"eh-dir ['ad-ra] able

'eh-khir ['ukh-ra] other

'eh-la kat-ba typewriter

'eh-sif! ['as-fa!] sorry!

'eyh? what?

'ibn son

'il-ti-hehb infection, inflammation

'im-sehk constipation

'im-ta? when?

'in shaa' al-laah God willing (I hope so).

'in-ti-Zaar waiting, parking

"irsh (pl.) "u-roosh piastre

"irsh (pl.) "u-roosh shark

'is-boo^c (pl.) 'a-sa-bee^c week

'is-hehl diarrhea

'is-kin-di-ree-ya Alexandria

'is-lehm Islam

'ism (pl.) 'a-seh-mee name

'is-wid [soh-da] black

'is-^{c}ehf ambulance service

'i-sharb scarf

"ish-Ta cream

"i-zehz glass

"i-zeh-za (pl.) "a-zeh-yiz bottle

'oh-Da (pl.) 'o-waD room

'ud-dehm in front (of)

"uf-Taan (pl.) "a-fa-Teen caftan

'ug-ra fee, rent

"ul-lee ["u-lee-lee] tell me ...

'umm mother

"u-ray-yib soon

"u-ray-yib (min) near (to)

'us-loob style

"u-Say-yar short

'u-teel hotel

'u-tu-bees (pl.) 'u-tu-bee-seht bus

"uTn cotton

a

a-loh hello

a-na I

af-reeq-ya Africa

a-ghuS-Tus August

al-man-ya Germany

al-meh-nee [al-ma-nee-ya] German

am-ree-ka America

am-ree-keh-nee [am-ree-ka-nee-ya] American

ar-ba-ᶜa four

as-ban-ya Spain

as-bee-reen aspirin

as-beh-nee [as-ba-nee-ya] Spanish

ayr-lan-da Ireland

ayr-lan-dee [ayr-lan-dee-ya] Irish

ays kreem ice cream

b

baʺ-ʺehl grocery store

baʺ-sheesh tip, gratuity

baar bar

bad-la suit

bad-ree early, sooner

baHr sea

ba-laH dates

ba-lad town, country

bal-Too overcoat

ban-Ta-lohn pants, trousers

ban-yoo bath tub

ban-zeen gasoline

bank (pl.) bu-nook bank

ba-ra-zeel Brazil

ba-ra-zee-lee [ba-ra-zee-lee-ya] Brazilian

bard cold (noun)

bar-dehn [bar-deh-na] cold

bar-Doo also

ba-reed post, mail

bar-ra outside

bas-boor passport

bas-ka-weet biscuits, cookies

bass only, just

bash-ra skin

ba-Sal onions

ba-Taa-Tis potatoes

ba-Tee' slow

baT-Ta-nee-ya blanket

baT-Ta-ree-ya battery

baT-Teekh watermelon

baᶜd after

baᶜ-deyn afterwards, later

baᶜ-di buk-ra the day after tomorrow

baᶜd iD-Duhr in the afternoon

baᶜD— some of—

bee-ra beer

bee^c sale

beh-"ee remainder, change

behb door

beh-rid [**bar**-da] cold

beyD eggs

*beyt (pl.) bu-**yoot*** house

*bi ba-**lehsh*** free, for nothing

*bi-din-**gehn*** aubergine

*bi-**doon*** without

*bil-"**aTr*** by train

*bil-ba-**reed** ig-**gaw**-wee*
  by air-mail

*bi-**lehj**, plehj* beach

bi-nas hairpins

*bint (pl.) ba-**neht*** girl, daughter

*bi-**sur**-^c a* fast

bi-teh ^c - - belonging to —

*biS-**Sud**-fa* suddenly

*bi-**Taa**-qa (pl.) bi-Taa-**qaat***
  card

*bi-^c**eed*** far

bloo-za blouse

*boo-jey-**heht*** spark plugs

*bri-**Taa**-nee [bri-Taa-**nee**-ya]*
  British

*bri-**Tan**-ya* Britain

*bu-**feyh*** dining car

*bu-**Hey**-ra* lake

*bu-**leeS*** police

*bu-**loh**-var* sweater

bunn (ground) coffee

bun-nee brown

*bur-**ney**-Ta* hat

*bur-tu-"**aan*** oranges

d

da"n chin, beard

da-hab gold

*da-**jehj*** chicken

*da-**leel*** guide, guidebook

*da-**leel** 'al-**wehn*** color chart

damm blood

da-ra-ga class

*dars (pl.) du-**roos*** lesson

da-wa (pl.) 'ad-**wee**-ya*
  medicine

daw-la (pl.) **du**-wal* state

daw-sha noise

day-man always

day-ya" tight, narrow

dee-zil diesel fuel

dek-fee warm

*dib-**behn*** flies

*dil-**wa**"-tee* now

*di-**rch**^c* arm

*di-**sim**-bir* December

dohr (pl.) 'ad-**waar*** floor

*do-**laar** (pl.) do-la-**raat*** dollar

dugh-ree straight on

*duk-**kehn** (pl.) da-ka-**keen***
  shop, store

*duk-**toor** [duk-**too**-ra]* doctor

*du-**khool***   entry

dush   shower

D

Daa-*nee*   mutton, lamb

Dahr   back

DakhT id-**damm**   blood pressure

*Da-**ree**-ba (pl.) Da-**raa**-yib*   tax

*Deyf (pl.) Du-**yoof***   guest

Duhr   noon

f

*fa-"**eer** (pl.) **fu**-"a-ra*   poor

faa-*Dee [**faD**-ya]*   free, unoccupied

faD-*Da*   silver

fak-*ha*   fruit

fak-*ka*   small change

*fukh-**khaar***   pottery, ceramics

*fal-**lehH** (pl.) fal-la-**Heen***   peasant farmer

*fa-**loo**-ka*   sailboat

*fa-**nil**-la*   T-shirt, undershirt

*fa-**raa**-mil*   brakes

*fa-**ran**-sa*   France

*fa-ran-**seh**-wee [fa-ran-sa-**wee**-ya]*   French

*fa-**raw**-la*   strawberries

far"   difference

far ᶜ   branch

*far-ᶜ**oo**-nee*   Pharaonic

faSl   season, class, classroom

*fa-**Sul**-ya*   beans

*fa-**Zee**ᶜ*   dreadful

fee   there is/are

*feh-righ [**far**-gha]*   empty

*feh-tiH [**fat**-Ha]*   light (colored)

feyn?   where?

fi   in, at

*fib-**reh**-yir*   February

fik-*ra (pl.) 'af-**kaar***   idea

fil-*fil*   pepper

*fil-ma-ᶜ**ehd***   on time, punctually

*film (pl.) 'af-**lehm***   film

*fi-**loos***   money

*fi-**rehkh***   chicken

fis-seh-ᶜa   per hour

*fi-**shaar***   popcorn

*fi-**Taar***   breakfast

foh"   above, on top

foo-*Ta (pl.) **fo**-waT*   towel

foo-*Ta SiH-**Hee**-ya*   sanitary napkin

fool   pureed beans

*fool su-**deh**-nee*   peanuts

fun-*du"*   hotel

furn   oven, bakery

fur-*Sa*   chance, opportunity

fur-*sha*   brush

fus-*Ha*   outing, break

fus-**tehn**   dress

g

ga-*bal (pl.) gi-***behl**   mountain

gud-*wal il-ma-wa-*ᶜ**eed**   timetable

gadd   serious

   bi **gadd**   seriously

gal-*la-***bee***-ya*   galabiyya

ga-*mal*   camel

gam-ᶜ*a*   university

ga-**noob**   south

ga-**ree** *da (pl.) ga-***reh***-yıd*   newspaper

ga-*wa-***hir***-gee*   jeweler's

ga-**weh**-*hir*   jewelry

ga-**wehb** *[ga-***weh***-beht]*   letter

ga-**wehz** *is-***sa***-far*   passport

gaww   weather, atmosphere

gayy   coming, next

gaz-**zaar**   butcher's

gaz-*ma*   shoes

gaz-**ma**-*gee*   shoemaker

ga-ᶜ**ehn**   hungry

geh-*hiz [***gah***-za]*   ready

geh-*mi*ᶜ *(pl.) ga-***weh***-mi*ᶜ
   mosque

gib-*na*   cheese

gidd   grandfather

gid-*da*   grandmother

gi-**deed**   new

gi-**hehz** *ka-***sitt**   cassette player

gild   leather

gi-**ney**   pound (currency)

gi-**ney**-*na (pl.) ga-***neh***-yin*
   garden, park

gi-**neyn**-*t il-Ha-ya-wa-***neht**   zoo

gin-**see**-*ya*   nationality

gi-**zee**-*ra (pl.) ***gu***-zur*   island

gohz   husband

gow-*wa*   inside

gum-*ruk*   customs

gu-**nil**-*la*   skirt

gh

gha-*bee [gha-***bee***-ya]*   stupid

gha-*da*   lunch

gha-*laT*   wrong, mistake

gha-*nam*   sheep (and goats)

gharb   west

ghar-*bee [ghar-***bee***-ya]*
   Western

gha-**seel**   laundry

gheh-*lce [***ghal***-ya]*   expensive

ghi-**wey**-*sha*   bracelet

ghur-*fa (pl.) ***ghu***-raf*   room

h

*ha-**dee**-ya (pl.) ha-**deh**-ya* gift

*han-**da**-sa* engineering

hee-ya she

heh-dee [**had**-ya] quiet, calm

hi-na here

hin-dee [**hin**-dee-ya] Indian

*hi-**nehk*** there

*ho-**lan**-da* Holland

*ho-**lan**-dee* Dutch

*hu-**doom*** clothes

huw-wa he

H

Haa-Dir certainly

Hadd someone

Had-sa accident

Haf-la party, concert

Haf-la *mu-si-**qee**-ya* concert

Ha-ga thing, something

Ha-gar stone

Hagz reservation

*Ha-la-wee-**yeht*** desserts

*Ha-la-**weh**-nee* confectioner's

*Ha-**leeb*** milk

*Hal-**leh**″* barber's

*Ha-**mehm*** pigeons

*Ham-**mehm*** bathroom

*Ham-**mehm** si-beh-Ha*
  swimming pool

*Han-**Toor*** horsedrawn carriage

*Ha-**raa**-ra* temperature

*Ha-**reer*** silk

Harr hot

*Ha-sha-**raat*** insects

*Ha-**weh**-lee* about

Hashw filling

*Ha-**zeen*** sad

Heh-mee hot, spicy

Heh-mil pregnant

*Hi-**keh**-ya* story

Hilw sweet, lovely

*Hi-**sehb*** bill, check

*Hi-seh-**beht*** accounts

*Hi-**zehm*** belt

*Hu-**boob*** pills

*Hu-**boob** mi-naw-**wi**-ma*
  sleeping pills

*Hu-**moo**-Da* acidity,
  indigestion

*Hur-**ree**-ya* freedom

i

*ig-ti-**meh**ᶜ* meeting

iH-na we

il — the —

*il-'**eh**-ni-sa —* Miss —

*il-**hind*** India

il-lee   who, which

il-qaa-hi-ra   Cairo

il-wi-la-yeht il-mut-ta-Hi-da
   the United States

il-ya-behn   Japan

il-yu-nehn   Greece

im-beh-riH   yesterday

im-ti-Hehn (pl.) im-ti-Heh-neht
   exam

in-floo-in-za   influenza

in-gi-lee-zee [in-gi-lee-zee-ya]
   English

in-gil-ti-ra   England

in-ta [in-tee]   you (sing.)

in-tum-ma   you (pl.)

ir-ri-yaa-Da   sport

is-maH-lee   pardon me

is-ra-'eel   Israel

is-ra-'ee-lee [is-ra-'ee-lee-ya]
   Israeli

is-say-yid —   Mr. —

is-say-yi-da —   Mrs. —

is-ti-raad   import

*is-ti*ᶜ*-la-meht*   information

is-tiq-lehl   independence

is-Ti-waa-na   disk, record

iS-Seen   China

iS-SubH   (in the) morning

ish-sharq il-'aw-saT
   the Middle East

ish-ti-raa-kee   socialist

it-shar-raf-na   Pleased to meet
   you.

i-Taa-lee [i-Taa-lee-ya]   Italian

i-Taal-ya   Italy

iz-zayy?   how?

iz-zay-yak? [iz-zay-yik?]   How
   are you?

j

ja-kit-ta   jacket

jehk   jack (mechanical)

k

ka-ba-rey   floor show

kab-reet   matches

kah-ra-ba   electricity

kalb (pl.) ki-lehb   dog

kam?, bi kam?   How much/
   many?

ka-mehn   also

ka-me-ra   camera

ka-na-da   Canada

ka-na-dee [ka-na-dee-ya]
   Canadian

kart (pl.) ku-root   card

kart bus-tehl   postcard

ka-sitt (pl.) ka-sit-teht   cassette

kash-shehf   headlight,
   flashlight

*ka*ᶜ*b*   heel, ankle

kee-loo   kilo

kee-*lott*   briefs, panties

keh-mil   complete

keh-tib   clerk

keyf   how, like

keyf il-**Hehl**?   How are you?

ki-**beer** [ki-**bee**-ra] (pl.) ku-**baar**
   big, old

ki-da   thus, so

ki-*feh*-ya   enough

ki-*leem* (pl.) 'ak-*li*-ma   woven
   rug

kis-wa   suit

ki-*teer*   much, many

ki-*tehb* (pl.) **ku**-tub   book

kitf   shoulder

koh-ra   ball, football

ko-*lon*-ya   Cologne

kreym   (cosmetic) cream

kreym li 'i-**zeh**-lit il-mak-**yaj**
   cold cream

kreym li Hi-**meh**-yit il-**bash**-ra
   suntan cream

kri-dit kard   credit card

kub-**beh**-ya   glass

kub-ree (pl.) ka-**beh**-ree   bridge

ku-*fee*-ya   headscarf

kuH-Ha   cough

kull   each, every

kul-li **Ha**-ga   everything

ku-*reek*   jack (mechanical)

ku-*rumb*   cabbage

kushk (pl.) '*ik*-**shehk**   kiosk

kwa-*feer*   hairdresser

kway-yis [kway-**yi**-sa]   good,
   well

kh

khaaS   private

khad-*deh*-ma   servant (fem.)

kha-*feef* [kha-*fee*-fa]   light
   (in weight)

kha-**laaS**!   That's enough!
   I've finished.

kham-ra   liquor

kham-sa   five

kha-*reef*   autumn

kha-*ree*-Ta   map

khass   lettuce

kha-*shab*   wood

kha-*Tar*   danger

kha-*Teer*   dangerous

khaTT (pl.) khu-**TooT**   line

khay-**yaaT** [khay-**yaa**-Ta]
   tailor, dressmaker

khaz-na   safe (noun)

khehl   (maternal) uncle

kheh-la   (maternal) aunt

kheh-tim   ring

khib-ra   experience

khid-ma   service

khi-*yaar*   cucumber

khohkh   peaches

khubz   bread

khu-Daar   vegetables

khu-roog   exit

khu-Saa-ra   pity

l

la'   no

la-bun   milk

laHm, laH-ma   meat

laH-ma ba-"a-ree   beef

lam-ba   lamp, light bulb

lam-ma   when

la-moon   lemon

la-Teef [la-Tee-fa] (pl.) lu-Taaf
kind, nice

law sa-maHt ...   Excuse me ...

lu-zeez   delicious

leh-zim —   it is necessary,
must —

leyh?   why?

ley-la   night

li   to, for

li waH-dee   on my own

lohn (pl.) 'al-wehn   color

lohz   almonds

los-yohn   lotion

m

maa-Dee   past (noun)

ma-"aSS   scissors

ma-"ehs   size, measurement

ma"-fool   closed

ma"-lee   fried

mab-lool   wet

mab-rook!   Congratulations!

ma-dee-na   city, town

ma-dehm —   Mrs. —, madam

mad-ra-sa (pl.) ma-deh-ris
school

ma feesh   there isn't/aren't
(any)

maf-tooH   open

ma-gal-la (pl.) ma-gal-leht
magazine

mag-geh-nan   free, for nothing

mag-noon   crazy

magh-sa-la   laundry,
launderette

ma-HaT-Ta   station, stop

ma-HaT-Tit 'u-tu-bees
bus stop

ma-HaT-Tit ban-zeen   gas
station

ma-Hat-Tit il-"aTr   railway
station

ma-Hall (pl.) ma-Hal-leht
shop

ma-Hall zu-hoor   flower shop

maH-fa-Za   wallet, pocketbook

maH-roo"   burned

mak-soor [mak-soo-ra]   broken

mak-tab   office, desk

mak-tab il-ba-**reed**   post office

mak-tab Sarf   money exchange

mak-**ta**-ba   bookshop, library

mak-wa   iron

mak-**wa**-gee   ironer

mak-**yaj**   makeup

makh-baz   bakery

makh-**SooS**   special

ma-**leh**-hee   entertainment

malH   salt

ma-lik (pl.) mu-**look**   king

mal-**yehn** [mal-**yeh**-na]   full

mam-**noo**^c   forbidden

man-ga   mangoes

ma-ni-**keer**   manicure,
nail polish

man-**Ti**-qa   area

man-**Zar** (pl.) ma-**naa**-Zir   view

ma-ra (pl.) ni-**seh'**   woman

ma-**raD** (pl.) 'am-**raaD**
disease, illness

ma-**reeD** [ma-**ree**-Da]   ill

mar-**Ha**-ba!   welcome

mar-kaz   center (institution)

mar-kib (pl.) ma-**reh**-kib   boat

mar-ra **waH**-da   once

mar-**wa**-Ha   fan

ma-sa-lan   for example

mas-**'ool**   responsible

mas-**loo**"   boiled

mas-raH   theater

mas-ra-**Hee**-ya   play

maS-na^c (pl.) ma-**Saa**-ni^c
factory

maSr   Egypt, Cairo

maS-ree [maS-**ree**-ya]
Egyptian

mash-**ghool**   busy

mash-**hoor** [mash-**hoo**-ra]
famous

mash-roo-**beht**   drinks

mash-wee   grilled

mat-Haf   museum

matsh (**koh**-ra)   (football) match

ma-**Taar**   airport

ma-Tar   rain

maT-^cam (pl.) ma-**Taa**-^cim
restaurant

maw-"af (pl.) ma-**weh**-"if   stop

maw-"af tak-**see**   taxi stand

maw-**good**   present (adj.)

may-ya   water

maz-za   "mezza," appetizers

maZ-booT   exact, precise

ma-^ca   with

ma-^ca l-'**a**-saf   unfortunately

ma-^ca-**lish**!   Never mind!

ma-^ca s-sa-**leh**-ma   Good-bye.

ma-^c**ehd**   appointment

ma^c-mal   laboratory

ma^c-raD   exhibition

meen?   who?

mee-na   port, harbor

mee-ya (pl.) mee-**yeht**
hundred

meh-ris   March

mi-*dehn*   square (place)

mi-*fal*-lis   bankrupt, broke

mif-*tehH* (pl.) ma-fa-*teeH*   key

mi-*khad*-da   pillow, cushion

mi-*khal*-lil   pickles

min   from

min faD-lak [*min faD*-lik]
   please

mi-*nab*-bih   alarm clock

mi-*neyn?*   Where from?

min-yoo   menu

mi-*reh*-ya   mirror

mi-*seh'*   evening

mi-*seh' il*-*khevr*   Good evening.

mis-*ta°*-gil [*mis*-ta°-*gi*-la]   in a
   hurry

mis-*ti*-wee   ripe, cooked

mish   not

mish baT-*Taal*   not bad

mish-*mish*   apricot

mishT   comb

mit-'*ak*-kid   certain, sure

mit-*gaw*-wiz [*mit*-gaw-*wi*-za]
   married

mitr   headwaiter

mitr   meter

mi-°ad-*dee*-ya   ferry

mi°-da   stomach

mohz   bananas

mo-*toor*   engine

mu-"*ab*-la   interview, encounter

mu-'*al*-lif   writer, composer

mu-*beh*-shir   direct

mu-*dar*-ris [*mu*-dar-*ri*-sa]
   teacher

mu-*deer*   manager, director

mu-*fakk* ma-sa-*meer*   screwdriver

mu-*feed*   useful

mu-*ghan*-nee [*mu*-ghan-*nee*-ya]
   singer

mu-*han*-dis   engineer

mu-*himm*   important,
   interesting

mu-*Haw*-wil   adapter plug

mu-*Heh*-mee   lawyer

muH-tamm (*bi* —)   interested
   (in —)

mu-*kal*-ma   phone call

mu-*khay*-yam si-*yeh*-Hee
   campsite

mukh-*ta*-lif [*mukh*-*ta*-li-fa]
   different

mu-*lay*-yin   laxative

mu-mar-*ri*-Da   nurse

mum-*tehz*   excellent

mi-*nab*-bih   alarm clock

mu-*nch*-sib   suitable

mu-*rab*-ba   jam

mu-*rat*-tab   tidy

mur-*gehn*   coral

mu-*see*-qa   music

mus-lim [*mus*-*li*-ma]
   (pl.) mus-li-*meen*   Muslim

*mus-**tash**-fa* hospital

*mush-**ki**-la (pl.) ma-**sheh**-kil*
  problem

*mu-**Tah**-hir* antiseptic

*mu-**waZ**-Zaf [mu-waZ-**Za**-fa]*
  employee, official

n

na"d cash

*na"-**leht*** gears

*na-ba-**teht*** plants

*naD-**Daa**-ra* eyeglasses

*naD-Da-**raa**-tee* optician

*naD-**Daa**-rit shams* sunglasses

*na-far (pl.) 'an-**faar*** person,
  individual

nafs il — the same —

nahr river

*na-**moos*** mosquitoes

*na-**See**-Ha* advice

*na**S**-ya* (street) corner

nayy raw

na-^cam yes

neh-dir rare

*neh-shif [**nash**-fa]* dry

*ni-**beet*** wine

*ni-**Deef** [ni-**Dee**-fa]* clean

nim-ra number

*nim-rit ti-li-**fohn*** telephone
  number

*nis-ba mi-'a-**wee**-ya*
  percentage

nohm sleep

noh-ta notebook

noor light

nus-kha copy

nuSS half

*nu-**vim**-bir* November

o

*ok-**too**-bar* October

*os-**tral**-ya* Australia

q

*qa-**moos*** dictionary

*qa-**naah*** canal, channel

*qa-**noon*** law

qar-ya village

*qa-wee [qa-**wee**-ya]* strong

qaw-mee national, nationalist

*qun-Su-**lee**-ya* consulate

r

ra-'ees president

ra's mehl capital (finance)

ra"S   dance, dancing

*ra"S **ba**-la-dee*   belly dancing

raa-gil *(pl.)* rig-**geh**-la   man

raa-gil *'a^c-**mehl***   businessman

raas   head

*ra-**bee^c***   spring

radd   reply (noun)

rad-yoo   radio

*ra-**maa**-Dee*   gray

ra-qam   number

*ra-**Seef***   pavement, platform

raTl   pound (weight)

ray-yis   boss

reef (pl.) 'ar-**yehf**   countryside

rigl   leg

*ri-**gheef** (pl.)* 'ar-**ghi**-fa   loaf

*ri-**kheeS** [ri-**khee**-Sa]*   cheap

*ri-**seh**-la*   message

rohb   robe, dressing gown

roo-see   Russian

roos-ya   Russia

*ru-**baaT***   bandages

rukh-Sa   license, permit

*ru-**shit**-ta*   prescription

*ru-**Too**-ba*   humidity

ruzz   rice

S

sa-bab *(pl.)* 'as-**behb**   reason

sab-^c*a*   seven

*sa-**faa**-ra*   embassy

*sa-**fee**-na*   ship

sahl   easy

*sak-**raan** [sak-**raa**-na]*   drunk

sa-la-Ta   salad

sa-mak   fish

sa-na-wee   annual

san-dal (pl.) sa-na-**deel**   sandals

*san-**doo''***   box, chest

sand-witsh *(pl.)* sand-wit-**sheht**   sandwich

*sar-**deen***   sardines

*sa-**ree^c***   quick

sa-wa   together

*saw-**weh''***   driver

*say-**yaa**-ra*   car

seh-kit *[sak-ta]*   silent (of people)

seh-^ca *(pl.)* sa-^c*eht*   hour, time

*sib-**tim**-bir*   September

siDr   chest

*si-**fing***   sponges

*si-**gaa**-ra (pl.)* sa-**geh**-yir   cigarette

*sig-**geh**-da (pl.)* sa-ga-**geed**   carpet

*si-kir-**tcer** [si-kir-**tee**-ra]*   secretary

sik-ka *(pl.)* **si**-kak   road, way

sik-ka **Ha**-deed   railway

*sik-**kee**-na*   knife

s-*la* chain

n *il-***feel** ivory

i-*reer* (*pl.*) *sa-***reh**-*yir* bed

sitt (*pl.*) *sit-***teht** lady

sit-*ta* six

sit-*ti beyt* housewife

*si*ᶜ*r* price

soo″ market, bazaar

*soo-***tyehn** bra

*su-'***ehl** (*pl.*) '*as-'***i**-*la* question

*su-***gu***″ ″* sausage

suk-*kar* sugar

sukhn hot

*su-khu-***nee**-*ya* fever

sur-ᶜ*a* speed

sus-*ta* zip fastener

*Sar-***raaf** cashier

SatH surface, roof

*Say-da-***lee**-*ya* pharmacy

*Sa*ᶜ*b* difficult

See-*nee* [*See-***nee**-*ya*] Chinese

Seyf summer

Soof wool

Soo-*ra* (*pl.*) **So**-*war* picture,
photo

Soht (*pl.*) '*aS-***waat** voice

*Su-***baa**ᶜ (*pl.*) *Sa-***waa**-*bi*ᶜ
finger

SubH morning

*Su-***daa**ᶜ headache

*Su-***ghay**-*yar* [*Su-ghay-***ya**-*ra*]
small, young

*Su-*ᶜ*oo-ba* difficulty

S

Saa-*Hee* awake

Saa-*Hib* (*pl.*) '*aS-***Haab** friend

*Sa-***baaH** morning

*Sa-baH il-***kheyr** Good
morning.

*Sa-***boon** soap

Sa-*daf* shells

*Sa-***HeeH**? Really?

SaH-*ra* desert

*Sa-***lohn** *tag-***meel** beauty parlor

Sanf (*pl.*) '*aS-***naaf** kind, sort

sh

sha″-″a (*pl.*) *shu-″a* apartment

sha-″ee naughty

shabb (*pl.*) *sha-***behb** young man

sha-ga-ra (*pl.*) *sha-gar* tree

*shagh-***ghehl** [*shagh-***geh**-*la*]
worker, servant

shahr (*pl.*) *shu-***hoor** month

shakl appearance, look

*shak-***loo** [*shak-***la**-*ha*] —
he (she) looks —

shakhS (*pl.*) '*ash-***khaaS**
person

shakh-*See* personal

sha-**mehl** north

sham-**poo** shampoo

shams sun

sham-**see**-ya sunshade, umbrella

sha-nab mustache

shan-*Ta (pl.)* **shu**-naT bag, suitcase

sha-**raab** socks, stockings

sha-**raa**-yiT tapes

shar" east

shar-"ee Eastern, oriental

shaTT beach, shore

shayy tea

shay-**yehl** porter

shaᶜ-bee popular

shaᶜr hair

shcek [shee-**keht**] check

shee-**keht** si-ya-**Hee**-ya traveler's checks

shee-sha nargile, hubble bubble (water pipe)

sheh-riᶜ *(pl.)* sha-**wak**-riᶜ street

shib-**behk** *(pl.)* sha-ba-**beek** window

shib-shib slippers

shi-**mehl** left

shir-ka *(pl.)* sha-ri-**keht** company

shi-ta winter

sho-ko-**lua**-ta chocolate

shoh-ka fork

shu-naT bags, luggage

shur-ba soup

shur-Ta police

shway-ya a little, rather

shway-yit — a bit of —

t

ta'-**meen** insurance

ta-"**ree**-ban nearly, roughly

tad-**leek** massage

taHt under, below

taH-**weel** exchange (finance)

taH-**wee**-la detour

tak-see taxi

tak-**yeef ha**-wa air conditioning

takh-**feeD** reduction

talg ice, snow

ta-**mal**-lec always

ta-man price

ta-**man**-ya eight

tan-**Deef** cleaning

ta-qa-**leed** traditions

ta-**reekh** date, history

ta-**ree**-khee historical

tar-zee tailor

taS-**leeH** repair, mending

ta-**Taw**-wur development

taw-**zee**ᶜ distribution

ta-^ceh-la! [ta-^ceh-lee!]
  Come on!

teh-*gir* merchant, businessman

teh-*nee* again

teh-*nee [tan-ya]* another,
  second

ti-"eel heavy

*ti-**gaa**-ra* commerce, business

*ti-li-**fohn*** telephone

*til-li-**ghrehf*** telegram

*ti-li-viz-**yohn*** television

*til-**meez** (pl.) ta-**lam**-za* pupil

tis-^ca nine

tiS-*baH* ^c*a-la* **kheyr** Good
  night.

tohm garlic

*tuf-**fehH*** apples

*twa-**litt*** lavatory

T

Ta"s weather

*Ta"-**Too**-"a* ashtray

Taa-*lib [Taa-**li**-ba]*
  (pl.) **Ta**-*la-ba* student

Taa-*za* fresh

*Ta-**ba**" (pl.) 'aT-**baa**"* dish,
  plate

*Ta-**beeb** [Ta-**bee**-ba]* doctor

*Ta-**beeb** 'as-**nehn*** dentist

Tab-^can of course

*Ta-rá-**bèy**-za* table

*Tard (pl.) Tu-**rood*** parcel

*Ta-**ree**" (pl.) **Tu**-ru"* way, road

*Ta-**ree**" ra-'**ee**-see* highway

*Ta-**waa**-bi^c* stamps

*Ta-**waa**-ri'* emergency

*Ta-**weel*** long, tall

*Tay-**yaa**-ra* airplane

*Tay-yib [Tay-**yi**-ba]* good

*Tifl (pl.) 'aT-**faal*** child

Tur-*shee* pickles

u

*u-**rub**-ba* Europe

*u-**rub**-bee* European

v

vid-*yo* video

volt volt

w

waa-DiH obvious

waa-Tee [waT-ya] low

wa-ga^c pain

*wa-**Heed*** sole, only

*wa-**keel*** agent

wakh-ree late

wa-la **Ha**-ga   nothing

wa-lad (pl.) 'aw-**lehd**   boy

wal-la (in question)   or?

wa-**leh**-kin   but

wal-**leh**-ᶜa   lighter

wa-ra   behind

wa-ra" (pl.) 'aw-**reh**"
leaf, paper

ward   roses, flowers

war-sha   repair shop

waSl   receipt

wa-**zeer**   minister

wa-**Zee**-fa   job, post

weh-Hid [**waH**-da]   one

weh-si̇ᶜ [**was**-ᶜa]   wide, loose

wi   and

widn   ear

wi-ḷi̇sh [**wiH**-sha]   bad, ugly

wi-sikh [**wis**-kha]   dirty

wis-kee   whiskey

wiST, wuST   center

wishsh   face

wi-**zaa**-ra   ministry

wu-**Sool**   arrival

y

ya-**beh**-nee [ya-ba-**nee**-ya]
Japanese

yakht   yacht

yal-la!   Let's go!

ya-**neh**-yir   January

yee-gee   to come

yeh-kul   to eat

yeh-khud   to take

yi-"**ad**-dim X li Y   to introduce
X to Y

yi-'**ag**-gar   to hire, rent

yi"-dar   to be able

yi-"**ees**   to measure

yi-"**eh**-bil   to meet

yi"-fil   to close

yi-"**ool**   to say, tell

yi-"**oom**   to get up

yi"-ra   to read

yi-**beeᶜ**   to sell

yi-**boos**   to kiss

yib-**ti**-dee   to begin

yib-ᶜat   to send

yi-**dakh**-khan   to smoke

yi-**dar**-dish   to chat

yi-**dar**-ris   to teach

yi-**daw**-war ᶜa-la   to look for

yid-ris   to study

yi-**Deeᶜ**   to be lost (objects)

yiD-rab   to hit

yi-**faD**-Dal   to prefer

yi-**fah**-him   to explain

yi-**fak**-kar   to remind

yif-ham   to understand

yif-taH   to open

yif-**ti**-kir   to think, remember

yif-Tar   to have breakfast

*yi-**ghan**-nee*   to sing

*yi-**ghay**-yar*   to change (trans.)

***yigh**-sil*   to wash

*yi-**Had**-did*   to limit

*yi-**Ham**-maD*   to develop

*yi-**Haw**-wil*   to exchange (money)

*y**iH**-giz*   to book

*yi-**Hibb***   to like, love

*y**iH**-la"*   to shave

*y**iH**-ra"*   to burn

*y**iH**-Sal*   to happen

*yi-**kal**-lim*   to speak to

*yi-**kar**-rar*   to repeat

*y**ik**-sar*   to break

*y**ik**-tib*   to write

*yi-**kuHH***   to cough

*yi-**khab**-bee*   to hide (trans.)

*yi-**khal**-laS*   to finish

*yi-**kheh**-ni"*   to quarrel with

*yi-**khiff***   to get better, recover

*y**ikh**-laS*   to finish (intrans.)

*y**ikh**-la^c*   to undress

*y**ikh**-taar*   to choose

*y**il**-bis*   to dress

*yi-**leh**-"ee*   to find

*yi-**liff***   to wrap

*yil-^c**ab***   to play

*y**im**-Dee*   to sign

*yi-**meen***   right (direction)

*y**im**-kin*   perhaps

*y**im**-la*   to fill

*y**im**-shee*   to walk

*yi-**naD**-Daf*   to clean

*yi-**nehm***   to sleep

*yin-**saH***   to advise

*yin-**ti**-Zir*   to wait

*y**in**-zil (fi)*   to get off, stay (at)

*y**ir**-ga^c*   to return

*y**ir**-kab*   to get on

*yi-**rooH***   to go

*yi-**rudd***   to reply

*y**is**-'al*   to ask

*yi-**sag**-gil*   to record, check

*yi-**sal**-lif*   to lend

*yi-**sal**-lim*   to greet

*yi-**seh**-fir*   to travel, leave

*yi-**seh**-miH*   forgive

*yi-**seh**-^c*id*   to help

*yi-**soo"***   to drive

*y**is**-ra"*   to steal

*yis-ta-**Ham**-ma*   to bathe

*yis-**tan**-na*   to wait

*yis-ta-**ray**-yaH*   to rest

*yis-**ta**-^c-mil*   to use

*yi-**Sal**-laH*   to repair

*yi-**Sal**-lee*   to pray

*yi-**Saw**-war*   to photograph

*y**iS**-raf*   to spend, change (money)

*yi-**shag**-ga^c*   to support, encourage

*y**ish**-fee*   to get better

*yi-**shoof***   to see

yish-rab   to drink

yish-raH   to explain

yish-ti-ree   to buy

yit-far-rag (ᶜa-la)
   to watch, look (at)

yit-gaw-wiz   to get married

yit-ghad-da   to have lunch

yit-ghay-yar   to change
   (intrans.)

yit-kal-lim   to speak, talk

yit-mash-sha   to take a walk

yit-mat-taᶜ (bi —)   to enjoy

yi-tar-gim   to translate

yit-ᶜash-sha   to have dinner

yiT-Ti-Sil (bi —)   to contact

yiw-gaᶜ   to hurt

yiw-Sul   to arrive

yiw-ᶜid   to promise

yi-Zoor   to visit

yi-Zunn   to think

yi-ᶜeesh   to live

yiᶜ-mil   to do, make

yiᶜ-oom   to swim

yiᶜ-zim   to invite

yohm (pl.) 'ay-yehm   day

yoh-meyn   two days

(yohm) ig-gum-ᶜa   Friday

(yohm) il-Hadd   Sunday

(yohm) il-kha-mees   Thursday

(yohm) is-sabt   Saturday

(yohm) it-ta-leht   Tuesday

(yohm) lar-baᶜ   Wednesday

(yohm) lit-neyn   Monday

yu-"af   to stop

yu-"aᶜ   to fall

yu"-ᶜud   to sit down

yul-yoo   July

yu-neh-nee [yu-neh-nee-ya]
   Greek

yun-yoo   June

yur-"uS   to dance

yus-kun   to live

yuT-bukh   to cook

yuT-lub   to ask for, order

Z

za-kee [za-kee-ya]   intelligent

zaw-ba-ᶜa   sandstorm

zeyt   oil

zeyt zey-toon   olive oil

zib-da   butter

zi-meel (pl.) zu-ma-la
   colleague

zohg   husband

zoh-ga   wife

zu-hoor   flowers

zu-kehm   cold (noun)

Z

Za-reef   pleasant

*Zarf (pl.) Zu-**roof*** envelope

*Zu-**raar** (pl.) Za-**raa**-yir*
button

c

^ca"l mind

*^caa-**Si**-ma* capital (city)

^ca-dad number, quantity

*^ca-dam in-**nohm*** insomnia

*^ca-da-sa (pl.) ^ca-da-**seht*** lens

*^cad-**dehd*** meter

^cads lentils

^caDm bone

^cafsh luggage, furniture

^caf-wan Not at all, don't mention it.

^ca-ga-la wheel, bicycle

^ca-la on

*^ca-la **fik**-ra …* by the way …

*^ca-la **mah**-lak!* slow down!

^camm (paternal) uncle

^cam-ma (paternal) aunt

^cand with (= have)

*^ca-ra-bee [^ca-ra-**bee**-ya]* Arab, Arabic

*^ca-ra-**bee**-ya* car

^carD show (noun)

*^cas-**ka**-ree (pl.) ^ca-**seh**-kir* soldier

*^ca-**Seer*** juice

*^ca**S**-ree* modern

^ca-sha dinner

*^ca-**shehn**, li-**ann*** because

*^caT-**laan** [^caT-**laa**-na]* broken down, out of order

*^ca-wiz [^caw-za] (pl.) ^caw-**zeen*** want

^cay-yehn [^cay-yeh-na] ill

*^ca-**Zeem*** marvelous, magnificent

^ceed feast, festival

*^ceed il-mi-**lehd*** Christmas

*^ceed mi-**lehd*** birthday

^cey-la family

^ceyn eye

^cil-ba (pl.) ^ci-lab packet, can

*^cilm (pl.) ^cu-**loom*** science

^cil-mee scientific

*^ci-**maa**-ra (pl.) ^ci-maa-**raat*** building, block

^ci-nab grapes

^cin-wehn address

^cum-la currency

^cum-la Sa^c-ba hard currency

*^cu-**zoo**-ma* invitation

FOREIGN PHRASE BOOKS Series

Barron's new series gives travelers instant access to the most common idiomatic expressions used during a trip—the kind one needs to know instantly, like "Where can I find a taxi?" and "How much does this cost?"

Organized by situation (arrival, customs, hotel, health, etc.) and containing additional information about pronunciation, grammar, shopping plus special facts about the country, these convenient, pocket-size reference books will be the tourist's most helpful guides.

Special features include a bilingual dictionary section with over 2000 key words, maps of each country and major cities, and helpful phonetic spellings throughout.

Each book paperback, 256 pp., 3 ¾" x 6"

ARABIC AT A GLANCE, Wise (0-8120-2979-8) $6.95, Can. $8.95
CHINESE AT A GLANCE, Seligman & Chen (0-8120-2851-1) $6.95, Can. $9.95
FRENCH AT A GLANCE, 2nd, Stein & Wald (0-8120-1394-8) $5.95, Can. $7.95
GERMAN AT A GLANCE, 2nd, Strutz (0-8120-1395-6) $6.95, Can. $8.95
ITALIAN AT A GLANCE, 2nd, Costantino (0-8120-1396-4) $6.95, Can. $8.95
JAPANESE AT A GLANCE, 2nd, Akiyama (0-8120-1397-2) $7.95, Can. $10.50
KOREAN AT A GLANCE, Holt (0-8120-3998-X) $8.95, Can. $11.95
RUSSIAN AT A GLANCE, Beyer (0-8120-4299-9) $6.95, Can. $8.95
SPANISH AT A GLANCE, 2nd, Wald (0-8120-1398-0) $6.95, Can. $8.95

Barron's Educational Series, Inc.
250 Wireless Blvd., Hauppauge, NY 11788
Call toll-free: 1-800-645-3476
In Canada: Georgetown Book Warehouse, 34 Armstrong Ave.
Georgetown, Ont. L7G 4R9, Call toll-free: 1-800-247-7160

Books may be purchased at your bookstore, or by mail from Barron's. Enclose check or money order for total amount plus sales tax where applicable and 15% for postage and handling (minimum charge $4.95). Prices subject to change without notice.
Can. $ = Canadian dollars

(#25) R 4/97

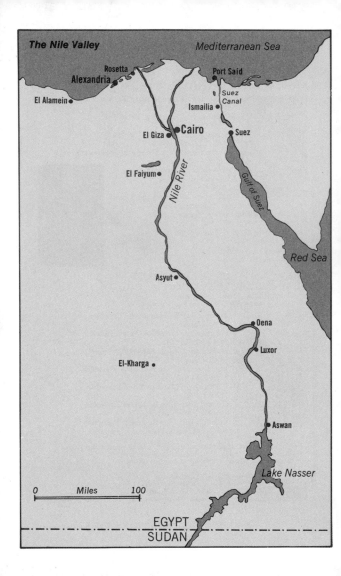